Winifred Coombe Tennant

A Life through Art

Winifred Coombe Tennant

a life through art

Peter Lord

**LlGC
NLW**

Llyfrgell Genedlaethol Cymru
The National Library of Wales
www.llgc.org.uk

Text copyright © Peter Lord 2007

First published by The National
Library of Wales, Aberystwyth, 2007

Designed by Olwen Fowler
Printed by Cambrian Printers, Aberystwyth

ISBN: 978-1-86225-065-9

Noddir gan
Lywodraeth
Cynulliad Cymru
Sponsored by
Welsh Assembly
Government

'I am like a violin string,
vibrating to every touch of the
bow, and I can't change my nature
and temperament, but must carry
it with me, God helping me.'

The Diary of
Winifred Coombe Tennant,
28 July 1935

Pressed leaf from the Diary of Winifred Coombe Tennant
J.D. Innes, *Decoration*, 1907
Frontispiece: Evan Walters, *Still Life: Flowers*, n.d.

CONTENTS

Introduction

INTRODUCTION

Winifred Coombe Tennant was more closely involved with the evolution of Welsh visual culture than any other patron of the twentieth century. Her involvement was both direct, through her friendships with the painters and craftspeople of the period, and indirect, through relationships established with other patrons, art institutions and the wider establishment. This book is about Winifred's love of visual images and artefacts, and the light which the expression of that love sheds on the evolution of visual culture in Wales. However, Winifred Coombe Tennant was a complex person, and the range of activities which she undertook in parallel to those involving visual culture reflects that complexity. Winifred was a political activist. She campaigned for women's suffrage and for Welsh home rule, and she took a radical position in public on many social issues. During the last years of the coalition government of David Lloyd George she was a frequent visitor to 10 Downing Street, and she stood for parliament. She was active in the movement for international peace, and represented Britain as a delegate to the League of Nations. She was among the first women

magistrates to be appointed. Side by side with this public life, Winifred's inner world was truly remarkable. It was dominated by religious experience. She was a devout Christian, much attracted to the practice of the Roman Catholic and the Russian Orthodox churches, but also with a sincere respect for Nonconformist tradition. Furthermore, she was a spiritual medium, who experienced vivid trance-like states which led her to believe firmly in the continuity of the life of the individual after death.

This book is not a full biography, and does not attempt to give an account of all aspects of Winifred's life. Some of these, and in particular her psychic experiences, have been documented in detail elsewhere. That said, the many facets of Winifred's complex character all had a direct bearing on her engagement with visual culture. The extraordinary value of the large collection of her papers which survives is that in the intimate juxtaposition of politics, social observation and religious experience they reveal, we perceive the deep penetration of the visual image into every aspect of her own life and, indeed, into the life of the nation. It would be impossible to understand the centrality of the visual image to her understanding of the world without drawing into the discussion other aspects of her experience. Certainly, Winifred often asserted that the artist was a special kind of person, who stood apart from the rest of humanity. She was strongly attracted by the idea of genius. She believed that art was a transcendent medium and that the artist created a channel through which ordinary people might pass beyond the tensions, anxieties, imperfections and frustrations of the material world. Nevertheless, especially in the years between the two world wars, the very proximity in her papers of the discussion of visual culture to that of politics, social issues and religious experience demonstrates how art and artists were rooted in the realities of daily life. The fate of the spirit and the state of the world were intimately related matters for Winifred. Pictures were a functional element in her daily existence, as well as a way to pass beyond it. The visual image was the point at which the material world and that of the spirit met.

The effects of Winifred Coombe Tennant's long engagement with the Welsh art world would be apparent even if her correspondence and diary had not survived. However, the archive which she took pains to ensure would be available for posterity provides a unique insight into its evolution over a period of half a century. There are over five hundred letters to and from Winifred which are of direct relevance to the visual culture of Wales. Over half of these remain in her own

archive, though some she donated to The National Library of Wales. Clearly, these are letters sent to her in the main, by patrons, painters, and art administrators, though Winifred occasionally kept copies of her side of an exchange, when she regarded it as particularly important. Fortunately, many more letters written by Winifred were preserved by their recipients, and some of these have found their way into public collections. In addition to her extensive correspondence, Winifred wrote many articles, reviews and letters to the press on a wide range of matters of concern to her, including visual culture.

The diary of Winifred Coombe Tennant covers the period from 1909 until 1956. A few fragments of an earlier diary, at present untraced, were published shortly after her death. She generally wrote her diary at home at the end of each day, only occasionally revising her entries with hindsight. When she was away from home, sometimes she kept a record of events and thoughts on separate sheets, which were subsequently inserted in the diary volumes. It is clear that she intended the diary to survive and for it to be read. Like many documents of this kind, written by a person engaged in public affairs, occasionally a degree of self-consciousness, even of rhetoric, colours the entries. On the other hand, Winifred certainly also used the diary as a medium to externalise her intense inner life, in response to her immediate emotional needs. Many entries were impulsive and, as a consequence, were sometimes erratically formed and punctuated.

In transcribing them I have simplified and standardised punctuation and capitalisation. I have expanded most of her contractions, where their meaning is not obvious. The date of diary entries is generally given in the text. Where further explanation is required the date is given in the footnotes, as are all the other sources.

My thanks go to John Barnie, who edited the text, to Olwen Fowler, who designed the book, and to the staff of Cambrian Printers, who printed it. The photography of the paintings from Winifred's collection is the work of Gareth Lloyd Hughes and Mark Davey of The National Library of Wales, and I would like also to thank those many other members of the staff of the National Library, and of the Glynn Vivian Art Gallery, who assisted me with my research, and with the practicalities of publication.

Finally, my thanks go to the Coombe-Tennant family for their generosity in making this book possible. Alexander Coombe-Tennant (1909-2003) first granted me access both to his mother's collection of pictures and to her letters, which he allowed me to reproduce and to quote in an earlier series of publications. He shared with me his memories of his mother, and his observations on her personality and life. Subsequently, Mark Coombe-Tennant has granted me continued access to the letters, and extended that access to include his grandmother's diaries, for which I am deeply grateful. Most importantly, my thanks go to Jenifer Coombe-Tennant, daughter-in-law of the central character of this book. Jenifer married Alexander Coombe-Tennant in 1954, and so knew Winifred during the last years of her life. Without Jenifer's enthusiasm, her generosity and her practical assistance, this book would not have been written and published. I look back with affection on many long conversations with her about Winifred, and to the discoveries about her life which we made together. I thank her for her support of my work over recent years, and for her continuing friendship, which I value highly.

Peter Lord
August 2007

Chapter One

TO THE GREAT WAR

By any standards Winifred Coombe Tennant had an unusual upbringing. It was shaped by her father's insatiable appetite for travel. George Edward Serocold Pierce-Serocold was brought up in Cambridgeshire but travelled widely throughout Europe as a child. He attended Eton College and then joined the Royal Navy, so that by the time he was twenty he had also visited China and west Africa. He then resigned his commission and went to Australia, where he made money as a sheep farmer. In 1862 he returned to England but immediately began to travel again. In Rome he met his first wife, Amy Richardson, daughter of a Swansea ship-owner, with whom he promptly returned to Australia. They then came back to Europe, and by 1871 there were four children. However, his wife died in childbirth in August 1872 at a family house, Tawelfa, at Langland Bay in the Gower Peninsula. Eighteen months later, in Sketty Church, he married his first wife's cousin, Mary Clarke Richardson, the daughter of Jeremiah Clarke Richardson of Derwen Fawr, Glamorgan. The couple departed on a continental tour without his children. On their return they lived at Rodborough Lodge, Stroud, an 'old manor house of Cotswold stone'. The only child of their marriage, Winifred Margaret, was born there on 1 November 1874.[1]

As a child Winifred lived in a bewildering succession of countries with no settled home. In 1877 her parents left Gloucestershire and

Unknown photographer,
George Edward Serocold Pierce-Serocold, 1908

10

moved to Langland Bay, which would become the most stable point of return for Winifred during the peripatetic childhood that ensued. In 1878 the family took a house in Bologne, where they lived until 1880. Winifred and her siblings attended a Catholic school and learnt to speak French. However, during this sojourn her father again took off, this time for an extensive tour of Portugal, Spain and north Africa. His travelling companion was the Rev. John Parker, whose abilities as an architectural draughtsman had already resulted in an important visual record of church buildings in Wales, in addition to his

records of English and continental buildings.[2]

In 1881 the family moved to Montreux, where they were based for three years, though they travelled widely in the meantime. At the end of this period they went first to London, then to Langland Bay, and finally to Clevedon in Bristol, where Winifred was left with two of her step-sisters, Violet Amy and Mildred. Her father and mother went round the world, via Australia and the United States of America. It is reported that at Clevedon 'Winifred felt sadly ill at ease for after her long sojourn on the Continent she felt herself something of a foreigner among her English schoolfellows'.[3] Subsequently, she was educated by governesses. In 1886, when Winifred was eleven, the family was established at Cherryhinton in Cambridgeshire, her father's ancestral home. In 1889, while still living there, she sat to a painter for the first of many times. He was Herbert Arnould Olivier, who had completed his training at the Royal Academy Schools a few years earlier, and was setting out upon what would become a moderately successful career. Not long after the painting of the portrait, Winifred's travels resumed. Following a period of ill health and a doctor's recommendation that she would benefit from a bracing climate, in January 1890 she was taken by her mother and father to Lausanne. They travelled on to the baths at Schwaldbach for Winifred to take the waters.

There followed an interlude at Torquay, from where the family left for Naples in 1892 to spend three years. By this time Winifred was twenty

H.A. Chapman,
Mary Clarke Richardson, c.1870

Herbert Arnould Olivier,
Winifred Coombe Tennant, 1889
Oil on canvas, 22×18

years old. The final episode in this story of extraordinary familial mobility took place in 1895. Winifred's father again departed for Australia, taking Violet, Mildred and their brother Edward with him. In their absence Winifred and her mother travelled in Italy, thence to Innsbruck and Munich, into Austria and back to Italy:

They descended to Chiavenna, and by Lake Como to Bellagio about the 16th September, where the Tennants, Mrs Tennant, her daughter Mrs Stanley, wife of the celebrated African explorer, and Mrs Tennant's only son were staying. After a few days Winifred became engaged to Mr Tennant.[4]

Winifred's father received the news in a letter from his wife which he collected at Suez, *en route* from Australia.

While such an unsettled early life does not appear conducive to the creation of a sense of security and identity in a child, in retrospect Winifred clearly valued highly her exposure to continental cultures, especially in France and in Italy. Her childhood left her with a strong sense of history, a love of visual art and music, and an international outlook. By the time she married she had first-hand experience of much of the canon of European high art, with which she had been engaged at a more intense level than that acquired by the average Grand Tourist of the eighteenth and nineteenth centuries. She had lived on the Continent and her observations of its cultures were facilitated by the ability to speak fluent French and Italian.

Winifred's father had not only led an extraordinary life but was gifted with the verbal and literary ability to pass on his experience. The effects of his story-telling went beyond the inculcation in his daughter of a romantic sense of the exotic. Some fundamental attitudes to life, which arose from his wide experience of cultures other than his own, clearly affected Winifred's beliefs and would inform her engagement in maturity with social, political and artistic matters. For instance, while on the Continent her father was exposed to strong anti-British sentiment during the Boer War and, perhaps in response to experiences of that kind,

12

Unknown photographer,
Charles Coombe Tennant, c.1895

his attitude to Imperial power was unusual for a man of his class. In 1906 he wrote, in a memoir of his life:

> *Where is the dreamed of peace and the hope of disbanding armies and navies? We have ten times the amount of men under arms in Europe now than we ever had in the Napoleonic wars. It is a strange idea that peace can only be obtained by every nation being armed to the teeth.*

International peace would become a central concern of Winifred's public life. Similarly, Winifred's attitude to the most fundamental questions about the meaning of human existence would carry a strong resonance of the view which her father expressed in closing his memoir:

> *To me the only explanation of human life, with all its joys and all its sorrows, is that it is an education to higher things, and when we pass beyond the Veil we shall know the reason 'Why?' of our earthly experience.*

George Pierce-Serocold rejoined his wife and Winifred at Naples on his way from Australia to England. Charles Coombe Tennant accompanied the party as they travelled through Switzerland, and stayed with the women alone as they took a detour to Paris. The family were united again in London, where Winifred married Charles on 12 December 1895 at St Margaret's Church, Westminster.

Charles Coombe Tennant was 22 years older than his bride. His home was Cadoxton Lodge, Neath, an elegant three-storey country house, essentially of the eighteenth century though older in origin and with architectural accretions of a later date. He was the third generation of Tennants to live there. His grandfather had been celebrated in the area as the builder of the Tennant Canal, an entrepreneurial venture whose initial success had been limited by the development of the railways, which took away much of its traffic.[5] However, George Tennant and his son, Charles, invested widely, and their estates and other interests provided the family with a substantial income, though one which was by no means on a par with that of the great industrial families of the period. By the time of Charles Coombe Tennant's marriage the family could mix socially with the squirearchy and gentry of the area but, equally, they could not have been considered entirely conventional. Charles Coombe Tennant's mother, Gertrude Barbara Collier, was an urbanite, who maintained a London home of some repute. Though English, she had grown up and lived largely in France until she was in her mid-twenties. In Paris she had moved in the most fashionable artistic circles, coming to know Gustave Flaubert, Alphonse Daudet and many others. Looking back on her long life Winifred later remarked that her mother-in-law 'to the last … retained a warm admiration for French ways of life and thought, the experiences of her early days having, indeed, stamped her whole personality with something of the charm and distinction of the great ladies of the *ancien régime*.'[6]

On moving to England Gertrude Collier married Charles Tennant, Liberal Member of Parliament for St Albans. Her husband died in 1873, but their London home at 2 Richmond Terrace, Whitehall, maintained its well-established position as the resort of an equivalent intellectual circle to the one within which she had moved in Paris. On the model of a Paris *salon* she entertained many prominent politicians, from Gladstone down. Mixing with them were eminent writers, who included Browning, Tennyson, Huxley, Herbert Spencer, George Moore and George Eliot, and the painters G.F. Watts, Burne-Jones and Whistler. By her marriage to Charles Coombe Tennant, Winifred gained access to this circle, as well as to the accumulated memories and experience of her mother-in-law. Her own continental orientation and extensive awareness of painting, music and literature enabled her to fit into such a sophisticated milieu, notwithstanding her youth. Moreover, in addition to the excitement of meeting her mother-in-law's circle, two of her husband's siblings were, in themselves, of great interest to her.

Dorothy Tennant had studied at the Slade School of Art and was established in London as a painter and illustrator. She drew for *The Quiver* and for the children's magazine *Little Folks*, specialising in depictions of street children. They were sufficiently popular for Cassell to publish a collection, in the introduction to which Dorothy sought to distance herself from artists motivated by the social reform movement, popularised by the work of Dickens:

Eveleen Tennant [Myers], *Dorothy Tennant*, 1890

Most of the pictures I had seen of ragged life appeared to me false and made up. They were all so deplorably piteous - pale, whining children with sunken eyes, holding up bundles of violets to heedless passers-by: dying match-girls, sorrowful water-cress girls, emaciated mothers clasping weeping babies. How was it, I asked myself, that the other side is so seldom represented? The merry, reckless, happy-go-lucky urchin; the tom-boy girl; the plump untidy mother dancing and tossing her ragged baby; who had given this side of London life?[7]

Dorothy Tennant [Stanley], *Despair*, 1880s Pencil, 5x4

Nevertheless, her observation of 'ragged life' was not entirely picturesque, and among her drawings are a number which stood closer to the emerging documentary tradition. Some, such as *Out of Work*, which was reproduced in the Cassell collection, clearly reflect the works of critical social commentary familiar from the illustrated newspapers of the 1860s and 70s.[8] Dorothy produced paintings in the same genre, one of which, *His First Offence*, painted the year after Winifred and she became sisters-in-law, achieved the great accolade, for a late Victorian painter, of purchase by Sir Henry Tate. In complete contrast, Dorothy also produced small, minutely painted female nudes in Classical settings.

16

Dorothy Tennant
[Stanley], *His First
Offence*, 1896
Oil on canvas, 25x14
Tate Gallery,
London

In 1890, Dorothy Tennant married the Welsh explorer Henry Morton Stanley. The wedding took place with great pomp in Westminster Abbey. The bride was 39 years old at the time. Six years later, in the first year of her brother Charles' marriage, Dorothy painted Winifred on the terrace at Cadoxton Lodge. The two women became friends as well as sisters-in-law, notwithstanding the fact that the painter was over twenty years older than the sitter. Winifred always referred to her as Dolly, and they spent much time together. The portrait may well have been painted on one of the visits Dorothy made to her family home in the company of her husband:

> *We spent many happy summer days at*
> *Cadoxton Lodge and took long walks together*
> *up the lovely Vale of Neath. Another favourite*
> *walk was up in the hills behind the village of*
> *Cadoxton - undulating hills of short, dry grass,*
> *where sheep browsed. We used to climb over low*
> *walls which divide the pasture lands. Stanley*
> *loved the quiet and loneliness of those hills.*
> *Yes, he cared for Wales.*[9]

A single anecdote survives to suggest the nature of Winifred's relationship with Stanley himself. Dorothy had been unwilling to leave her mother on her marriage, and had brought her husband to live with her at Richmond Terrace. This arrangement had the compensatory advantage of convenience for Stanley in the five years

Dorothy Tennant [Stanley], *Winifred Coombe Tennant*, 1896 Oil on canvas, 20x15

W.M. Chaffin, *Eveleen Tennant*, c.1880

during which he
was a Member of
Parliament. Winifred was
fond of recalling Stanley's part in
a conversation with her which took place there:

*I have lived many years and travelled much in
many quarters of the globe and I have come to
the conclusion that there is no more than five
per cent. of efficiency among human beings. And
I should put you into that five per cent.*[10]

Henry Morton Stanley died in 1904.
Winifred was present at his death, and
recorded her feelings in her diary:

*Oh this process of
dying, how bitter it is!
This dying by inches ... is
there any spring for human beings
... is there a beyond ... when the mechanism
breaks up does anything survive?*[11]

For Winifred, the posing of this large question
was more than a commonplace speculation
stimulated by proximity to the death of a relative
and a famous man. Her second sister-in-law,
Eveleen Tennant, had married Frederick William
Henry Myers, a Cambridge psychologist. In 1882
Myers had been among the founder members
of the Society for Psychical Research, a group

Eveleen Tennant [Myers], *Frederick Myers and Leo Myers*, early 1890s

Eveleen Tennant [Myers], *Adelaide Passingham*, early 1890s
National Portrait Gallery, London

interested in demonstrating by scientific method the continued existence of the individual after bodily death. Myers was a president of the Society and its most prominent theorist, writing works that attracted widespread attention among the intellectual and scientific communities of the period. He died in 1901 and it may have been that event which brought Winifred to the point of joining the Society in the same year. She left in 1905, but rejoined and became a crucially

important participant in its work from 1908 until her death. However, of more immediate relevance when Winifred joined the Tennant family in 1895 was probably the fact that Eveleen was a photographer.[12] She produced portrait photographs of distinction, no doubt initially gaining access through the good offices of her mother to the great and the good who sat for her. Among them were Gladstone, Joseph Chamberlain, Arthur Balfour and Robert Browning. Eveleen also produced whimsical costume portraits, a popular genre in the period, and studies of beautiful young women. No photograph of Winifred by Eveleen has been identified, but even if she did not sit to her sister-in-law Winifred was certainly familiar with her work.[13]

Winifred's first child, Christopher, was born in 1897, but given a liberal provision of governesses the event does not seem to have constrained her social life. Based on a reading of Winifred's diary for these years, Signe Toksvig concluded that in the last years of the Victorian age 'Travelling, racing, fashionable dinners and doings were part of her life. She disliked the country in winter':

*How can one wilfully pass one day in
the country in England in winter! It is the
abomination of desolation ... Tomorrow
I go to London, thank Heaven!*[14]

In 1901 Winifred cruised on the yacht *Aphrodite* with its owner Sir George Goldie, a most celebrated Victorian Imperialist. He was regarded as the founder of Nigeria, and had been that country's governor until the previous year. Sir George was nearly thirty years Winifred's senior, but promptly fell in love with her. However, his sense of decorum prevailed and he soon fled from her life. Winifred continued to travel extensively, often in the company of Christopher. She was given to strong enthusiasms for places with artistic resonances. In 1905 Robert

Unknown photographer, *Winifred Coombe Tennant with her son Christopher, her Mother (Mary Richardson), and her grandfather (Jeremiah Clarke Richardson), at Cadoxton Lodge,* 1898

H.A. Chapman, *Winifred Coombe Tennant and a Friend in Welsh Costume,* date uncertain

Louis Stevenson's villa at Hyères, where he had written the *Child's Garden of Verses*, made a considerable impression on her.[15] Equally, she was impressed by the historical resonance of the places in Wales to which she was introduced after her marriage. Not far from Winifred's new home at Cadoxton Lodge was the ancient house of Aberpergwm, the home of the Williams family, reputed to have been the last in Wales to keep a family bard.[16] Subsequently it had been the home of Maria Jane Williams, the collector of folk songs and close friend of Lady Llanover. Maria's brother, William Williams, had also been a leading figure in Welsh cultural revival at the beginning of the nineteenth century. Both had died within living memory of the members of the family who Winifred came to know. Their values were carried forward by the younger generation, and their continued identification with tradition exposed Winifred to rooted notions of national culture:

> *It was a large and pleasant house inhabited by Morgan Stuart Williams and his wife, a daughter of William Herbert of Clytha, in Monmouthshire, and their family of four sons and two daughters. I remember my first visit there and my delight at finding the mother and daughters dressed in Welsh costumes made from home-spun wool clipped from their own sheep and dyed in varied colours with vegetable dyes. The boys were wearing kilts of the same materials.[17]*

Under the influence of Mrs Williams, from about 1898 Winifred too wore Welsh dress at Cadoxton every morning until after lunch, and continued to do so for ten years – 'apron, skirt, bed-gown, fichu'. [21 June 1924] The young Vicar of Aberpergwm was also much engaged

Unknown photographer, *Cadoxton Lodge*, c.1900

with notions of national tradition. In 1909 he played the part of St. David in the National Pageant created on an enormous scale in Cardiff by Owen Rhoscomyl.[18] In the absence of the diary which Winifred kept for those years, the detailed record of her reaction to life at Aberpergwm is lost, but the evidence of her subsequent attitudes, and occasional retrospective observations, suggest that the deep respect for Welsh cultural tradition which she encountered there had a profound influence upon her.

Winifred rapidly developed an affection for Cadoxton Lodge, evinced by many lyrical descriptions of the nearby countryside and seashore, the house itself and its gardens:

The house is surrounded by one of those old-world gardens where old-fashioned flowers lift year by year familiar faces in the same spot. The large walled kitchen garden is not so much an adjunct to as an integral part of the flower garden, from the fact that a terrace walk some two hundred yards long stretches past the house and on through the kitchen garden to a bright patch of flowers and an ivy-canopied seat. The house faces south, wreathed in vine and rambling rose ...[19]

Unknown photographer,
Daphne with Charles Coombe Tennant, 1907

Inside the house, relations with her husband were not always easy. On some important matters of principle Charles Coombe Tennant stood with Winifred, in particular on the question of gender. Winifred could say honestly and inclusively that hers was 'a home where belief in the equality of the sexes, and the equality of opportunity which forms its natural corollary, had always been an article of faith'.[20] On the other hand, there were tensions on matters of practical politics. Describing the home in which Christopher grew up, Winifred remarked that 'political discussions were part of the atmosphere ... partly due to the fact that while his Father leaned towards a Toryism of the old school, his Mother was what a friend described, more in sorrow than in wrath, as "a fanatical Liberal"'.[21] Nevertheless, she and Charles achieved a *modus vivendi*, even if it was secured increasingly on the basis of the pursuit of interests which did not substantially overlap. Their divergence was sharply intensified by the consequences of two personal tragedies which disrupted the pattern of their existence, and which would dominate the rest of Winifred's life.

At Cadoxton in January 1907 Winifred gave birth to a daughter, whom she called Daphne. Eighteen months later the child died suddenly.[22] The trauma of this event was manifested by Winifred in two ways. Firstly, she was thrown into a deep depression from which she never fully recovered, but of which only a few of the people in her circle were aware. Periods of depression alternated with bursts of optimism, as her experience of overwhelming physical lethargy alternated with energetic activity, sometimes on a daily basis. The long public life into which she entered at the end of the first decade of the twentieth century represented a remarkable triumph of will over the debilitating effects of depression.

Secondly, under the influence of those of her circle who were involved in psychical research, she attempted to contact her lost daughter. To her surprise and, at first, bewilderment, this she believed she could do. Winifred was able to enter a trance state in which she wrote down communications which emanated, she became convinced, from the living spirits of the departed. In time, Winifred came to be regarded as the most important psychic medium of her period, and the chief subject of study by members of the Society for Psychical Research, whose leading light, Oliver Lodge, she met first in 1909. In January 1911 she was introduced to another prominent figure in the field, Gerald Balfour, brother of the Prime Minister, Arthur Balfour. The Balfours' sister, Elinor, had married Henry Sidgwick, first president of the Society. Winifred's activities were observed and analysed in detail by these prominent theorists of psychic phenomena, and by other mediums with whom Winifred corresponded. However, the most frequent of her sitters (that is, the observers who sat with her in her trance state) was Gerald Balfour, to whom Winifred became deeply attached. Their

Unknown photographer, *Gerald Balfour*, c.1925

relationship would last until his death. Notwithstanding the often daily frequency of her trances and her other, shorter visionary experiences, the details of this part of her life were known only to a small inner group of colleagues in the Society for Psychical Research, and to her husband and first child, Christopher. Winifred's psychical experiences were extensively published, but her identity was hidden behind the pseudonym Mrs Willett – a name which she did not much like.[23]

Winifred reacted to her private tragedy and depression with the decision to become engaged in public affairs, or service, as she thought of it. Her decision was first manifested by her identification with the campaign for women's suffrage, a cause to which she became firmly committed in 1910. In that year she met Emmeline Pankhurst at Fisher's Hill in Surrey, the home of Gerald and Betty Balfour. 'I honour her and wish her God-speed', she reflected in her diary.[24] After attending a meeting in November 1911 at the Albert Hall, which was addressed by Chrystobel Pankhurst and several of her colleagues, Winifred came to the conclusion that militancy was counter-productive. Nevertheless, her views on the issue were passionately felt:

Read Fabian tract on prisons as affecting women prisoners ... Many thoughts [on] man's inhumanity to man and still more man's inhumanity to women. I feel more than ever the vital necessity of women having the vote if material righteousness is ever to be reached. Women should sit on the Prison Commission, should form an element in all magisterial benches in cases in which women are concerned. Public opinion must be aroused. One half of the world must have it driven into them how the other half lives. Sheltered lives must be disturbed mentally and the pain must bring to birth a new state of things. Nothing can be done without women's power, insight, co-operation ... [17 March 1912]

Two years later she gave her first public speech, and in June 1915 she was elected to the executive of the National Union of Women's Suffrage Societies.[25] Throughout the Great War she worked closely with the leading figures of the movement, notably Millicent Fawcett and Eleanor Rathbone. Winifred shared many of the broader feminist ideas of these women. In particular, frequently she expressed the view, especially associated with Rathbone, that motherhood should be recognised

Unknown photographer, *Christopher Tennant at Cadoxton Lodge*, August 1917

as a service to society, and that women must be enabled both to bring up children and to engage fully in public affairs. Winifred's first identification with feminist ideas, immediately prior to, and during, the war, coincided with the years in which she was a mother to small children. She gave birth to her third child, Alexander, in 1909, and her fourth, Augustus Henry, in 1913:

These days spent in his [Augustus Henry's] company, looking into his starry eyes, make me feel the appalling European war - Servia running in blood, innumerable atrocities to the whole Armenian race, massacre of mothers and children, Belgium, everywhere slaughter and destruction - and my work in life giving life and the human body - maternity - and then the contrast of this frenzy of bloodshed, cruelty and hate. Say what you will, that is a man's world and maternity is a woman's. These horrors could not be in a world where women were equal in stature and power to men and the unit was the human being, regardless of sex. Women must enter into public life and wrestle there with the male blindness. [29 November 1915]

It was the great misfortune of Winifred's eldest son, Christopher, who was known affectionately to her as 'Cruff', to have been born into the generation of children whose lives were shaped by the Great War. He was sixteen years old when the war began and so he chose to go to Sandhurst rather than to Cambridge, as he had wished. He joined the Welsh Guards and crossed to France in August 1917. He was killed in action at Ypres less than a month later. His death was no less devastating to Winifred for the fact that it was expected. She had discussed the strong possibility of this outcome with him before he left and had agreed with him that, should he be killed, he would seek to communicate with her from the other world. The origins of her extraordinary relationship with her son were documented by Winifred herself and by Oliver Lodge in the biography entitled *Christopher, A Study in Human Personality*, which was published in the last year of the war. In her own contribution to the book, Winifred made plain her belief that it was possible for the living to communicate with the dead and vice versa, and strongly suggested her own ability to establish such communication. Nevertheless, although the book was widely reviewed in 1918, this aspect of Winifred's life does not appear to

have attracted great public attention, perhaps because of the considerable number of bereaved parents who reported similar experiences in the period.[26]

In public, the most apparent outcome of Winifred's response to the war was her campaigning for the peace movement. After a meeting of the Suffrage Union in Birmingham in 1915 she stated her belief that 'God knows I am a Pacifist heart and soul'. [17 June 1915] She railed against 'The crimes which are being committed against conscientious objectors, and scarcely a voice lifted. No fair play anywhere, and in Ireland rebels shot in cold blood after "court martials", while Carson, the arch-rebel sits in the House. Who would fight for such a country'. [4 May 1916] At a political level the idea that small nations like Wales and Ireland might stand for peace against the great empires appealed strongly to her imagination. Her commitment grew to Welsh home rule and the strengthening of what she regarded as the particular cultural characteristics of the nation. More deeply and personally, she felt that Christopher's death had been for Wales. Despite scholastic exile in Winchester, her son had become deeply attached to the idea that Wales was his country. He identified himself as Welsh in a way in which earlier generations of the Tennant family had not. Among Winifred's most abiding memories of him was his appearance in the Gorsedd circle at the proclamation of the National Eisteddfod at Neath in 1917, shortly before his departure for France. For Winifred, displays of national sentiment, and in particular Gorsedd ceremonies in connection with the Eisteddfod, would always be deeply resonant of her lost son. Her support for Welsh political development, and for the cultural continuity of the nation through art and craft, was certainly, in part, an expression of her commitment to what she believed were Christopher's ideals.

The details of Winifred's psychic life would only occasionally have direct implications for her patronage of painters. However, the beliefs and principles which underlay her pursuit of psychic phenomena were the source also of her belief in the spirituality of art. The idea that artists had special gifts of access to the spiritual domain, and that they could mediate it for others, coupled with her strong identification with Wales, was fundamental to her patronage.

Winifred Coombe Tennant's visits to Italy and, occasionally, to Germany during her adolescence had occurred within recent memory of the *Risorgimento* and of German unification. The idea that the bond between a people, its language and its history should be expressed in all aspects of national life, from art to government, was an important part of the European intellectual ambience of her period. Because of the loss of her early diaries it is unclear to what extent the idea had impressed itself upon her before her marriage, at a European level. However, through her mother-in-law, she subsequently gained access

to leading figures in the Liberal Party and to the liberal-minded establishment in general, within which circles the idea was alive and contentious in a British context. Although it was toward the end of the active pre-war campaign for Welsh home rule, from 1895 Winifred was in a position to hear informed talk about the place of national groups within Britain and the British Empire, and to witness the political consequences of the increasing importance of the issue, both in London and in Wales. During the last Gladstone administration of 1892-4 the Liberals had come under pressure from a group of young Members of Parliament, elected from 1886, who were strong proponents of home rule for Wales. Their leader was Tom Ellis, and his most energetic supporter was David Lloyd George. The evidence of her own reflections, although written after the Great War, suggests that Winifred had, indeed, been impressed by the ideas of these two men in particular. In 1921, while working on a speech about home rule, she noted that 'Always in speaking on that subject I feel as though standing in an Apostolic Succession, Tom Ellis in spirit beside me, young Lloyd George of the 80s and 90s ...' [23 January 1921] The expression of such a sentiment placed Winifred firmly in the mainstream of the pre-war Nationalist consciousness.

A collection of the speeches and addresses of Tom Ellis, published posthumously in 1912 in English (and so available to Winifred) presented the breadth of the national agenda with which she identified herself in public. Prominent among the issues of concern to Ellis was art, upon which subject he had addressed the Cymmrodorion Society in 1897. In the context of an affirmation of 'a season of awakening' in Wales, Ellis nevertheless observed:

I think one may say at the start - and one admits it with sorrow as well as with frankness - that not the most patriotic of us can claim for Wales the possession of a native school of art, as is possessed in other small countries which have obtained and enjoyed the priceless gift of self-government. I remember well in 1887 spending a few days in the great Exhibition at Paris. I have forgotten most of what I saw there: I have a vague recollection of the crowd and of watching many who came from the various provinces of France, and a vague recollection of the enormous wealth exhibited, the wealth of industry and of art and of commerce and of the various activities of the great country of France. But the one thing which stands out in my memory and which, I think, will stand out so long as I live, is the fact that, not alone had the great countries, - France, Germany, Great Britain, - their separate rooms for the exhibition of the products of their art, but that Denmark, Servia, Greece, and countries very much the same as Wales in population and in ordinary material wealth, had each one of them, even distant Finland, separate rooms in that great Exhibition, in order to show, as show they did, the splendid products of the

Unknown photographer, *The Unveiling of the Statue of Tom Ellis at Bala*, 1903. Seated on the platform, from left, the father and son of Tom Ellis, and David Lloyd George. In white coat at foot of statue, the sculptor, William Goscombe John. The National Library of Wales.

native art of each country. I wondered then, as I often wonder whenever I think of these nationalities now, whether it is possible that in the times to come our own country may claim a place in the galleries which, from time to time, will show the collective activities of the nations of the world.[27]

The belief of Tom Ellis that there was no 'native school' of art in Wales reflected the received wisdom of the period, and lay like a dark shadow behind national rhetoric. If national characteristics arose from the racial distinctness of the people, as was generally believed, they should manifest themselves naturally in the style and content of the work of a nation's artists. The absence of art might be construed, therefore, as revealing a congenital inadequacy in the people, a condition which undermined the case for nationhood. Such inadequacies demonstrated that the Welsh would always be a dependent appendage of the fully rounded nationality of the English.[28] In response, Ellis and his like-minded contemporaries pointed to a history of individual native genius in painting, sculpture, architecture and design in the persons of Richard Wilson and John Gibson, both Welsh-born, and Burne-Jones, Inigo Jones, and Owen Jones, all deemed to be of Welsh blood. However, in two respects the thinking of Tom Ellis was unusual, and marked the beginning of a more creative reaction to the perceived problem of Welsh art. Firstly, he linked the apparent absence of a native school of art to the fact that Wales lacked its own government and, by implication, associated structures of power and patronage. Secondly, he took a broader view of visual culture than that of those for whom high art alone was the definitive factor in determining national worthiness. He turned his attention in an affirmative spirit to the domestic visual culture of Welsh people, manifested in their building and in their crafts. Ellis recognised early the emergence of a stream of thought that would become central in discussions of Welsh visual culture throughout the period of Winifred's own engagement with the issue.

In some ways, the broad view of visual culture, as opposed to an exclusive concentration on high art, sat squarely within contemporary English ideas, and those of William Morris and the Arts and Crafts Movement in particular. The assertion of the dignity of the common people in their labour, and the reaction against what was regarded by many socialist thinkers as the dehumanising influence of industrial production, inspired Ellis. To his mind there was a close linkage between the arts and both the spiritual and social progress of the common people. Following Ellis, Winifred, too, found in the message of William Morris 'a special significance for industrial Wales at this time of revival in national art and literature':

For him art and labour were never divorced. He saw in the art of a people the expression of its moral values and social ideals, and it was because he found himself in a world where ugliness reigned supreme, where the craftsman was entirely cut off from the artist by the interposition of the capitalist with his machinery, and men toiled in joyless labour to produce things which carried with them no single joy-giving element to the consumer, that he passed from aesthetic discontent to a deep discontent with the whole social fabric of a world in which such things could be accepted as inevitable.[29]

It did not escape the attention of Tom Ellis and other Welsh intellectuals in the period that William Morris was of Welsh parentage. Furthermore, it comes as no surprise to learn that Ellis and his contemporary, O.M. Edwards, had attended lectures given by John Ruskin while they were students at Oxford. Ellis, especially, held Ruskin in the highest regard, habitually referring to him as 'the Master'. Nevertheless, in their thinking Ellis and Edwards used the ideas of Morris and Ruskin to reinforce a particularly Welsh construct, which presented the common people (and especially the rural and Welsh-speaking common people) as the foundation of the new Wales – *Cymru Fydd* or Young Wales – which they promoted. *Cymru Fydd* was formally initiated as a movement in 1886, modelled on the Young Ireland movement. After the Great War, Winifred would become closely associated with several of those who had been its most active promoters, notably Beriah Gwynfe Evans, the secretary from 1895. The common people, known as *Y Werin*, who were the bedrock of this concept of nationhood, were characterised in particular by their religiosity and their belief in education as the means to spiritual and material progress. The concept of *Y Werin* would achieve the status of a new national foundation myth in the early twentieth century, a myth which Winifred internalised thoroughly and which guided her art patronage until the end of her life. Tom Ellis himself was its greatest embodiment. He had risen by his own efforts from the mountain smallholding of his father to the post of chief government whip in London. His death in 1899, only four years after arriving at the pinnacle of his career, and when still a young man, facilitated the development of the idea of his martyrdom for Wales. Winifred's perception of her position as standing in 'an Apostolic succession', when writing on home rule, the central plank of the political platform of Tom Ellis, was more than the private expression of a person much given

to religious metaphor. It clearly reflected Welsh public rhetoric on the subject of Tom Ellis as the apotheosis of *Y Werin*, just as her underlying sympathy for his ideas reflected her frequent reading of Ruskin.

In the early years of the twentieth century, the aspiration of Tom Ellis to address the perceived deficiency of the visual culture of Wales was taken up by a number of cultural nationalists, most notably the writer Thomas Matthews. His essays in O.M. Edwards' magazine *Cymru* engaged with contemporary Welsh painting and sculpture in depth. These writings were not directly accessible to Winifred (who did not learn to read or speak Welsh fluently) though Matthews did publish some work in English, notably his biography of John Gibson in 1911.[30] In *Cymru*, Matthews promoted Welsh painters and sculptors, especially a new generation mostly emanating from the urban south of the country, prominent among whom were William Goscombe John and Christopher Williams. On Matthews' early death in 1916, Williams wrote to O.M. Edwards of him in terms which not only paid personal tribute to the writer but which encapsulated the spirit of the age. An important aspect of that spirit was the internationalism of the nationalists who were involved in visual culture, an outlook wholeheartedly shared by Winifred:

We have lost one of the best, and genuine nationalists. I feel the loss of Tom Matthews keenly. Perhaps I knew him as few did. He always had an enthusiasm for Wales. When we were in Morocco or Holland, it was the contrast of those countries and peoples to Wales and the Welsh that interested him, - the similarities or differences of their manners and customs, their poetry and art and music, and he always attempted to get what he thought was good out there, and see if it were not possible that Wales should have it too. He was always striking out for fresh soil, and had he lived, I believe, he would have struck it in such a way that others at any rate would build well on it, even if he would not himself. It was the Wales that you and I are interested in, that was his; not clubroom - whether in London or elsewhere, but the love of the mountains and the woods, the sunshine and storm of the people's lives, the something that is and will be Hen Wlad fy Nhadau when ambitions and honours are forgotten ...[31]

By 1911, fifteen years after Winifred made her home in Wales, and at the peak of Mathews' critical activity, Welsh artists were flourishing as never before. Not only were there painters and sculptors practising successfully in London, but also it could be said that for the first time there was a Welsh art world. Resident painters were at work in several parts of the country, most notably at the two centres of Cardiff and Betws-y-coed, and they were in touch with each other. Albeit largely emanating from one writer, there was art criticism, published in a national journal, which attempted to notice all contemporary activity.

There were national art institutions in the form of the Royal Cambrian Academy, founded in 1882, and the Art Department of the National Museum of Wales, founded in 1907. The first attempt at a comprehensive historical survey of Welsh art, *Welsh Painters, Engravers, and Sculptors*, was being compiled by T. Mardy Rees and would be published in 1912. On Winifred's own doorstep, the Glynn Vivian Art Gallery in Swansea had opened its doors the previous year. Its first curator, William Grant Murray, had been appointed in 1909 as Principal at the School of Art, which he would transform into an institution of high repute. From its opening Winifred would be a regular visitor to the gallery, and after the war Murray would become her closest associate and friend in the Welsh art world.

Of the artists themselves, by 1911 the sculptor William Goscombe John had been commissioned extensively to make portraits of establishment figures, and had produced a series of large scale public memorials, notably that to Tom Ellis in Bala. In Cardiff, Winifred thought his equestrial statue of Viscount Tredegar 'splendid' when she saw it in 1914. Most importantly for national self-respect in the period, Goscombe John had achieved recognition in England. His impressive career was crowned by a knighthood, conferred at the Investiture of the Prince of Wales at Caernarfon. John designed the regalia for the ceremony and his younger contemporary, Christopher Williams, painted a large group portrait of the event.[32] For the majority of nationalists, who saw Welsh revival and the achievement of home rule from within the tradition of Tom Ellis, the Investiture was a positive event, which acknowledged the place of Wales as one of a family of nations in the British Empire. Williams' evocation of the spirit of the last native Prince of Wales in his *Wales Awakening*, painted in the same year as the Investiture, did not seem inconsistent with this view. This most ambitious of all images of national revival was based on the idea that Gwenllian, daughter of Llywelyn, had not died in the late thirteenth century, but merely slept, to awake when Wales itself stirred. In another genre, but also self-consciously national, Carey Morris recently had painted *The Welsh Weavers*. His subject was contemporary but old-fashioned rural life among the *Gwerin*, so much celebrated by Tom Ellis. After training in Carmarthen and London, Morris had chosen to work at Newlyn in Cornwall, which was, by this time, more fashionable among the avant-garde than the older artists' colony at Betws-y-coed. Nevertheless, the leading light of the painters of the Conwy Valley, Clarence Whaite, was still at work there. Whaite had been the central figure in the emergence of the Welsh art world. He had been elected the first President of the Royal Cambrian Academy in 1885 and provided the main link between the activity of the painters working in the Conwy Valley and the artists centred in Cardiff. Whaite's colleagues in the Academy, T.H. Thomas and the architect Edwin Seward, had been prominent in the failed attempt to establish its headquarters in Cardiff. Following the failure, both men had turned their attention to the successful promotion of a National Museum in the city.[33]

In his essays Thomas Matthews drew attention both to the Cardiff artists and to the landscape tradition at Betws-y-coed. Many of the painters there, like Whaite himself, had not been born in Wales, a fact which had caused Tom Ellis some difficulty a decade earlier, given the contemporary understanding that national schools of art should arise from the expression of congenital characteristics, rather than from cultural empathy. In 1897 Ellis had noted:

> *... the change which has come over Wales in one respect during the last thirty or forty years in the fact that artists - not, I am sorry to say, as a rule Welsh artists but artists from outside - have, from time to time, lived and settled down in Wales in order to interpret the life and scenery of Wales. My feeling with regard to them is one rather of sadness that the interpretation of the beauty of the landscape and of the life of Wales should be left to artists from outside, and that their products should be for a public outside Wales. Their pictures do not pass through the heart or mind of Wales, and this must be so, until we have a municipal gallery or galleries, or national gallery or galleries, where the products of these artists, who have seen the loveliness of Wales, can be exhibited for the wise enjoyment of the Welsh people.*[34]

The point made by Ellis was not that the pictures were un-Welsh as a consequence of the ethnic origins of the painters, but that they failed to infiltrate the national consciousness because of the absence of what might be described as art infrastructure. The generation of Thomas Matthews would begin to address that problem. Nevertheless, they did not abandon a residual adherence to the linkage between race, culture and landscape. Matthews was often at pains to point out the ancestral association with Wales of painters such as Benjamin Williams Leader, born in Worcester of distant Welsh descent. Where there was no such association he tended to resort to a mystical Celticism to blur the issue, as in the case of David Cox, or Dafydd Coch, as he would have it. Furthermore, his writing was characterised by frequent lyrical suggestions of a direct association between what he saw as the godly purity of the mountain landscape of north Wales and the character of the people who had lived in it since time immemorial, as it seemed to him. At first in the uplands of her own part of south Wales, and later, with even greater emotional potency, in the mountains of north Wales, Winifred Coombe Tennant made the same association between mountain landscape, godly purity, and the Welsh nation. To look at the mountain landscape was to look at the goodness of creation, and so to experience closeness to God. Its quality of natural grandeur, unsullied by human corruption, had been defined by generations of painters. The virtues of the common people, projected as the archetypal virtues of the nation as a whole, arose as a result of their closeness to the landscape.

Welsh writers placed great emphasis on the morality of the common people, which was implied in the pictures of David Cox and Clarence Whaite.[35] O.M. Edwards was passionate in expressing his appreciation of the virtues of *Y Werin*:

> *In the loneliness of my meditation I rejoice to think of the common people of Wales, and I thank God for them, - for their faithfulness and their honesty, for their desire to do that which is right, for their love of thought, for their correctness of opinion, for the tenderness of their feelings and the strength of their determination ...*[36]

Even when writing in praise of landscape paintings in which the people were scarcely apparent, Thomas Matthews made liberal use of images of godliness and cleansing, often reinforcing his views with the authority of bursts of poetry: '*O llawer paradwysaidd lyn/A olcha draed y creigiau hyn*' – 'Oh! the many lakes of paradise/Which wash the feet of these crags'. Eifion Wyn was a particularly fruitful source of such images. In his poem '*Crefyddolder Cymru*' the poet tightly bound together the people, the mountains and godliness:

> *Yn egwyddorion yr Efengyl gu*
> *Mor hyddysg ydynt ei thrigolion hi!*
> *Y gair Efengyl yw y cyntaf bron*
> *A ddysgir iddynt dan fynyddau hon ...*

In the principles of the dear Gospel
Her inhabitants are so learned!
The word Gospel is almost the first
Which is taught them under these mountains ...

For O.M. Edwards, Tom Ellis and Thomas Matthews, the mountains were a metaphor for the soul of the nation. Along with countless other nationalists, Winifred Coombe Tennant absorbed the idea which they had expressed with such power. When Edwards died in 1920, Winifred would note his death with the words 'a great Welshman, God bless him!'. [17 May 1920] The following year, at Cadoxton School, on St. David's Day, she unveiled a portrait of him, which she had donated, remarking in her diary how well she remembered her initial sighting of him at an Eisteddfod. When she visited Snowdonia for the first time, she was predisposed to understand her intense emotional reaction to the place in precisely his terms.

In 1911 most of the painters of this landscape who were celebrated by Thomas Matthews were growing old. However, even as he wrote in *Cymru* his lyrical celebrations of Clarence Whaite and Benjamin Williams Leader, the much younger Augustus John and his friend J.D. Innes were painting the same mountain landscape in new ways. Both these young painters were dividing their time between Wales and France, where they were in touch with the latest trends in painting. Indeed, John had met Picasso as early as 1904. In

1911 Matthews certainly knew of Augustus John. He and Winifred became aware of his new work, and that of Innes, at about that time as a result of the exhibitions of their pictures at the Chenil Gallery in London, which caused a stir in the English art world. Winifred did not meet John until much later, and it seems unlikely that Matthews ever met him, but he responded in print to John's pictures within three years of the Chenil Gallery exhibitions:

There is nothing more difficult than understanding the work of Augustus John - but the best way to understand it is to see that he is trying to protest against the smooth and finished style of academic painting, and instead give us painting in its bare simplicity ... Simplicity is his aim, his slogan 'Let us be as children'... In his romantic protest he tries to paint with the simplicity of primitive art.[37]

Important as the work of John and Innes may have been in the context of the English art world, in Wales it had limited implications.[38] It was the work of Evan Walters, a still younger painter, which more accurately predicted the direction that the visual culture would take, and which would most immediately affect Winifred. Again, in that remarkably fruitful year of 1911, the work of Walters attracted critical attention for the first time. Writing for a local audience in the Swansea newspaper the *Cambria Daily Leader*, an equally youthful critic, John Davies Williams, drew attention to the exploration of 'A new artistic idea!':

Not that all these water colours and oils that picture the [Gower] peninsula are not interesting: only that we are getting very used to them, and just a little tired of them.

Right among them is a painting of a pit head - the familiar lines of Cefn Cyfelach! And not far away is another of Tirdonkin Colliery, and another of The Night Shift at the Boilers ... Evan J. Walters is going to make a name for himself ...[39]

Such radical subject matter was difficult for the older Welsh establishment to embrace. At root, it was industrialisation that drove the national revival, but to many nationalists it represented Paradise Lost, the antithesis of the mountains of Snowdonia. Art might only act as an antidote to, or as a means of escape from, what they regarded as its dehumanising ugliness. Speaking in 1912 on behalf of an Eisteddfod committee in his home town of Maesteg, Christopher Williams reminded his audience that 'Man does not live by bread alone':

It was with the full knowledge of the meaning of this phrase that they had attempted to bring art into their colliery districts to help those who toiled hard for their living in the bowels of the earth to realise and partake of the beauties and glories of the world.[40]

Williams could not see industrial society in positive terms and it entered his work only as social criticism. In 1911 he had completed the large painting *Why?*, depicting 'the outcasts of society sleeping under the electric light with Charring Cross bridge and the trams in the background'.[41] Two years later Williams was represented by this picture and by his *Ceridwen* at the 'Exhibition of Works by Certain Modern Artists of Welsh Birth or Extraction' organised by the new National Museum. *Why?* was the only work in the exhibition which suggested the existence of urban or industrial society.

The creation of the National Museum in 1907, and within it a Department of Art, seemed at the time to go a long way towards meeting the aspiration of Tom Ellis for a National Gallery. The Museum's first two exhibitions, held in 1913, defined its sense of purpose and its methodology.[42] The opening exhibition comprised loans from private collections, including that of Gwendoline and Margaret Davies of Llandinam, which provided the most famous names – Corot, Millet, Manet and Whistler among them. It was the first occasion on which the late-nineteenth-century French works, still considered radical, had been shown in Wales. The sisters' collecting of such pictures was in full swing, having begun only five years earlier with the purchase of two works by Corot. Hugh Blaker, their art adviser, was among the exhibition organisers. The second exhibition, of works by 'Certain Modern Artists of Welsh Birth or Extraction', expressed the prevalent idea that ethnicity rather than cultural empathy or commitment to working in Wales defined a Welsh artist. Thus Benjamin Williams Leader, who worked for only a few years in Wales, was represented by virtue of his Welsh ancestry, but Clarence Whaite, who had lived over half a century in the country and had made an outstanding contribution to its visual culture, was not. In the illustrious company of Watts and Burne-Jones, the works of some younger artists were shown, but Augustus John, whose reputation as a leader of the avant-garde was at its height, was included only at the insistence of the influential figure of Howard de Walden. The works representing John had all been shown at the celebrated Chenil Gallery exhibitions.

In January 1914, in its review of the Cardiff exhibition of Welsh art, the first issue of the magazine *The Welsh Outlook* established an attitude to art consistent with its wider modernising inclinations by devoting more space to the works of Augustus John than to those of any other artist. Winifred probably read the review, and was certainly familiar with a subsequent group of essays in the magazine about visual culture, written or encouraged by the editor, Thomas Jones. In the tradition of Tom Ellis, Jones set the discussion of visual culture on the national agenda, and related it closely to the discussion of social issues. However, he chose not to concentrate on the presentation of new Welsh art, as O.M. Edwards had done in *Cymru* through the writings of Thomas Matthews. Jones preferred to draw attention to work from elsewhere, which he believed to have particular relevance to the lives

of the common people of Wales and which might provide appropriate models for aspiring Welsh artists. In particular he presented for the first time to a Welsh public the work of Belgian Realist painters and sculptors, notably Laermans and Meunier. Jones was driven to do this partly because he was not aware of Welsh artists who addressed what he considered to be the appropriate agenda, but also as a consequence of his relationship with the Davies sisters, whose brother, David, funded his magazine. At the outbreak of the war the sisters had despatched Jones to organise the evacuation of Belgian artists to Wales. *The Welsh Outlook* had raised public awareness of the presence of these artists and had suggested the possible improvement they might make to the 'deplorably backward condition' of painting and sculpture in Wales.[43]

The congruence between the artistic, social and political agenda of *The Welsh Outlook* and that of Winifred was very close. Its supporters 'rejected the old-fashioned Welsh Liberal consensus and aimed at promoting credible alternatives to the militant ideas of the extreme members of the Labour movement in industrial south Wales. In effect they hoped to preserve what they saw as the worthwhile elements in Welsh society, its culture, its Christianity, and link them to the new ideas of social reform'.[44] Winifred was involved as a contributor to the magazine from its first year of publication. She met the editor, Thomas Jones, when she addressed a suffrage meeting at Barry in July 1914. Jones drove her home, and

I n 1911, that remarkably creative year for Welsh visual culture, Winifred became aware of an unusually talented student at Swansea School of Art. Frank Alford was from Neath, and had begun his tuition at the School three years earlier, at the age of only twelve. Winifred invited him to Cadoxton Lodge:

For Frank, at the age of fifteen, being summoned to Cadoxton Lodge for a first meeting with her was something of an ordeal; he later related that he was so nervous that as he was shown into her impressive drawing room, he held out his hand, blurted out 'How do you do Mr Alford?', slipped on a rug and slid towards her flat on his back.[45]

Neither Alford's career nor his relationship with Winifred was fatally damaged by this inauspicious beginning. Winifred followed his progress to the St. John's Wood School of Art in London, where George Murray, brother of William Grant Murray, his teacher at Swansea, was Principal. Early in 1915 she inspected a ceiling decoration which he had painted at the Castle Hotel in Neath and in July she commissioned him to paint her portrait. 'It looks well', she noted. 'It makes me look older than I am and it doesn't flatter me and my eyes are larger – but it is a pleasant sort of picture and I am well satisfied with it'. It was her first act of specifically Welsh patronage, and one which set the tone for the forty years of encouragement of young painters which ensued.[46]

in the car she 'praised *The Welsh Outlook* quite unconscious that he was connected with it'. [18 July 1914] They talked all the way to Neath, and Jones commissioned the first of her many contributions to his magazine, on a particularly pertinent subject. She was to review Arthur Clutton-Brock's new book about William Morris. Although Jones resigned the editorship for a post in the cabinet secretariat in London in 1916, where he soon rose to serve the Lloyd George administration as deputy secretary, Winifred maintained her relationship with him until the end of his life.

Frank Alford, *Winifred Coombe Tennant*, 1915
Oil on canvas, 47x35

Chapter Two

THE TWENTIES

In January 1917 Winifred Coombe Tennant took the chair of the Arts and Crafts Committee of the National Eisteddfod, to be held at Neath in August of the following year. The work of organising the event did not always go smoothly. Winifred's vision of what might be achieved was rather wider than that of many of her committee:

To Eisteddfod Committee. People seem so indifferent to National, that is, Welsh industries and crafts - the women among them, I mean. They seem void of any form or focus - afternoon tea cloths and embroidered screens the objects beloved of their minds! 'Genteel' in all the hideousness of that word. [17 February 1917]

The considerable difficulty for Winifred of organising a national event in war-time was deepened by the death in France of her son Christopher in September. Nevertheless, like many other people of her generation and class at this time, Winifred found the strength to continue her public life despite her personal loss. Indeed, through the Eisteddfod she achieved some degree of catharsis, which helped her to sustain her life after bereavement.

Winifred pointed out in her speech at the opening of the Art and Craft Exhibition, nearly a year later, that 'entries had not come up to expectation in the painting section owing to the great difficulty in sending pictures by rail, and because so many artists were doing war work'.[1] Nevertheless it proved possible to mount an exhibition of competition entries in many art and craft categories which satisfactorily repeated the pattern established before the war. Reporting of Winifred's speech suggests that the rhetoric of the opening ceremony also stood in a well-established tradition. In 1895, speaking at the opening of the Arts and Crafts Exhibition at Llanelli, the painter Hubert Herkomer had caused controversy when he criticised the low status given to visual culture in the National Eisteddfod. Herkomer's comments found a strong echo in Winifred's speech in August 1918:

It had been said that the arts and crafts section was the Cinderella of the National Eisteddfod, but she felt that it had great opportunities to foster and encourage art in all its branches. Although music was the natural expression of the Welsh genius, she did not see why it should be limited to music. It would be a wonderful thing to train the rising generation in art, and to let them realise the joy of making and designing things that were beautiful. [That was] the natural outlook of the intellectual, religious and commercial life of the people ... When they regarded that grand national institution - the Eisteddfod - as the foster-mother of art, that would come to pass.[2]

Later on that opening day, in her diary, Winifred recorded the private thoughts that lay behind the public rhetoric, as the vote of thanks to her was proposed by the Mayor of Neath. It was still less than a year since Christopher had been killed in France:

I was so moved that for a few moments I felt almost unable to respond ... when I did I told them all my work for Neath was a labour of love - but oh! My Cruff it was who filled my heart! - and for you I wore my lovely new black dress and feather hat - just for you! [1 August 1918]

Winifred's Eisteddfod committee organised a small loan exhibition of works by well-known artists to accompany the competitions. There were pictures by Margaret Lindsay Williams, and the display of Carey Morris' *The Welsh Weavers* attracted particular attention in the press. It had recently achieved celebrity as a result of being reproduced as a coloured print in the United States.[3] Frank Alford, now working as assistant to Frank Brangwyn, represented the kind of young artist to whom Winifred had made reference in her speech. Among the established locally-based practitioners was Harry Hall, the jeweller and sculptor. Of the older generation of artists invited to exhibit, F.J. Kerr was as renowned for being the first teacher of Christopher Williams as he was for his own work, since by this time Williams was generally perceived as the leading Welsh painter of the day. During 1917 he completed his large painting of *The Charge of the Welsh Division at Mametz Wood*, a work which was facilitated by David Lloyd George.[4] Williams completed his third portrait of the Prime Minister in the same year. Lloyd George had also sat to Augustus John, but John was still considered wayward by most of the establishment and Williams received many more Welsh portrait commissions than he.[5]

Christopher Williams and Isaac Williams, Curator of Art at the National Museum, were appointed painting adjudicators at the Neath Eisteddfod. They awarded one of the prizes to Percy Gleaves who, like Harry Hall, was a teacher at Swansea School of Art. The award of the prize had a substantial if less than satisfactory outcome for Gleaves, who was commissioned to paint a large group portrait in celebration of the impending award of the Freedom of the Borough of Neath to Lloyd George. Winifred both sat for her own portrait in this picture and helped Gleaves to obtain sittings from some of her acquaintances. Notwithstanding Winifred's impression that the

Unknown designer, *The Cover of the Programme for the National Eisteddfod of Wales at Neath*, 1918
The National Library of Wales

painter was 'a pleasant person', who regarded her face as 'interesting to sketch', the omens were not good. She thought Gleaves' preparatory drawing not very like her. [14 August 1918] Less than a year later Winifred sat for Gleaves again, with even more depressing results: 'He makes me look like a buxom heavy florid young country woman in a Sunday hat!! Amazingly *un*like me.' [8 July 1919] The large finished work, described somewhat defensively by Gleaves himself as 'first and foremost a human document', proved a debacle, in Winifred's opinion at least.[6] It was a further eighteen months before she saw the 'awful and absurd' picture again: 'No one could recognise either I or CCT [Charles Coombe Tennant] – and the P.M. has his toes turned in and looks like a dwarf. It is a fearful production!'[7]

With the exception of the delightful design which adorned its literature, the Eisteddfod of 1918 was not regarded, at the time, as memorable for its contribution to the visual culture. However, in retrospect it can be seen to have had lasting consequences, because of its effect on Winifred. She was inspired by what she often later described as the 'democratic spirit' of the institution. She had caught sight there of the great leaders of pre-war Welsh intellectual life, in particular O.M. Edwards, and she established the relationships which would direct the course of her public life for the ensuing decade. She became woven into the network of the intellectual establishment, not only through the Eisteddfod itself, but through the associated activities of the

Percy Gleaves, *The Granting of the Freedom of the Borough of Neath to David Lloyd George*, 1918. Oil on canvas, detail. Charles Coombe Tennant and Winifred, in mourning, centre. Neath Port Talbot County Borough Council

Cymmrodorion Society and the Gorsedd. Her new friends were active over the wide range of issues which comprised the patriotic national agenda of the period – the development of national institutions, Welsh history, literature, music and visual culture. They were also involved with social reform, and interested in the points at which social concerns and the arts met. In her speech at the opening of the Arts and Crafts Exhibition Winifred drew particular attention to the architecture section, which the press regarded as one of the more successful aspects of its work.[8] Winifred's committee had organised a competition to design housing for rural workers, and a number of wealthy individuals, notably Sir Alfred Mond, the Swansea industrialist and Member of Parliament, had provided substantial premiums of £50 for the winners.[9]

The improvement of housing for the common people had been an issue throughout the nineteenth century, and one of which Winifred was frequently made aware in Neath.

Returning from the town in the sumer of 1913, she noted her 'Thoughts of sadness that any human life should be set in the midst of dirt, ugliness and degradation – industrialism! – and what it means'. [3 July 1913] A year later she was given a 'terrible account of housing conditions in poorest parts of Neath – terrible dens built round airless courts'. [21 June 1914] At this time she conceived the building of a 'garden city' on land she owned on a hillside above the Neath Valley, which she proposed to provide at an agricultural rent. She discussed her plan with those involved with the development of Rhiwbina in Cardiff, and with Thomas Jones, who devoted considerable space in the pages of *The Welsh Outlook* to the problem of workers' housing.[10] The decision of Winifred's Arts and Crafts Committee to campaign on the same issue reflected the considerable overlap that existed between those who wrote for and read the magazine, and those who worked on behalf of the Eisteddfod and its associated bodies. The Committee organised its competition in association with Edgar Chappell, founder and secretary of the Welsh Housing and Development Association, which subsequently published the results with an introduction written by Daniel Lleufer Thomas, the chairman.[11] Thomas was perhaps the most influential and energetic public servant of the period, and a founder of the Cardiff Workers' Co-operative Garden Village Society which created Rhiwbina. Winifred's acquaintance with him was marked a few months after the

Eisteddfod when she wrote an article for the *Welsh Housing and Development Year Book*.[12] Similarly, the adjudicator for the architectural competitions at Neath was Patrick Abercrombie, Professor of Civic Design at the University of Liverpool. Abercrombie was already a distinguished figure and would come to dominate the field of planning in Britain until after the Second World War.[13] He was already known to Winifred, and stayed at Cadoxton while adjudicating the competition.

By 1917 the problem of housing was beginning to be addressed in the particular context of post-war reconstruction, with the prospect of the release of young men and women from the armed forces and war work. The Eisteddfod's contribution to this wider debate also brought Winifred to the attention of the intellectual community. Under the guidance of Sir Vincent Evans, the Cymmrodorion Society had regained the prominent position in the intellectual life of Wales which it had occupied in the eighteenth century. Since 1893 the Society had used the Eisteddfod as an annual platform to raise a wide range of issues of national concern. Winifred presented a paper to the Society meeting on the Wednesday of the Neath Eisteddfod on the subject of 'Rural Reconstruction in relation to the Rural Working Class Woman'.[14] Evans was clearly impressed and a relationship which would last for many years was established. The following evening Winifred dined in the company of Evans and David Lloyd George:

*Vincent Evans told the P.M. of the
Cymmrodorion meeting and my speech in great
praise, so that when later I was introduced to
him he said at once 'I hear you have been
making a great speech' ... [8 August 1918]*

This was the first time that Winifred had met
Lloyd George. The following day she was again
acknowledged by the Prime Minister, and by
October she had been drawn into active Liberal
Party politics. Their meeting had taken place in
the context of the extension of the franchise to
women and the passing by parliament of the bill
which permitted women to sit as members.[15] It
seemed obvious to Lloyd George that recruiting
able women like Winifred into an active
campaigning role and having them stand
as candidates would be of crucial importance
in winning the new votes. He immediately
recognised the potential of Winifred in both roles,
and they would meet many times in Downing
Street and at Chequers during the remaining
years of his incumbency as Prime Minister in
the Liberal-Tory coalition. Winifred was soon
adopted as the Liberal Party parliamentary
candidate for the Forest of Dean constituency.

Clearly Winifred's close association with Lloyd
George gave her a privileged view of public affairs
in Britain as a whole, but since the Prime Minister
was surrounded by the Welsh intelligentsia, her
interest in the arts in Wales was also affected by
people she met through him. For instance, in
February 1920 Christopher Williams and she

spoke in Downing Street about *Christopher*,
which the painter had read. Like Winifred,
Williams had detested the war. His *Charge
of the Welsh Division at Mametz Wood* was a
condemnation of its brutality. Winifred and he
had much in common, therefore, in their attitudes
to the events of the past and also to art. They
shared a love of the work of the painter G.F. Watts.
Williams had known Watts, in his old age, and
memorably described him as 'Love in Love
Triumphant'. Winifred was a frequent visitor
to the Watts Gallery, at Compton in Surrey,
and to the painter's mausoleum there, 'grave
and sedate', which had strong emotional
associations for her.[16]

Winifred's network of associates among the
elite of the Welsh establishment – Thomas Jones,
Daniel Lleufer Thomas, Vincent Evans, Lloyd
George – was extended yet further when she met
Gwilym Davies. In 1911 Davies, who was a Baptist
minister, had been among the founders of the
Welsh School of Social Service, an organisation
of Christian intellectuals and activists who met
to discuss and promote social reform. From its
origins within Davies' own denomination,
the School had expanded into an ecumenical
movement by the time of Winifred's post-war
involvement. She rapidly became a leading
contributor to its activities, especially to those
of its women's section, and spoke at many of
its conferences in the early 1920s.[17]

During the National Eisteddfod at Neath, Winifred was initiated into the Gorsedd as 'Mam o Nedd'. The proceedings were described in the pages of *The Welsh Outlook* by a mildly cynical Spanish observer:

I was up early, for I was anxious to be present at the Gorsedd. In truth I cannot say that it impressed me. The Sun was kind to us, and the Park, fresh from the night showers, was pure and luminous. The rough-hewn Gorsedd Stone, and the dolmens arranged in a circle round, seemed out of place on the well-groomed grass. And, moving among a crowd of twentieth-century sombre-clothed people, the Archdruid, the Druids and the Bards were out of tune. The costumes struck me as poorly designed. The colours were not very pleasant individually: the blue and the pink very shallow, and the green, though better, unable to stand the competition of the vivid grass. The combination of the four tones, white, blue, pink and green, was somewhat acid and unwelcome, an impression further strengthened by the quality of the stuff, which was hard and thin ...

The ceremony struck me as a little fluctuating. There was a mixture of past and present which did not allow the mind to rest. A man in khaki blew his bugle to the four winds, and the Archdruid, in somewhat popish robes, was presented by two ladies (in twentieth century attire) with an obviously ornamental and unblowable horn. The Nightingale of the North sang in mufti, and the bards climbed up the stone and said their poems clad in Druidical robes. Yet the ceremony undoubtedly supplies an outlet for the tendency towards the enjoyment of light and colour, otherwise suppressed in Wales. That the inspiration behind all this pageantry should come from the chapel leaders is truly illuminating. 'Chassez le naturel, il revient au galop.' I saw yesterday excellent acting in Chapel. Here is Church pageantry in the Park. For what is the Archdruid but a Pope; what are the Druids but his Cardinals, and what is the Gorsedd but a High Mass?[18]

Winifred's view from the inside of the same event was couched in very different terms, since it was deeply coloured by memories of Christopher:

Started at 7.30 for the Gorsedd ... Inside the Circle I stood and heard Llewellyn Williams speaking in Welsh and towards the end I heard Welsh Guards, and then 'Christopher Tennant' ... he spoke, I understood later, of his having been in that circle last June and two months later his body lay in a soldier's grave ... Then Sir Vincent Evans escorted me up on to the Logan Stone and the Archdruid initiated 'Mam o Nedd'. It was a great moment ... [8 August 1918]

Winifred's first Gorsedd, and all the many that succeeded it, contained within them the resonance of a high mass for her dead son. That resonance underlay her life-long commitment to the ceremonies, and also to her determination to dignify them. Notwithstanding the deep emotional impact of the Gorsedd ceremony of 1918, at a more superficial level Winifred, like the Spanish observer, had been dismayed by its visual tawdriness:

I felt that here was a ritual which could be full of beauty and which held something precious to Wales, but was marred by the absence of a sense of pageantry as a whole and of due decorum in the case of a number of those taking part. The procession of the Bards was a strange sight. Many were clad in soiled and torn robes, some reaching little below the knee, others pinned up with safety pins to keep them off the ground. Many carried large umbrellas, others had cameras and miscellaneous impedimenta, including scarcely extinguished pipes. Bards rushed out of the procession to talk with friends and raced back just in time to enter the circle, where hoods were freely removed, snap-shots taken and each became a law unto himself ...

As a girl I had lived much abroad. I had watched the great religious and civic ceremonies in Italy and France and Spain. I knew how moving pageantry which expressed a tradition and a spiritual ideal could be ...[19]

Winifred's response to the state of affairs was entirely typical of her. She set to work to dignify the ceremonies, and in particular to improve their visual quality, by lobbying her new acquaintances in the hierarchy. In 1921 Winifred had her own

robe and head-dress made, copied from that owned by the Vicar of Aberpergwm, 'very beautiful – graceful, glorious in colour'. [21 June 1921] She wore it in public for the first time at the Proclamation of the National Eisteddfod at Ammanford. In October a committee of female grandees was established, with Winifred as chairperson, to oversee reform. Although the process proved surprisingly contentious and caused her much irritation, at the Ammanford Eisteddfod itself, the following August, new robes were on view.[20]

Before the war Winifred had become a habitual visitor to the new Glynn Vivian Art Gallery in Swansea. Subsequently she maintained her interest, notwithstanding the memories of Christopher which the place evoked, since he had often been her companion there. Sometimes she noted visits in her diary, such as that in January 1920 when she much enjoyed an exhibition of Turner oils and watercolours of Wales. However, later that year she visited an exhibition of the work of Evan Walters which would transform her relationship with the Glynn Vivian Gallery and which would have consequences for the practice of young Welsh artists for over thirty years. After first being brought to the attention of the public in 1911 by John Davies Williams, Walters had won a variety of scholarships and prizes, and had concluded his formal training at the Royal Academy in London. By 1916 he was working

Chapman,
Evan Walters, c.1920
The National Library
of Wales

in New York but was
unable to avoid the war,
finding himself conscripted
in the United States.[21] On
his return to Wales at the end of hostilities,
Walters struggled to restart his career. The turning-
point came when he was offered the exhibition
at the Glynn Vivian by William Grant Murray –
the first of his former students to be assisted
in this way by their teacher. Winifred knew
of Walters, but the tone of her diary entries in
response to the exhibition suggests that she was
not closely familiar with his work. She was both
surprised and excited by the discovery of it:

*On to Art Gallery to see Evan Walters' paintings.
I much liked a man's portrait, an exquisite small
half-finished picture called 'Mother and Baby' -
and two sepia drawings which reminded me of
Blake, one 'Cleanse me in Deep Waters' and one
'Weep for Joy'. How I long to buy the 3 latter. I
left a note for the painter asking if Mother and
Baby were for sale - and what his charge would
be for a Portrait.[22]*

Over the next two months Winifred's diary
was dominated by expressions of her mounting
excitement as a relationship with Walters was

established. Two days after seeing the pictures
a letter from the painter arrived asking twelve
guineas for *Mother and Babe*. Four days later
she met Walters at the gallery and recorded her
impressions of him:

*A young dark typical Welshman. Very intelligent
and pleasant. Had a long talk. I found the 2
drawings I liked so much in the Blake manner
were 'Cleanse me in Deep Waters', 5 gns. and
'Weep for Joy', 3 gns. so I decided to buy these
in addition to the Mother and Baby. He will paint
my portrait this summer - 15 to 20 guineas - and
charcoal heads of the children would be 5gns. He
has genius. He then introduced me to the Director
of the Gallery, Mr. Murray and we had a long
talk on Welsh Art, Augustus John, Eisteddfod
exhibitions etc ... Oh! How refreshing to meet
kindred spirits. And to think I shall have these 3
heavenly things to live with. CCT very appreciative
of my Mother and Baby, and much struck by
Evan Walters work in general.[23]*

On Sunday 23 June Walters visited Cadoxton
Lodge for the first time:

*What a wonderful thing Genius is! It makes all
my hum drum wrestling with things and people
shrivel up into a landscape of dust. I believe in
Genius one sees Man as God meant him to be.
This young man has it - and it is wonderful to
watch. He is highly nervous, vivid, unaffected -
he functions on a different plane to the ordinary*

being - his reactions are other, other his joys and his sorrows. Through his eyes another world is open to him, and what he sees enters the crucible of his spirit - and then he gives it back, laying it on canvas that all may see. Can we make the world possible for Genius? [23 June 1920]

Winifred's choice of works from the Evan Walters exhibition of 1920 expressed the two levels of her understanding of the world which drove her life. Her radical social ideas derived from a fundamental mysticism, a conjunction which she immediately identified in the painting of Evan Walters. After the death of her first two children, Winifred experienced human existence as a trial from which, she believed, men and women were only released by divine will to join God in an unsullied eternal life. God had granted complete revelation of divine purpose in the life of Jesus, and had provided glimpses into paradise itself through chosen people in all subsequent ages. Her own psychical experience was a part of this provision. Furthermore, those granted such vision might also perceive God's own view of the human condition. In this way human beings might know how to act rightly in the world. People of all kinds were used by God as channels, but foremost among them were artists – that is to say those painters, writers and musicians who rose above the commonplace by virtue of possessing genius: 'I think genius is something *shining through* the individual from beyond him – it looks something like focussing

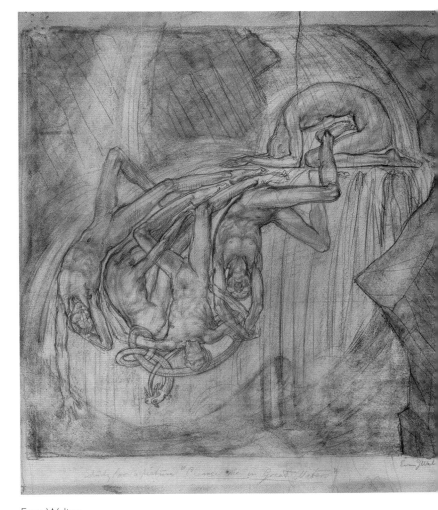

Evan Walters,
Study for a Picture,
'Cleanse Me in Great
Waters', 1915
Pencil and colour wash
on paper, 15×14

a ray of God-light ...' She was convinced that her psychic mentor, Frederick Myers, would have 'seen God' in Evan Walters. [24 and 23 June 1920] Winifred's essentially mystical and religious view of art would set her against many aspects of Modernism, yet her ideas were not outmoded in the sense that, although deeply rooted, they continued to evolve at the hands of contemporary art historians and aestheticians. Her view of the privileged nature of the artist – and, by implication, of those who appreciated art – had been influentially expressed by Clive Bell in his book *Art*, published in 1914. It is surprising that Winifred seems not to have read *Art* until 1926, but when she did so her enthusiastic annotations and underlinings, especially of Bell's 'Metaphysical Hypothesis', reveal how closely her views were in accord with his. The book was a gift to Winifred from Evan Walters.[24]

Thinking within this philosophical framework it is not surprising that Winifred admired the work of William Blake and, therefore, that Evan Walters' two early drawings, *Weep for Joy* and *Cleanse Me in Great Waters*, were the first of his works that she chose to buy. *Weep for Joy* had been made in 1915 and taken with him to New York, and the other he made when newly arrived there. The influence of Blake is apparent in both the style and the philosophical content of the drawings. Walters gave Winifred detailed interpretations of their meaning with which she identified closely, particularly so in the case of *Weep for Joy*. Looking back to 1915, through

her experience of the Great War – a war made by men, in her view – Walters' work must have seemed to her prescient. Looking forward, it identified, as did she, the central place that women must take in the defeat of evil and the restoration of love and joy to God's creation:

The woman's figure symbolises Love and Joy grown to womanhood, and risen in revolt against the destroyer, sin. In mortal combat the woman slays the Devil, thereby liberating the elemental powers of Nature that are the appointed protectors of the Garden, symbolised in the picture by strange prehistoric beasts that have risen from sea and land, and stand guardian to exclude all further intruders from the sacred precincts of the Garden of Love.

In the upper portion of the picture is seen a group of three figures, Motherhood, symbolised by a mother and babe, sorrowing womanhood, and a figure with drooping head typifying redeemed and liberated womanhood, who weeps for joy at the defeat of evil.

To the left in the lower portion of the picture appears a group of three figures typifying human love, father, mother and child, the parents with arms interlaced, the child, her back turned to the spectator, reaching up both hands towards them, whilst beside the figure of the triumphant woman, who stands with one foot upon the prostrate figure of Evil, are seen two other female forms, one standing and one in an attitude of complete exhaustion after long endurance in struggle.[25]

Evan Walters,
Weep for Joy, 1915
Pencil and colour
wash on paper, 15x9

"WEEP FOR JOY"

Evan Walters,
Mother and Babe,
1919
Oil on canvas,
18×21

The suffering of women in their giving of love was also central to the appeal of the third picture which Winifred bought from Walters' exhibition. In a retrospective version of the experience of seeing his work for the first time, she made clear that she had understood his 'tender and beautiful' picture, *Mother and Babe,* as a Christian metaphor:

The first picture which my eyes fell on as I stood looking into the room took me by surprise and storm, and has been one of the jewels of this house for the last seven years. It was a small oil painting entitled 'Mother and Babe', showing a dark haired, rather weary-looking collier's wife, sitting beside her kitchen fire and suckling her baby, the typical Madonna and Child of Industrial Wales.[26]

Winifred's understanding of the Madonna and Child was deeply layered. Two days after first seeing Walters' painting, she spoke at the Cardiff Conference of the Welsh School of Social Service. From the left wing of the Liberal Party Winifred expressed views close to those of Christian Socialists, for whom the birth of Jesus in poverty formed an essential part of the ideological framework within which they engaged with society.[27] Whether or not Walters had painted his image of working-class motherhood within this same framework, Winifred certainly perceived it in that way. At the same time, and with equally political implications, the Madonna represented the sacrifice of women in the world. Winifred knew both the pain of loss after the death of a child, and the loss occasioned by the tension between the demands of motherhood and the complete expression of self. Indeed, her life was dominated privately and publicly by her attempts to come to terms with these profoundly difficult issues. She regarded the Madonna with awe. For Winifred, the Mother's sacrifice was as important as that of the Son. Most deeply and mysteriously of all, as the mother of a child known to her as the Wise One, that is, her youngest son, Henry, Winifred identified personally with the Madonna. Winifred and Gerald Balfour envisaged for Henry a messianic role in the world.

On 24 June 1920 Walters began to paint his first portrait of Winifred:

In the Music Room ... I in a black crèpe de Chine teagown - sitting. ¾ face. I sat from 10.45 to 1 - and he works very rapidly, so that here I am all sketched in and beginning to breathe - a very happy likeness I think and very much me - Wonderful to watch him at work - creative genius. And most of us, bound upon the wheel of things, hardly lift our heads from our tasks, whilst this man moves among the stars and is in the company of the Sons of God who shout for Joy. [24 June 1920]

Walters worked at Cadoxton Lodge on the portrait for three weeks, also making vivid charcoal drawings of Alexander and Henry. Winifred noted in detail the evolution of the picture, including her panic when Walters briefly lost the likeness, and her amazement when he 'announced at lunch that he had decided to change the background ... from dull gold to a soft grey'. [10 July 1920] In the evenings they talked about art – the Renaissance, Blake, Cezanne 'and the modernists of Wyndham Lewis type' [28 June 1920]:

Intensely interesting mind he has. Oh! The refreshment of the companionship of genius. 'Take off the shoes from off thy feet for the ground whereon thou standest is Holy.' [4 July 1920]

Vandyk, *Winifred Coombe Tennant*, c.1920

believed it was manifested. The intensity of her excitement resulted from the fact that she felt herself in some way closer to God in his presence. Notwithstanding her growing affection for Walters himself, at less emotional moments Winifred's observations of the painter, then aged twenty-seven, and so a generation younger than she, could verge on the patronising:

Today E.W. began to work at my picture in a black mood - shooting intent and displeased glances at my face and painting, working in dead silence. At the rest found the me I had got accustomed to in the picture had somehow changed. I was disconcerted ... the eyes had changed. After the rest he worked away again, the cloud gradually lifting ... the total result of the morning's work according to CCT is a vast improvement and more like me. I hardly feel the latter but see it is more interesting as a painting. However E.W. has quite regained his serenity and declares it is going to be a masterpiece. He is a most loveable youth. [13 July 1920]

Winifred's tendency to gush when admiring Evan Walters at work obscures a distinction of importance that existed in her mind between two aspects of what she observed. Winifred was celebrating genius as a phenomenon almost independent of the painter in whom she

On 16 July Walters finished the portrait:

Sitting all morning and all afternoon, finishing touches. How much I have entered into this picture - a happy sitter. Certainly this young Welshman will go far. The things he does know about life and the things he doesn't equally interesting to

Evan Walters,
*Winifred Coombe
Tennant*, 1920
Oil on canvas,
25x20

watch! I feel that [to be] the Divine Right of Artists: somehow they form a separate category of human beings, and while one is a model one is lifted for a moment to the outer courts of their world. Often sorrowful in heart they pour out things that give joy to others, possessing nothing they have all things, they pass us by these Kings, sometimes unguessed - and their name is a living flame in later generations. Two poems come back to me 'And did you once see Shelly plain' - and AE's 'I pitied one whose tattered dress'.

Sitting all day from 10 am to 3 pm except for lunch. Much good talk the while. There is something very Cinquecento about E.W. and he is very loveable and very Welsh. I think he has enjoyed painting this picture.[28]

During the painting of the portrait Winifred took advantage of Walters' presence to invite his two most important supporters to Cadoxton for the first time. William Grant Murray toured the house, dutifully admiring the ancient cast lead water cisterns outside and the family portraits within. The Principal expressed the view that the portrait of Winifred by Walters was the best thing his former student had done, an opinion which may have been influenced by his sense of social propriety. Walters had not long before produced an equally elegant portrait of Margaret Murray, his wife. On the whole, Winifred's reflections on Murray's visit suggest that his formal manner constrained the exchanges between them. Her reaction to the subsequent visit of John

Davies Williams, who had first brought Evan Walters to public attention in 1911, and predicted his future success, was quite different:

John Williams, Editor of the Cambria Daily Leader came over to lunch, Mr Taylor, the Neath Leader man accompanying him. J.D. Williams a most interesting man - strange blend of modernist under the drug of Calvinistic Methodism! He saw over the house, adored the lead pipes and the vast old kitchens - and spent some time over E.W. paintings, including my portrait which, he said, showed that E.W. had it in him to be quite a 'sedate painter'! to the huge amusement of E.W. and self. Followed 2 hours of brilliant thrilling talk and argument the Artist's point of view versus the ascetic - religion - puritan point of view - marvellous quick flash of thought and wondrous the juxtaposition of, as it were, Bard and Friar - Hebrew ideal and Greek ideal. I always knew I was pure Greek! Deeply interesting. E.W. on the future development of Painting and J.D.W. on the facts of religious experience. Oh! What a glorious afternoon.
[5 July 1920]

Unknown photographer,
John Davies Williams, 1913
The National Library of Wales

The contrast of attitudes which had stimulated such lively discussion was that identified by Matthew Arnold as 'Hebraism' and 'Hellenism' – or 'strictness of conscience' and 'spontaneity of consciousness'. Winifred identified herself emphatically with the Hellenistic spontaneity of the artist.[29]

Shortly after Walters' departure at the end of July Winifred received the news that she was among the first group of women to be appointed magistrates. The painter wrote to congratulate her, reporting that he had 'danced for joy' since 'though it was raining outside the sun shone!' Renewed contact with Walters prompted a characteristic exclamation from Winifred: 'Art – the moving of the spirit above the waters of life!' [20 and 22 July 1920] Given the heightened sense of the centrality of art in her life at this moment it is surprising that Winifred did not attend the National Eisteddfod at Barry in the first week of August 1920. The Eisteddfod included one of its most ambitious and successful Arts and Crafts Exhibitions, and the fact can hardly have escaped her attention. Under the direction of F.J. Kerr the Committee made a rigorous selection from the large number of competition entries and separately displayed the work of established Welsh artists to the public in an invited exhibition. In addition, the location of the Eisteddfod at Barry presented the opportunity to display a group of pictures from the collection of the Davies sisters, whose grandfather, David Davies of Llandinam, had built the docks on which the town's prosperity, and the sisters' immense wealth, was based. For the first time since the inaugural exhibition of the National Museum in 1913, a substantial number of what were still regarded as modern continental paintings were displayed to the public, including works by Monet and Gaugin.[30]

In all probability Winifred was simply too much absorbed with her own life to require further stimulation at this time. She was at work on a speech which she was to make at the impending Llandrindod Wells conference of the Welsh School of Social Service, and with Liberal Party affairs, especially the internal but angry debate on the question of political devolution to Wales.[31] More agreeably, Winifred had commissioned Evan Walters to paint a further two pictures for her. In the middle of the Eisteddfod week he returned to Cadoxton and began to paint a portrait of Charles Coombe Tennant. The following day, he faced the more challenging task of drawing the two children in preparation for a group portrait with their mother. This proved to be a 'rather trying experience' since the children were restless and Charles 'very disagreeable'. Walters became depressed and Winifred took to her bed.[32]

Walters continued to draw Winifred and the children but did not begin to paint the group until September. In the meantime he produced a portrait of Charles Coombe Tennant which was acknowledged by most who saw it, including Winifred herself, as outstanding:

Evan Walters,
*Charles Coombe
Tennant*, 1920
Oil on canvas, 24×20

*speaking likeness and a forcible
virile bit of work. He complains
that mine is too flowerlike and
sweet, and wants to do me again.
CCT's is the finer picture. E.W.
is a strange and wondrous being,
capable of cruelty and roughness,
yet intensely sensitive. He is full
of undisciplined power!*
[13 August 1920]

By the Autumn of 1920
Winifred's relationship with
Walters had become close and
easy. In the daytime he would
sometimes accompany her on
outings to the coast, and in the
evenings they would talk or read
together.[33] His friends came to the
house – Peter Keenan, a young
Irish artist, then Henry Dixon
'a nice very reserved cryptic

*Evan Walters made a charcoal sketch of
Alexander, making him look like a Bolshevik
anarchist and a ditto of me making me look
like a Revolutionary - no doubt 'strong and
unacademic' which seems to be the highest goal,
but marvellously repellent! He had his 5th sitting
of CCT and the portrait is a marvel. It is a*

creature' who also thought Charles' portrait
finer than Winifred's.[34] Grant Murray visited
again, eliciting a warmer response from Winifred
than he had on his first visit: 'Much good talk. He
is such a delicious Scotsman – very calm, but with
eyes that fill with amusement and then pleasure
and then surprise and then kindness and then

amusement again.' [15 October 1920] Equally, Walters was fully a part of Winifred's circle. She recommended him to new patrons. In October Winifred visited Admiral Walker Heneage and his wife and young children at Parc le Breos, where Walters had been painting, almost certainly at her instigation.[35] Walters was included in the company even of those people involved with the most private aspect of Winifred's life. At the end of August Oliver Lodge arrived at Cadoxton. Walters drew a portrait of him in the music room, while Winifred read aloud to them of Arthur Eddington's ideas on the interior substance of the stars. Eddington was Director of the Cambridge Observatory, a physicist and mathematician who made important contributions to the General Theory of Relativity, but also one of those Cambridge academics of the period, like Lodge, who were deeply interested in mystical experience.[36] There can be little doubt that the painter was acquainted with his patron's involvement in psychical research. Equally her political views must have been clear to him. The intimacy of her daily sittings with Walters for the group portrait coincided with the most intense social and political experiences of Winifred's life, after the Great War. In early October Winifred spoke at the Llandudno conference of the Welsh National Liberal Council on the subject of Home Rule. There she met and talked at length with George M.Ll. Davies, by whom she was deeply impressed. Davies was a pacifist who had been imprisoned for his views during the Great War.

Evan Walters,
*Admiral Walker
Heneage*, 1920
Oil on canvas,
54x38
City and County
of Swansea: Glynn
Vivian Art Gallery

As an intermediary between De Valera and Lloyd George he was presently attempting to achieve a peaceful resolution of the Irish crisis. Since Winifred's detestation of British rule in Ireland was longstanding, her attraction to Davies was natural. He was 'A man like unto Christ', who was engaged in furthering the cause of Irish independence by peaceful means.[37] Soon after her return to Cadoxton Lodge and to sittings with Walters she heard of the death of Terrence McSweeny, Lord Mayor of Cork, on hunger strike in Brixton Prison. Her diary entry for 26 October not only makes clear her attitude to the death of McSweeny, but underlines how closely integrated in her mind were her religious beliefs, her attitude to social issues, her politics and her need for art:

God's blessing go with a brave man. 'Not even in death thou diest'.

The utter shame of England - and the misery of helpless passion, of pain - Lord God of Hosts!! What can one say or do. I do not feel I can follow Lloyd George much further - it secures the parting of the ways.

Evan Walters arrived and began working again on my head and shoulders. [26 October 1920]

Exactly a month later Winifred was in London and there witnessed the aftermath of Bloody Sunday:

At 10.30 am went out onto the Terrace and watched the crowd assembled to see the sad procession of the bodies of the officers killed in Dublin last Sunday. Soon it hove in sight ... guards, more guards, bands - then the gun carriages with their flag strewn burdens. The sorrowfulness of man's inhumanity to man - 'Kings must have victories'. It seemed to me that I was watching the procession of the ages - the common people used as pawns by old and wicked spiders in power ... Old men make wars and young men die in them. The Black and Tans escorting one of the gun carriages looked to me about as villainous a set of men as I have seen in my life - man after man with a bad face. This struck me most, and made me believe that the stories one hears of their outrages are true enough.

The cenotaph was looking ghostly white in the winter sunshine ...[38]

Winifred thought and expressed herself in the language of visual images, both as an observer and as a vicarious creator. She commissioned and bought pictures which embodied her state of mind, and she contemplated them daily. They were a living presence, indeed, a necessity in her life. Notwithstanding her feminist views, Winifred's intellectual and practical engagement in matters beyond domesticity aroused in her a deep guilt. She conceived Evan Walters' group portrait as a reassuring sign that she adequately fulfilled the role of mother. Sitting on the floor, she has been playing at dominoes with her children. Behind untroubled motherhood, the picture masked her intense emotional experience of the politics of national and social injustice. It was an exercise in self-deception. In truth Winifred regarded motherhood as sacrifice – not only the sacrifice of the loss of children through death or estrangement, but the sacrifice of personal expression, which she felt that caring for their needs required. This sense of sacrifice was the source of Winifred's devotion to the Madonna, of the need she felt for Her image, and for this image of herself in the place of the Madonna. In his composition and his use of disturbing colour, Walters painted a picture which subtly disclosed the tensions between the sitters, of which he was surely aware. Although she acknowledged it as among his finest paintings, Winifred was never at ease with the picture.

Evan Walters, *Dominoes (Mrs Coombe Tennant and Her Sons, Alexander and Henry)*, 1920. Oil on canvas, 60x50 City and County of Swansea: Glynn Vivian Art Gallery

Returning from a visit to Downing Street in January 1921, Winifred was absorbed again into the smaller but not unconnected world of Welsh art by the visit of the engraver Fred Richards, in the company of Evan Walters. Richards, who was a contemporary of Winifred's, had been born in Newport and trained there before attending the Royal College of Art. By the end of the Great War he counted a number of influential individuals in the Welsh establishment among his supporters, including Thomas Jones. Presumably as a result of his influence, the work of Richards had been the subject of a substantial essay in *The Welsh Outlook* in 1917.[39] The following year he was commissioned to write a report on the state of art education in Wales. No doubt

the largely unhappy conclusions of that report were prominent in the 'most excellent talk on Art matters' with Winifred that took place at Cadoxton Lodge two years later. [6 January 1921] In his report Richards had quoted the remarks made by Tom Ellis in 1897 on the condition of art in Wales and noted his belief that in the meantime nothing had changed, citing as evidence the fact that art had not been mentioned in the most recent report of the Board of Education. 'The time has surely arrived when such a reflection on a nation's interest in its Art Education should be made impossible':

Art in Wales has been relegated to two or three Art Schools and to one or two picture galleries - to live a short life in the one or to die a lingering death in the other. To make it possible to obtain a smattering of any subject or merely to make opportunities for seeing pictures by means of sporadic exhibitions is not enough.

In Art, as in other things, a little knowledge is a dangerous thing. What are wanted are more creative opportunities; more opportunities to practice the Arts and Crafts. The vital creative faculty in the soul of the nation has had little or no opportunity to make itself evident. It has received little or no encouragement from Educationalists. It is true there are a few enthusiastic Welshmen who have the subject at heart, but it must be remembered that the Arts of a nation can truly flourish only when they concern all. The interest of a few enthusiasts,

Unknown photographer, *Fred Richards (right) and Norman Keene in their studio in Newport*, c.1907-8 National Museum of Wales

dilettanti, amateurs, collectors, connoisseurs or critics is a poor substitute for a National Interest. No nation can be truly happy whose labours consist chiefly in supplying the raw materials for the craftsmen of other countries. The joy of creation should be the heritage of every people.[40]

In his report, Richards drew on the experience of Winifred's Art and Craft Committee at the Neath Eisteddfod of the year in which he wrote. His concentration on the architecture section emphasised the importance of what appeared to his generation of patriotic intellectuals, under the influence of Ruskin and the Arts and Crafts movement, to be the desecration of natural beauty by urban building. Richards believed that 'Any nation which permits its natural beauty to be desecrated should cease to boast of its patriotism.'[41] Nevertheless, and perhaps as a result of his acquaintance with Evan Walters, Richards was able to point to Swansea as an example to be followed in its appreciation of the importance of the role of Grant Murray as an expert overseer of visual culture in the town.[42]

By the end of January Walters had all but finished the portrait group of Winifred and her children, and in February she left Cadoxton to campaign in the Cardiganshire parliamentary by-election. This was her first direct experience of the hustings. However, the account of her travels which appeared subsequently (under a pseudonym) in *The Welsh Outlook* was concerned not with her politics but with what she saw in the people she met in Cardiganshire. In the strictest sense Winifred's response was picturesque. A landlady at Llanddewi-brefi was 'a cinque cento Madonna – the eternal type of the peasant woman the world over'. Her account of the people she met at a meeting in a village near Lampeter was a late eulogy to the *Gwerin* of Tom Ellis and O.M. Edwards:

Llanfair schoolhouse, sweetest and strangest of meeting places, with the six wax candles that were the sole illuminant shining out in the darkness, and but half revealing the gathering that had assembled there that fine February night. Two adorned the Chairman's table, and two stood on the harmonium on the right, and one shone out in each of the two windows that faced us, little tongues of fire that seemed to rest in pentecostal blessing on the dark heads beneath them. An old man was speaking when I entered, and I had leisure to watch the scene. How a painter would have rejoiced in it! The roof lay in darkness above our heads: the candles broke but did not destroy the gloom: the wooden forms were filled with country men and women: and groups of men who could find no seats stood round the sides. It was the heart of Wales I had reached - or so it seemed to me: it was the unchangeable genius of the Welsh peasant I was watching. Happy the boys and happy the girls who drank of the waters of knowledge in that pleasant place.[43]

Geoff Charles,
Gwendoline Davies, 1937
National Library
of Wales

*Such pictures in this house! Monet, Millet,
Alfred Stevens, Whistler, Turners - oh! The joy
of them! I wander as in a Temple standing
before each.* [20 February 1921]

Two days later, the inspection resumed:

*Spent the afternoon going over Gwen's pictures,
such genius, marvellous the Eugene Carrière,
Daumier, very wondrous and new to me,
Augustus John drawings, Whistler etchings,
Manet, etchings by Friant, Monet, Whistler,
Diaz. This is a marvellous collection and thank
God it is in Wales!* [22 February 1921]

At the end of her campaign in Cardiganshire
Winifred travelled to Shrewsbury for a Liberal
Party meeting. Among those attending was
Gwendoline Davies, whom she had met under
similar circumstances at least as early as August,
1919, but on this occasion the two women
travelled on together to Llandinam, the Davies
family home. Winifred's initial impression of
Llandinam, where Gwendoline lived with her
sister, brother and step-mother, was less than
favourable. It was 'a large cold house full of fine
things but dead in spirit – a sort of prison for
rich people'. However, the following day, a more
detailed study of the fine things revealed the
collection of pictures assembled by Gwendoline
and Margaret, the extent of which apparently
came as a surprise to Winifred:

In the meantime Winifred had been taken to
Gregynog, a house that she had visited before
the war, when it had been the property of the
Joicey family of coal-owners. David Davies had
bought the Joicey estate during the war and, in
the process, had acquired Gregynog, which seemed
initially to be a 'white elephant'.[44] However, in
1919 Thomas Jones became involved in the
problem of what to do with the house, and
proposed using it as a centre for the discussion
of ideas and the practice of the arts in Wales. The
organist and composer Walford Davies, newly
appointed Professor of Music under the Davies
sisters' patronage at the University College
of Wales, Aberystwyth, also seems to have
contributed his thoughts at an early stage. The
concept that emerged stood squarely within the
intellectual tradition of William Morris and the

64

Arts and Crafts Movement, but was also informed by ideas arising from the presence of the Belgian artists who the Davies sisters had enabled, through the agency of Thomas Jones, to live in Wales during the war. In particular, the de Saedeleer family, who had settled near Aberystwyth, had ideas about the development of craft culture in their adopted community. Two of Valerius de Saedeleer's daughters had taught weaving and bookbinding at the new Department of Arts and Crafts at the University in Aberystwyth, a project promoted by the Davies sisters.[45] The idea of establishing a rural community of artists and craftspeople was in the air from that point, and Gregynog seemed to Thomas Jones an ideal setting for such a project. When Winifred went there in February 1921 the conceptual development of Gregynog was at its height, drawing on the ideas of many of *The Welsh Outlook* circle. Among them, George M.Ll. Davies was in residence on the day of Winifred's visit, and they lunched together.[46] On their return to Llandinam, the two women walked in the gardens and glasshouses 'talking Gregynog – Tom Jones – Young Wales'. Winifred concluded that the shy but able Gwendoline was 'a precious soul'.[47]

In May 1921 Winifred visited Caernarfonshire for the first time. Her immediate purpose was to address meetings in support of the political agenda of the Prime Minister. In mid-May she stayed at Garth Celyn, his family house at Criccieth, at which point the visit turned into

something of a Lloyd George pilgrimage. Much of what she saw she related to what she imagined to have been his youthful experience. The drawing room at Garth Celyn, for instance, was 'redeemed by a beautiful portrait of a Miss Thomas of the Lleyn Peninsula by Sir W. Beauchamp, a pupil of Sir Joshua Reynolds … the P.M. grew up with it'. [15 May 1921] On her return to London at the end of the month she hastened to the Army and Navy Stores and 'chose a large portrait of Lloyd George to be framed and sent anonymously to the schoolmaster at Llanystumdwy':

I sent a note, unaddressed and unsigned, saying it was sent to be hung in the school there, and of Lloyd George 'God gave him to Wales. Wales gave him to the world. Cymru am byth'. [30 May 1921]

However, in the longer term the visit was of importance because of Winifred's intense reaction to the landscape of Snowdonia. Informed as she was by the ideas of Tom Ellis and O.M. Edwards, the mountains seemed to her icons of the culture of Wales:

What a God-steeped country this is. 'What lovely things Thy hand hath made'. The mountains feed my soul - and to be here alone, mistress of my own time and movement, is such a rest and benediction.
Walked up to the Castle - a grand impressive pile. Climbed to the Battlements and spent nearly two hours sitting in the sunshine and adoring

Snowdon, Hebog and Moelwyn - a Holy Trinity if ever there was one - and the great plain stretching up to them with Portmadoc nestling to the left, the castle of Criccieth, the Carnedd Goch, the Rivals and all those lovely hills. Far far below me the golf links and beyond them the sea, as blue as the Mediterranean. Thank God for such beauty, such peace, and such solitude. Please God I shall return to this land ...

Oh! give me mountains in the next world - what on earth so loved, so longed for, as the hills of Home.

No one ever loved Wales more than I do, not those ancient great ones of Gwynedd even. [18 May 1921]

The intensity of these patriotic feelings, aroused by a landscape in which she sensed the immediacy of God, found almost immediate symbolic expression in her participation in the quasi-religious Gorsedd in June. Wearing her new robe and headdress she walked in the procession at Ammanford behind the banner designed in 1895 by an earlier reformer of the ceremonies, T.H. Thomas:

A day of intense heat and brilliant sunshine. The Gorsedd ceremony very fine - Dafydd, Vincent Evans ... and me there, and oh! My dear Cruff - he and his 1917 ceremony - God bless him. Suddenly I was told I was to speak from the Maenllog. I felt overwhelmed. Dafydd called me, and I mounted the sacred stone. I

spoke, of course, in English - just what was in my heart, very briefly. Then the descent in Procession to the Town - tea - and the drive back. I felt the honour done me. It has been a happy day ... [23 June 1921]

Winifred's happiness with the ceremony and procession was in stark contrast to the emotion she felt a few days later in London, when she watched the trooping of the colour, remarking there only on 'The fearful mechanical precision of it all'. Winifred was in London once again at the behest of Lloyd George. She was being drawn into the British political system by the magnetic personality of the Prime Minister and her own sense of service. 'I am so utterly bewildered by all this', she confessed to her diary on 4 July.

Unknown photographer, *Winifred Coombe Tennant in London*, 23 October 1922. Winifred is walking away from Downing Street, where she had breakfasted with the Prime Minister, David Lloyd George.

Her involvement reached both its highest and lowest points in the last months of 1922. On the 14 August she received a personal message from Thomas Jones at Downing Street:

He hoped I would accept an invitation from the government to act as one of the members of the British Delegation to the League of Nations Assembly at Geneva ... I am the first woman to be appointed to represent Great Britain. I go to Geneva on Sep 2nd and shall be there a month. Dear Cruff: he is my first thought. To help the cause of Peace, oh the joy of it ...[48]

Nine days later her exhilaration collapsed in the face of the violence of the civil war in Ireland:

Oh! Absalom my son! Lord God of Hosts how do human hearts live and beat on through hours like these. I was sitting with Miss Davies Llandinam, Mary Ellis and Rose Davies about 6.30 p.m. discussing further work of the [Welsh] School [of Social Service] when Gwilym Davies arrived. 'Michael Collins was assassinated this morning' he said. And my heart stopped. I laid my head down on my hands, stunned. I loved that man, I worked for him, he was my hero, from Llandudno onwards right through he ran like a golden thread through my life - 'whom having not seen, we love'. His face was as familiar to me as those with whom I lived ... and now he is gone and I shall never stand in his presence ... The awful waste the awful tragedy of his loss crushes me ...[49]

Unknown photographer,
Winifred Coombe Tennant in Geneva, 1922

67

Winifred had been at Downing Street during the negotiation of the Anglo-Irish Treaty in October the previous year.[50] She had become a passionate supporter of Collins because of his willingness, as she saw it, to lay aside violence for the honourable compromise of partition. She pasted his photograph in her diary. Now that image of Collins would be replaced by Sir John Lavery's posthumous portrait, *Michael Collins (Love of Ireland)*, painted as the assassinated Commander-in-Chief of the forces of the Irish Free State lay in the chapel of St Vincent's Hospital, Dublin. In the summer of 1923, Winifred was given by Sir Alfred Cope, one of the negotiators, a coloured print of the celebrated picture, which she hung, icon-like.[51]

Winifred was overwhelmed by political and social work. Her public life rose to a peak of intensity at the end of 1922 when, as a result of the resignation of Lloyd George, she fought the Forest of Dean constituency in the General Election. Her failure there was less a personal one than a particular instance of the general collapse of the Liberal Party. On reflection she defiantly described what had been a dirty campaign as 'a great experience',[52] but it was one she did not choose to repeat, notwithstanding periodic feelings of regret that she would never sit in the House of Commons. The experience of her social work, and especially prison visiting at Swansea, was equally distressing. It was often characteristically described in her diary in terms of visual images:

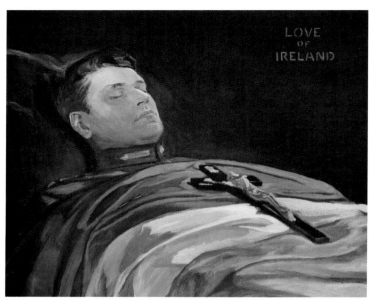

Sir John Lavery, *Michael Collins (Love of Ireland)*, 1922
The reproduction is of the print owned by Winifred.
The original oil painting is at the Hugh Lane Municipal
Gallery of Modern Art, Dublin

*A long morning in prison - so depressing ...
I feel drowned in the darkness of it - maimed
souls, stunted minds, broken lives. The picture
of a pale young man on remand for attempted
murder in an observation cell, seen through the
bars eating his dinner with a black cat sitting
at his feet comes back to me - why were we
ever made!* [27 October 1922]

Grant Murray was also working in the prison at this time, giving lectures on art to the prisoners – another instance of how the sense of Morrisian social responsibility remained strongly present in the art community of Winifred's generation. The powerful images in which Winifred encapsulated the contrast between the poor and disadvantaged and the wealthy and powerful were, however, inevitably coloured by the contradictions of her own social standing. A wealthy woman herself, who loved fine things, Winifred often observed the life of the rich with distaste. At Coryton, Whitchurch, she stayed 'with Sir Herbert Cory M.P. Appalling luxury – King Solomon like. I could enjoy it if there were no poverty in the world – as it is …' [30 November 1921] On the other hand, she noted with a suggestion of sadness the condition of Lady Bute, dwarfed by the exuberant excess of the medieval fantasy of Cardiff Castle, created by Burgess. She met Lady Bute alone 'in a small monastic sitting room'. To Winifred, whose taste was firmly for the Romanesque, with its associations of the piety of the early church, the castle was 'all poor Gothic'. [22 November 1921]

Unknown photographer, *Walford Davies*, c.1920 National Library of Wales

During 1921 and 1922 Winifred's need both for the immediate excitement and the underlying peace which she found in art was met only in brief interludes. Among the most important of these was her meeting with Walford Davies at the Llandrindod conference of the Welsh School of Social Service. The composer, lecturing on the worthy topic of 'Citizenship and To-morrow', 'swept us off our feet', though one suspects that Winifred may have been speaking primarily of her own reaction to the charismatic Doctor:

He is pure cinque-cento Florentine, lifted out of the Renaissance - for our deliverance - into this age. Before him shrivel all the ugly things of Wales - the bad architecture expressed in a thousand chapels, the poor art revealed in the average picture sent in for Eisteddfod competitions, the commercialised joyless furniture of its million homes, the dreadful so-called 'Music' of the 'Children's Operetta', a painful reminder that it is possible to feed them with crumbs left from the dog's platter - all these things fly from before the face of Walford Davies, and he creates for us a new Wales - by an act of faith we see it as he sees it - a Wales where the things of everyday life shall be beautiful, simple, real, sincere. He takes the common things of life and makes them holy, the humblest bush touched by him glows with the fire of God. Here is genius making its habitation among us - are we realising it, are we seeing Light in his light?[53]

Before this extraordinary eulogy was published, Walford Davies had visited Neath, at Winifred's invitation, and had stayed at Cadoxton Lodge, where a lasting friendship was established:

That great genius, Doctor Walford Davies came to Neath. Lecture concert on Beethoven, Schubert and Handel - trio giving examples. Oh the sweep and breadth and richness of this human man.
He slept here. I took him out to the music room. [28 November 1921]

In the music room Walford Davies saw the group portrait of Winifred and her children by Evan Walters, now hung between the earlier portraits of herself and Charles. Walters had applied some final revisions to the group in July 1921 in a brief space between visits by Winifred to Downing Street and to Chequers. The following year Winifred found it strange to see the picture at the Royal Academy, hung on the line and close to the portrait of George Bernard Shaw painted by Augustus John. Her earlier portrait by Walters made an appearance at the Ammanford Eisteddfod Art and Craft exhibition in 1922, where Winifred cooled somewhat towards it, viewed in the company of many other paintings. As ever, the highpoint of the Eisteddfod was the Gorsedd, notwithstanding continuing discontent about her reform proposals among the 'fierce red crotchety Band' of Bards. [7 August 1921] On the Thursday of the Eisteddfod Winifred participated in the ceremony of chairing the bard for the first time,

revelling in the 'dramatic moment when he stood up, a solitary figure in the vast assembly'.[54] The following day Winifred attended the male voice choir competitions:

The Dowlais choir magnificent. I took the boys up onto the platform and we sat there for an hour, the vast multitude filling the great Pavilion to its fullest extent. Met many folk I knew. The peace of music, after politics. I feel the atmosphere of politics rather irksome, indeed very irksome, and long for Peace ... Today the two men who murdered Wilson were executed. Brave men who were ready to die for Ireland - God rest their souls. In their new worlds they will see that violence is wrong and useless, that Love is the only conqueror. The long series of political crimes by oppressed races is a dark and sorrowful chapter in history.[55]

The electoral collapse of the Liberal Party in 1922 removed Winifred from the corridors of British power. As early as January 1923 she observed that 'The position of Liberalism in S. Wales seems to me to be a desperate one – the missionary spirit has passed to Labour and the young and the idealists are turning to them for light'. [6 January 1923] She was not unduly depressed by the fact. Her distaste for Toryism was much stronger than any reservations she had about Socialism. In November she came under heavy pressure to stand again for Parliament, but refused on the grounds that the seats she was

offered were impossible to win. She became convinced that 'women should not accept hopeless fights and thereby establish the legend that women never get in'.[56] In January 1924 Ramsay Macdonald became Prime Minister

Unknown photographer, *Winifred Coombe Tennant with David Lloyd George at Llandrindod Wells*, 1923. Lloyd George is greeted by Mrs Goodwin of White House, Builth Wells, on the way to the Gwalia Hotel from the Albert Hall.

in the first Labour administration and Winifred, with self-conscious symbolism, 'sorted and put into a tin box my whole collection of L.G. Papers, a list of visits to Chequers and Churt and 10 Downing St. Letters from L.G. to me'. She felt wistful as she put them by and saw 'that Big World rolling away from me', but nonetheless wished the new government God-speed. [22 and 23 January 1924]

The vacated political ground in Winifred's life was reoccupied by visual culture during the middle years of the decade. The National Eisteddfod exhibitions remained the main public focus for art and craft. They were exceptionally ambitious in this period, under the direction of professional organisers, including Isaac Williams, Curator of Art at the National Museum, and the painter Carey Morris.[57] In 1923 at Mold these two led a procession to the grave of

Unknown photographer, *Winifred Coombe Tennant (centre) in the Gorsedd procession to the tomb of Richard Wilson at Mold, August 1923*

Richard Wilson in which Winifred participated, clad in her green robes. Winifred stayed at Bryngwyn Hall, Caerwys, where her fellow house guest was T. Gwynn Jones. After their first meeting, Winifred glossed Jones as 'a Welsh Poet', clearly ignorant of the august presence in which she found herself. She rapidly became better informed and left the Eisteddfod discussing with the Professor an idea of hers to publish translations into Welsh of the works of Blake. Winifred's knowledge of the culture with which she so passionately identified was inevitably patchy, since she came to a large part of it without direct access through the language. Shortly before the Eisteddfod at Mold, she had visited the site soon to be occupied by the memorial to Hedd Wyn, clearly well-versed in a story that had already acquired mythic status, though unaware of T. Gwynn Jones' close involvement with the controversy surrounding the project:

> *... On then along a wild tract of country to Trawsfynydd, sacred from Hedd Wyn memories, the Shepherd Poet who fell on Pilkhem Ridge - God bless him. Great mountains of Merionethshire to the left of us, a ragged massive outline of wild glorious beauty. I got out at Trawsfynydd and walked to the spot where the memorial of Hedd Wyn will be erected, close to a little chapel, and looked up towards his homestead, a farm a mile away - of such is the Kingdom of Heaven.* [18 July 1923]

Leonard Merrifield, a student of Goscombe John, had been commissioned to create the memorial statue to Hedd Wyn, but controversy had arisen as a result of the opinion of some of the proponents of the project that the poet should be portrayed in his military uniform. T. Gwynn Jones had been angered by this proposal, and his view, that Hedd Wyn be portrayed both with realism and with deeper symbolic meaning as a shepherd, had prevailed.[58]

Clearly, Winifred depended heavily on her friends and associates in the Gorsedd for her knowledge of the literary culture. She felt less at a disadvantage in the field of art and craft, and during 1923 her involvement with the Robes Committee began to widen into a renewed interest in Welsh textiles, which would engage her for many years. Winifred had first become aware of the tradition of weaving in Wales through her friendship with the Williams family of Aberpergwm, and it may be that a sad reminder of earlier days played a part in the reawakening of her interest:

> *Opened Fête at Aberpergwm ... Saw the beloved old house in the distance through the trees and thought of the 90s, when I was so often in it, Mrs Williams of Aberpergwm in her Welsh dress, the long gallery with the Armour in it all gone and the house deserted, still surrounded by its beautiful woods.*
> [16 August 1923]

Winifred had recently begun a long correspondence with Pryce Jones, the emporium in Newtown which had pioneered mail order shopping in the nineteenth century. Pryce Jones was able to supply Welsh costumes, but Winifred's concern, both in acquiring a new dress for herself and in her ambition to reawaken public interest in the textiles, was with authenticity. This was a problematic concept in the case of a costume which had been at the very least heavily influenced by the taste of Lady Llanover in the first half of the nineteenth century. Winifred took the view that the costume as worn by the common people in some parts of Wales in the mid-nineteenth century represented customary practice. She regarded both the styles currently worn, and the patterns and colours of the materials available, as debased. Neither did she approve of the methods of manufacture. Chemical dyes and power loom production were not to her liking. In 1923 and 1924 she wrote dozens of letters to manufacturers all over Wales in search of supplies of traditional fabrics, and to experts seeking historical information. Among the respondents was W.H. Jones, Director of the Royal Institution of South Wales at Swansea:

> *I am much interested in your effort to restore to the women of Wales who wish to adopt the Welsh Costume as a spectacular dress, a correct knowledge of what they should wear: and I quite join with you in deploring the want of taste now displayed, and the wholly erroneous idea of*

what was the material used for the dress and even how it was made up. Really some of the efforts at dressing in the olden Welsh style are only burlesque, and bring the national costume into ridicule ...

We have several excellent photographs of the Welsh costume of sixty years ago of the women of Swansea Market, Penclawdd, Sketty, Mumbles and elsewhere in Gower, and although they are not coloured they were taken before the costume ceased to be very generally worn, and are therefore correct.[59]

In July 1924 Winifred visited Pryce Jones at Newtown to buy the luisey skirts for her new dress, and then drove to mills at Llanidloes:

I found the red traditional flannel like my own bedgown, also a perfect apron length in old design. Bought enough for my bedgown, also an apron length. If only I can get the Robes Committee to established a recognised design and materials and save the Welsh costume from modernising 'fancy-dress' deterioration.
[2 July 1924]

On her return to Cadoxton the materials were made up, with results which delighted her. For the first time since taking to black in 1908, she ventured out under a crimson shoulder shawl, 'all beautiful, comfortable, homely – and reminding me of happy days gone by. I shall take to wearing it again now'.

As a result of her search for traditional designs, Winifred accumulated a collection of sample textiles, some of which were made to her own specifications by mills and individual weavers who were both able and sufficiently interested to undertake the work. Given the association between Lady Llanover's early attempts to popularise Welsh textiles and costume, and so stimulate the rural economy, it is not surprising that John Jones of the Gwenffrwd factory at Llanover proved particularly accommodating:

As you are so anxious of getting the old pattern made I am prepared to do a piece say 50 yds 27in wide @ 4/- per yard. It will be poor pay but I hope it will be the means of getting once again a call for the handsome old designs and I am very pleased to find that the matter is in such noble hands. I will be pleased to have the pattern that I may make the piece exactly the same but I trust you will not press for the piece for a few weeks as I have a large order in hand at present.[60]

On her travels in all parts of Wales Winifred enquired after mills that were still at work, and visited those she found. However, even in the weaving centres of Carmarthenshire and Cardiganshire, she found the industry in decay:

On to Cardigan ... Went to the market, full of farmers. Nothing worth looking at in Welsh flannels. On to Aberayron and down to Felinfach on the road to Lampeter to look at Cwm Cafan Mills, only to find them shut down and machinery all sold. [11 July 1925]

Although Winifred's enquiries confirmed that the manufacturing of traditional textiles was in serious decline, they also revealed that she was not alone in her concern over the matter. In 1924 an article on the history of woollen manufacture, published in the antiquarian periodical *Archaeologia Cambrensis*, stimulated

a published exchange on the current state of the industry.[61] Furthermore, the Rural Industries Intelligence Bureau revealed that the School of Rural Economy at the University of Oxford was to produce a report late in the same year. The Bureau was a government funded organisation, the linear descendant of the Development Commission established by Lloyd George in 1909 to combat the effects of the agricultural depression of the period. It was but one of several organisations making efforts

Welsh Textile Samples Collected by Winifred Coombe Tennant, c.1924
City and County of Swansea: Swansea Museum Collection. Photographs by Graham Matthews

Unknown photographer, *Winifred Coombe Tennant in National Costume at Cadoxton Lodge*, 1924

to stem the decline, though apparently in a largely uncoordinated manner. The Welsh Industries Association had been the pioneer in the field. Since 1899 it had offered prizes annually at the National Eisteddfod in weaving, quilting and many other crafts. The Association ceased to function in the mid-1920s, but in 1928 the National Council for Social Service, with the help of grant aid from the Rural Industries Board, established an advisory service in south-east Wales and a sales outlet in London, offering items such as pottery from Ewenni and turnery from Henllan. Further grant aid, along with residual monies from the Welsh Industries Association and the

personal sponsorship of Lloyd George, enabled the University of Wales to appoint an officer to advise specifically on the textile industry.[62] The industry's own trade association proposed new marketing strategies, along the national lines pursued by the Scots in the successful promotion of Harris tweeds.[63] In October 1928 Grant Murray entered the debate on the matter with an appeal, published in the *Cambria Daily Leader*, for the establishment of what he defined as 'art industries' in the Swansea area. Winifred immediately threw her weight behind Murray's proposal. Her own article, published in the same newspaper under the title 'Beautiful

Unknown photographer, *The Pavilion of the Welsh Industries Association, National Eisteddfod at Carmarthen*, 1911
The National Library of Wales

Things Made in Wales', reveals the extent to which she manifested her patriotic sentiments in the material world of craft, alongside her already well-known support for painters:

I had slept well under the comfortable warmth of my 'carthen' (fringed woollen quilt), a thing of beauty woven for me by one of the few hand-loom weavers left in Cardiganshire. I looked down at its pleasant colouring - delphinium blue and maize, against a background of rich cream, and enjoyed once again the way in which the design played with the colours, now setting them one against the other, and now combining them, much as the notes of music in a Bach fugue.

Jumping out of bed, I stood on a large white wool rug, one of a number of which that prince of hand-loom weavers, the late Lewis Jones, of Lampeter, had made for me ten years ago. I had a busy day before me. I came down to breakfast in my Welsh dress, tying on my apron of 'two-blues' Carmarthenshire flannel as I ran down the stairs. In the hall the boys met me, both wearing suits of home-spun tweed made on a hand-loom in the Aberystwyth area, and which no Harris weaver could better for quality.[64] *Why does anybody in Wales wear Harris tweeds when Welsh tweeds of finest quality can be bought for a fraction of the price? I have shown these to some of the most famous tailors in London, and they have met with nothing but praise - except once. 'They have one defect, they will never wear out,' said one master-cutter!*

We ate our porridge out of two-handled bowls which the potter at Ewenny had made for me from a sample bowl I lent him and which I had brought home years ago from Spain, and the flowers on the breakfast-table were in a bright pot of his making also.[65] *On a table beside me were set the coffee pot and milk jugs - such a table! Well made, well proportioned, and solidly firm, the work of an old cabinet-maker whom Swansea folk should remember as a fine craftsman.*

After breakfast we adjourned to the drawing-room, gay with its large white wool rugs - these but lately come from a hand-loom weaver living near Tregaron. I drew up a stool to the peat and wood fire, which was making the room sweet with a countrified scent, and the stool, of beechwood with a seat of sea-grass, was the work of a women's institute in Montgomeryshire.

I could go through my day telling of things in daily use here which have been made by Welsh craftsmen. But I will admit that it has taken some hunting to find them. Now cannot we do something to preserve what is left of traditional craftsmanship in Wales, and hand it on to the next generation? If we do nothing, then in another ten or twenty years, much of beauty will have died out of the land.

Think of it! We have taken Lewis Jones' hand-loom and set it up in the National Museum at Cardiff, and put up a quilt of his weaving, in the intricate design he loved (but not so fine a specimen as the one of his weaving that I treasure here), and there is not a man in

Lampeter who is carrying on his work today.

There is a grand old weaver living in a white-washed cottage in a village in Cardiganshire whose skill is of the highest order. Quilts, travelling rugs, rugs for the floor, ask what you will, choose your own colours or leave it to him, you will have things of great beauty and well-nigh everlasting wear. When I was with him this August I tried hard to persuade him to train some boys to come after him. He was sitting at his loom in the tiny workshop at the back of his kitchen while we talked. He shook his head - his place was very small, he had but the one loom, he did not see how it could be done.

The weaver visited by Winifred in the summer of 1928 was Owen Davies of Llangybi: 'He is making me white rugs and a grey one, and I chose 2 lovely quilt patterns for him to make for me. He was at work in his little house in front of his handloom, most happy, and making lovely things.' After her visit to Llangybi, Winifred proceeded through Lampeter to visit the Pandy and Llanfair woollen mills. 'I bought at the former a quilt of Lewis Jones of Lampeter's weaving (his loom is now in the N. Museum at Cardiff) the last they had by that great weaver and a lovely thing! And at Llanafan Mills I bought a length of homespun for each boy, to their great delight.' [4 August 1928]

Winifred concluded her article with a call for urgent action to secure the skills of weavers such as Owen Davies for future generations:

Samuel Maurice Jones,
Trefriw, Old Flannel Mill, 1886
Watercolour on paper
National Museum of Wales

Now if we in Wales really cared for the old crafts, which - and this it is vital to remember - could well be carried on on a sound economic basis, we should see to it that such a man was provided with two additional hand-looms, and that two lads were set to learn from him the art of weaving Welsh wool in the traditional designs and colours. I do not know anyone in the whole of Wales who will make the things he makes once he is gathered to his fathers - and he is 'up in years'...

Unknown weavers,
Carthenni, c.1920

Unknown potter,
Soup Bowl, probably Spanish, c.1900

79

The urgent need of the moment is to set existing craftsmen to train younger men, in order that their own skill may not die with them. I repeat, ten years, or twenty years hence, it will be too late.

Can we do it now?[66]

The transfer of Lewis Jones' handloom to the National Museum had occurred shortly after the arrival of Iorwerth Peate as under-keeper in the Department of Archaeology in 1927. It was a sign of things to come. With the support of Cyril Fox, the Museum Director, Peate would be elevated to lead a new sub-Department of Folk Culture and Industry, which would eventually develop into the Welsh Folk Museum at St. Fagans, the most important creative venture in the Museum's history. It is not clear at what point Winifred was first introduced to Peate, though her meetings with Isaac Williams must surely have kept her abreast of developments at the Museum in a field in which she was deeply interested.[67]

Although the traditions of textiles, of national costume and of Gorsedd ceremonial to which Winifred devoted so much attention were largely modern constructs with only the most tenuous links to ancient customary practice, they provided in her daily life a feeling of historical continuity which helped to give it meaning. Historical continuity expressed God's design, and breaks in that continuity human failing, whether those breaks were caused by war or neglect. Notwithstanding Winifred's interest in ideas, it was through the material arts and the tangible practices of religion that she found reassurance about her place in the ultimate order, in the face of human destructiveness:

... to Neath Abbey in afternoon. Though I came here in Jan 1896 I have never been into it - 27 years, what an age! Fine remains but oh, the sadness of it. Recited the Ave and the Salve Requia as I walked over the grass grown nave of the great church - how often chanted there. The old Monks and Conversi seemed very near and comforted by one remembering. [11 January 1924]

The material evidence of religious practice reassured Winifred wherever she found it. In June 1924 she visited Stonehenge with Oliver Lodge:

I laid my cheek against one of those age-worn stones - thought of Maen Llia and Maen Madoc ... Man's search for God. My Welsh heart stole out to those vanished races who had worshipped there: I said the Gorsedd Prayer, larks overhead, winds blowing over the plain. Beauty. [5 June 1924]

Two months later she attended Nonconformist Sunday service at Zoar Chapel where she was inspired by the preaching of the Archdruid Elfed. Nevertheless, although open to religious experience of all kinds, the performance of Roman Catholic ritual was the most potent to her:

Motored to Ewenny, first to the pottery, then on to the Abbey, glorious in its loneliness and silence. I long to see such ancient buildings restored to the old faith that built them, to let the stones hear the blessed mutter of the Mass, to see incense rising. The historic continuity of such ceremonies, apart from any dogmatic implications, comforts me. [20 May 1925]

Although the range of her ecumenicalism was unusual, in the 1920s Winifred's nostalgia for Catholicism was not, and neither was its presence in her in the context of Romantic Nationalism and Welsh art. In 1921 the painter and poet David Jones had converted to the Roman church. Shortly afterwards he met the sculptor Eric Gill, and between Winifred's musings at Neath Abbey in 1924 and those at Ewenni Priory in 1925, he had come with Gill, his family and colleagues, to establish the religious art community at Capel-y-ffin. Gill had become aware of Capel-y-ffin and decided to move there as a result of a vist to the Benedictine monastery on Caldey Island. Drawings of the modern buildings of the Benedictine monastery on Caldey made by Peter Anson (who had been a visitor to Gill's previous community at Ditchling) were peopled with monks at work and in meditation just as Winifred imagined them present when she saw Neath Abbey. Again, it was in the mid-1920s that the medieval shrine of the patron saint was rebuilt at St David's (following the supposed discovery of his bones), which gave practical expression to the same desire for reconnection with ancient tradition that Winifred had experienced at Ewenni Priory.[68]

However, it would appear that Winifred did not become aware of the work of David Jones until early 1927. Her informant was Ifan Kyrle Fletcher, a bookseller from Newport. In January 1927 she bought from him a copy of *The New Broadside* with decorations by Jones, but immediately donated it to the National Museum:

I am glad that you like David Jones's illustrations. You did not seem very enthusiastic when I first told you of his work. He is immensely promising. I fear you will not find a great admirer of Jones in Isaac Williams. His exaggerated simplicity seems to repel at first but I think all his detractors will have to admit themselves in error.

If you wish I can keep you posted with particulars of his books. He does so much in semi-privacy that most booksellers never hear of them. He is doing illustrations for a book by Eric Gill to be called ART AND CHRISTIANITY.

This will be privately published, signed by the author and artist at 12/6. He is at work now on a great edition of THE ANCIENT MARINER. For this he is doing ten engravings on copper, a method which he has not previously used. Eight copies are being printed with an extra set of the engravings and an original drawing at 10 guineas, and three hundred ordinary copies at 2 guineas.[69]

David Jones,
Frontispiece to Eric Gill,
Christianity and Art, 1927
The National Library of Wales

Winifred ordered a copy of the proposed co-operation with Gill, which emerged as the pamphlet *Christianity and Art*. In it, Gill attacked the impact of industrialism on the artist, and affirmed the role of the church in 'maintaining the ideas and attitude of mind in which alone any great art is possible'.[70] In his frontispiece to the pamphlet Jones depicted the hand of God directing the artist, an idea beloved of Winifred herself. Given her faith, her aesthetics and her patriotism, it is surprising that the acute and well-informed Kyrle Fletcher's first impression of Winifred's lack of enthusiasm for Jones appears to have been correct. She did not buy his work.

Although Winifred was able to become unselfconsciously absorbed in the performance of ritual, whether collective or private, in church or Gorsedd, it was characteristic of her that she engaged also intellectually with the idea. Winifred reinforced her experience with analysis. In early 1924 she wrote a review of a book of essays about 'the place of art in human life', concentrating on a piece written by Percy Dearmer on the subject of ritual and religion:

The relation of music, drama, dance and ritual to the religious impulse is next examined and analysed. 'Is ceremonial an integral part of religion or just the baby-language of faith, which we must and ought to leave behind?' The traditional rite of the Eucharist and 'the dumb instinctive ceremonial of the Cenotaph' are pointed to as a warning that something stirs in the human heart which we have by our conventions too long made men forget. We recommend this chapter to the Bardic fraternity in Wales - too few of whom realise that in their ceremonies they are handling the children's bread.[71]

In October 1924 Winifred's sense of the relationship between art, memory and ritual, and especially her love of the Latin rites, came together in a visit to Rouen. She had conceived the idea of donating a relief of the Madonna which she owned, and which was believed to be by Della Robbia, to the Cathedral at Rouen in memory of Christopher. It was a bulky object and difficult to secrete, but passed through customs at Dieppe 'not discovered and no questions raised':

Took the Madonna to the Archevêché at 11 o'clock. Received by the Archbishop - I fell on my knees and blessed his ring. He was very kindly, a fine tall upstanding figure with clever kindly face - he is keen to have the Madonna actually in the Cathedral and bade us come back at 3.30 to see possible places, but the Minister des Beaux Arts is the final authority. I spoke to M. de Jouvenal with whom I had worked at Geneva - the Archbishop felt sure if I had his influence 'la chose sera faite'. At 3.30 went back and the Archbishop escorted us all over the Palace, a marvellous place, and the Cathedral ...[72]

Once the Madonna was installed Winifred attended services and religious processions at Rouen, visited the war-damaged cathedral at Rheims, and toured the Great War battlefields: 'All of it was holy ground, consecrated by the heroism of the un-numbered Dead'. [31 October 1924]

Winifred's visit to the Continent in Autumn 1924, her first since the death of Christopher in the Great War, was one of two events which appear to have contributed to a decision to formalise her sporadic art patronage for the benefit of the nation. The other event, rather more banal in itself, was a lecture given by Isaac Williams to the Neath Antiquarian Society, which she chaired. The Curator of Art at the National Museum showed interesting slides but was 'very slow and though showing good knowledge of Art his speech betrayeth imperfect general education which, unless made up for by inner light and warmth, always puts me off'. The next day Williams visited Cadoxton Lodge where he was impressed by a portrait of a Tennant ancestor painted by John Hopner 'But his greatest praise was for the Evan Walters' group of Emperors and self sitting on the floor …

Unknown photographer, *Isaac Williams (centre) with Carey Morris (left) and William Goscombe John (right), leading the Gorsedd procession to the tomb of Richard Wilson at Mold*, August 1923.

"A hundred years hence that picture will be worshipped as a great masterpiece" – He was amazed and excited over it'.[73] Though no doubt gratified by this observation, Winifred clearly found Williams limited in understanding and, in the context of her recent experience of religion and art united in French culture, formulated a plan which she believed would enrich the visual experience of the people of Wales:

Walked down Bond St to the Independent Gallery and saw some wondrous water colour drawings of French artists, Segonzac, Fre'laut, Jean Marchand. One, an old manor house by Jean Fre'laut I longed to buy - low buildings with a great noble tree in the foreground. Would the National Museum have accepted it? If I could afford £100 a year for 5 years and give a Tennant Collection of really good small modern things! Modern Wales knows nothing of International Art.

Telegraphed to the Independent Gallery that I would buy The Old Manor House of Fre'laut - and wrote to Gaggi of my scheme of collecting during the next 5 years pictures of modern, chiefly foreign, painters - to be given eventually to the Welsh National Museum's Art Gallery, the amount spent being £100 a year. I veritably believe a small good collection of little known painters could be got together with the assistance of P.M. Turner and Isaac Williams.[74]

85

Evan Walters,
The Laughing Woman, 1924
Oil on board, 15x12

To her distress, the Fre'laut picture was sold an hour after she had seen it, and so implementation of her plan was delayed, though only for a fortnight. Winifred decided to start the collection at home:

The Tennant Collection really began today when I motored over to Evan Walters' studio and bought 3 pictures, 1) a laughing woman, in oils, 2) a charcoal head of a miner, 3) an oil sketch of a sailor for a total of £9. Each in its way seems to me good - I feel happy about this. My idea is for 5 years to collect what I can of modern pictures up to a total of £100 a year of which I put in £50 and CCT and Gaggi £25 each - and eventually give the collection to the National Museum at Cardiff. Saw at Evan Walters' studio a fine portrait of a blind man playing the piano. Wrote to Isaac Williams about it - wondering if it could be bought for Cardiff.[75]

In retrospect it might seem significant that Winifred began her collecting in a deliberate way in the immediate aftermath of coming to know Gwendoline Davies and inspecting her collection, and that of her sister, at Llandinam. Certainly in 1913, with the exhibition of the collection in Cardiff under the aegis of the National Museum, and again in 1920, at Barry, the sisters had demonstrated a sense of responsibility to the public by making the works available to be shown. Furthermore, ultimately most of the pictures collected by the sisters would be

Evan Walters,
The Sailor, 1919
Oil on canvas, 21×17

bequeathed to the nation, in the care of the National Museum, but that was not their intended destination at the time of Winifred's first contact with Gwendoline. Indeed, in 1925 Isaac Williams wrote to Winifred on precisely that subject, observing that 'It does seem a pity – as you say – that all those lovely things at Gregynog are more or less shut away from the public eye …'.[76] The notion of forming a collection specifically to donate to the nation, in order to increase awareness of modern painting, was Winifred's. Most of her pictures were collected for that purpose, even though, in the end, the nation would not be the beneficiary. The nature of Winifred's collecting was, of necessity and by design, also very different from that of the Davies sisters, notwithstanding their common emphasis on French pictures. The resources available to Winifred bore no comparison to those available to the sisters, for although she was a wealthy woman by the standards of the common people, the capital demands of the family business interests and the maintenance of the London house of her mother-in-law absorbed a great deal of money. Winifred was not in a position to spend large sums on pictures. Her first purchase of French works was made in London on 27 February 1925 at the Independent Gallery. She bought landscape drawings by Marchand and Segonzac, and a portrait head of a young girl by Boussingault, for a total of £40, 'which seemed a very big plunge to make. But if I am to collect for 5 years and get something really fine together I must seize an opportunity to get a good buy when it comes – these are beauteous things'. [27 February 1925] The following day she visited the Goupil Gallery to inspect a collection of French drawings by many of the artists presently being bought by the Davies sisters, including Manet, Daumier, Cezanne, Rodin, Matisse and Vlaminck. The prices being asked – up to £400 – opened Winifred's eyes to the limitations that would constrain her own

buying, though she was consoled by having paid what she regarded as relatively low prices at the Independent Gallery. From time to time Winifred would regret not being able to buy as she would wish, but the confinement of her collecting to the works of contemporary and largely young painters reflected her attitudes as well as her means. The Davies sisters were shy and retiring, and on the whole were not inclined to engage with living artists. Like Grant Murray, whose opinions she regarded with increasing respect, Winifred was excited by the making of new art. In the autumn of 1925 she visited France twice, mainly with the intention of buying new works. After a visit to the museum at Caen, where she saw 'a few fine pictures', including 'a lovely Tintoretto', nevertheless Winifred observed that 'I find I care less for the old and more for the new, as time goes on, as far as painting goes'. [11 October 1925]

The visits to France in 1925 resulted in the acquisition of thirteen oil paintings, four drawings and a collection of over fifty Japanese prints, including examples by Utamaro. Many of the paintings were bought directly from the artists, as at Rouen in September, where she met Pierre Le Trividic:

Visited the Galerie Moderne and at last got in touch with a young painter of whom I had heard. I bought for 200fcs an oil of his of a vase of Dahlias - gorgeous in colour. I also bought a fine oil painting by Madelaine Hue of barges

Pierre Le Trividic, *Interior of Rouen Cathedral*, 1925
Pencil heightened with pastel, 9x7. The drawing for the painting
commissioned by Winifred. The Della Robbia relief given to the
Cathedral by Winifred is visible in the right foreground.

*describing his emotion at hearing of my
search and at my having bought the picture
that he had most highly prized among the six
that he had sent to the Exhibition. As a token
of reconnaissance he had gone out and done
for me a drawing of the Cour d'Albane, which
he there and then tore out of his sketchbook and
presented to me, a most exquisite little drawing.
Suddenly something happened, before I knew
exactly what I was doing I asked him if he
would undertake a commission for me and,
on his agreeing, I took him to the Cathedral
and there told him the story of Cruff and his
Madonna and asked him to paint for me an
oil painting of the Madonna just as he liked in
style and size. It was settled he would do it ...*
[16 September 1925]

In October Winifred visited the Salon in
Paris, where she was confronted with a mixture
of modernist pictures and more conservative
works in the Post-Impressionist tradition. Her
taste was for the latter:

*In afternoon to Salon d'Automne. Many
frightful and hideous pictures - ugly revolting
Nudes in figures sub-human, ill drawn and ill
painted specimens of the hideous in still life and
figure, but a few divine things. The one I liked
best was already sold ... but I made an offer
for two others, a boy watching three ducks and
a lovely landscape under snow. I wonder if the
painters will sell at any price!*[77]

*and boats on the Seine for 500fcs. I went
back to pay and fetch these at 5 o'c and a
few minutes later Le Trividic came in, a modest
looking young man. We launched into a wondrous
dialogue. I described my efforts to find him,
consulting directories, stopping postmen etc., he*

Joseph Fregier,
L'Enfant aux Canards, c.1925
Oil on canvas, 28×36

Both artists proved compliant, though the 2,000 francs paid for *L'Enfant aux Canards* by Joseph Fregier was an unusually expensive purchase for Winifred. The following week 'a most gorgeous Vlaminck' which she saw priced at 12,000 francs (about £97 at the exchange rate of the period) was well beyond her.

Before returning to Wales Winifred visited La Louvre, the Paris department store, and bought an easel 'on which to stand one of my Tennant Collection pictures at a time to comfort me when I am back in harness at Cadoxton!' The easel would be an important feature of Winifred's daily life and one which became familiar also to the many visitors who would view her pictures.[78] Nevertheless, important as the pictures were to Winifred's daily life, her own need was not allowed to stand in the way of her vision of them as part of an educational programme for Welsh artists and the Welsh public. Her vision was put into practice almost immediately. Firstly, Winifred discussed the collection of Japanese prints with Laurence Binyon of the British Museum and Isaac Williams at the National Museum, proposing that they be formed into an exhibition to be circulated around educational institutions. Williams was greatly excited by the collection and wrote to ask Winifred to 'go a step further' and donate them to the Museum. The Curator was much exercised at the time with efforts to 'penetrate the Wilderness of Wales, where there has never been any opportunities for the development of

Art Culture'.[79] Winifred agreed to give the prints, and by January 1926 they were mounted and ready to exhibit:

Isaac Williams showed me my 55 Japanese Prints most beautifully mounted (back sheet with cut mount folded over). They looked marvellously beautiful. The Utamaro of the woman holding up a transparent veil with a small child playing near her and a black lacquer workbox in the background looked marvellously lovely. I enjoyed seeing them - saw that my name had been printed as the donor on each of the mounts. [5 January 1926]

Next, it was agreed that all the French pictures from the Tennant Collection would be exhibited by Grant Murray at the Glynn Vivian Art Gallery in February 1926, and sixteen of them would be included in the large loan exhibition which he was organising for the National Eisteddfod at Swansea in July and August. By this time Winifred had made a second visit to Paris where, in a frenzy of gallery visiting, she bought nineteen pictures in twelve days. She added a further six in Rouen in September, and the enlarged group of French works from the collection was exhibited at the Technical College in Cardiff in November. They were dispatched to Newport for a showing after Christmas.

The purpose of Winifred's project was clearly outlined in the newspaper notices of the first exhibition. Having presented the conventional picture of Wales as a nation devoid of art, and

Kitagawa Utamaro,
Woman with a Veil, late 18th century
National Museum of Wales

cited the usual notable exceptions, the *South Wales News* reported on Winifred's attempts 'to foster art amongst our people':

For the last few years she has been endeavouring to encourage it in our National Eisteddfod, and by purchasing paintings by Welsh artists to add to her valuable collection. Mr Evan Walters, of Llangyfelach, the rising young painter, has received much encouragement from this lady, and his pictures now adorn the walls at Cadoxton Lodge. Mrs Coombe Tennant is convinced that Welsh thought and mentality are more akin to the French temperament than to English thought and mentality. For that reason she has in recent years been making a collection of French and Welsh modern paintings, etc. With the object of trying to illustrate her conviction, she has lent her collection of modern French pictures to the Glynn Vivian Art Gallery ...[80]

Of the individual pictures, the writer drew attention in particular to the works of Le Trividic and Boussingault, whose head of a girl was 'making good copy for students, one of whom, a miner, was a few days ago discovered to be studiously endeavouring to reproduce it'. Though his message was essentially the same, this residual note of nineteenth-century paternalism sounded in the *South Wales News* was avoided by the well-informed reviewer for the *Cambria Daily Leader*, probably the editor himself, John Davies Williams:

We have some young artists in Wales who are starting to do for our industrial life what Meunier did in Belgium. Mr Evan Walters I believe is engaged on a big canvas of life in the pit, and Mr Archie Griffiths, who is working at his scholarship in London, is engaged on a vast cartoon of a journey of trams drawn by a pony underground. In France art is much nearer everyday life than it is here. This little collection shows this strikingly. Our dock workers ought to go and see the picture of barges loading coal in Rouen harbour; our firemen the picture of a fire escape; our roadmen the picture of the sand shovellers on the Seine quayside; our carters the picture of the two horses and their cart. And then the country folk will find a French farmstead set in its clump of trees, and the cockle woman from Penclawdd will see what an old Normandy peasant woman looks like with her basket and traditional head covering.[81]

In 1927 the collection was shown in Merthyr but the press reaction to all the shows was less than enthusiastic. Winifred expressed her disappointment to Ifan Kyrle Fletcher who, in response, wrote a piece in *The Welsh Outlook* on the subject of 'The Appreciation of Art in Wales' in which he expressed his frustration:

During recent years I have noticed three glaring examples of the low state of art appreciation in Wales - the appalling standard of the art exhibitions of the National Eisteddfod; the studied contempt shown to Mrs Coombe Tennant's collection of French paintings when they were exhibited at Cardiff, Newport and Merthyr; the outburst of prejudice which greeted the recent publication of R.H. Wilenski's book on 'The Modern Movement in Art'...

When Mrs Coombe Tennant sent her French pictures on tour through South Wales it was both an opportunity and a test. The opportunity of delighting in the gaiety of young France was taken by a few and used to its utmost. But it must be confessed that the trial proved too exacting for most people. The newspapers were only vaguely critical, feeling, no doubt, that it is wise not to look a gift horse in the mouth. So the critics dipped their embittered pens in the milk of human kindness and wrote in veiled disapproval of the too riotous colours of de Segonzac and his friends. No such restraints, however, were felt by the general visitors and their comments were, at least, not hypocritical.[82]

Privately, Fletcher sought to reassure Winifred: 'I am delighted to be able to do something to draw attention to the value of your pictures. Some day Wales may be in a state to appreciate them. Until then the Brickbats must be suffered gladly.'[83] Winifred continued to buy new pictures on visits to the Continent until 1937. The range of the collection was widened with purchases made in Brittany and in Belgium. The pictures were shown again in Swansea in 1928 and in part in Eisteddfod loan exhibitions for several years. However, most subsequent showings of the collection were at public art galleries in provincial England.[84]

A week before her visit to Evan Walters' studio in December 1924, at which the first purchases for the Tennant Collection were made, Winifred had noted in her diary an event which may have had a bearing on her choice of the *The Collier* from among the painter's many drawings:

Great epic tale of heroism of two men who swam 75 yards in darkness with only 4 inches of airway between the water and roof in Killan Pit and rescued 2 men who had been entombed for days. The Welsh miner as he really is! As God made him - Housed often like a dog, with little to amuse or elevate him, he is at the root of him pure gold. [2 December 1924]

Even in the privacy of her diary Winifred felt the need to emphasise that this incident revealed the true nature of the miner because for a hundred years those outside the mining community had been unable to decide if he (and initially also she) was a heroic humanitarian or a barbarian. Public attitudes to the miner, expressed in the writing and visual imagery of the popular press, swung from intense sympathy when disasters occurred (or when the liberal press reported on the dire living conditions in towns such as Merthyr Tydfil), to hostility at times of strikes and disturbances.

Public mood swings had been particularly evident in the early 1870s but dramatic contrasts in the imaging of the miner were still evident in Winifred's own time.[85] She had lived in the Neath Valley through the Great Revival of 1904-5, when the image of the underground prayer meeting, purveyed by J.M. Staniforth, the *Western Mail* cartoonist, among others, had rapidly fossilised into the cliché of the pious collier. Five years later, during the Tonypandy disturbances, Staniforth presented the barbaric brother of this commendable individual stamping on a defenceless baby, symbolic of bravery, religion and orderliness, above the caption 'His own reputation'. As a social and political liberal, in 1924 Winifred was clearly pleased to have her instinctive sympathy for the collier reinforced by the events at the local pit.

Shortly after her visit to Walters' studio, the painter contacted Winifred offering to paint for her a portrait of Lloyd George, if she could persuade him to sit. The Prime Minister was an impatient man – 'a hot-arse', according to Augustus John, who had not enjoyed the experience of painting him.[86] Nevertheless, the number of portraits for which he had already sat suggested that he might be well disposed towards the further enhancement of his public image by a talented young painter. Two weeks later Walters was ensconced at Criccieth. After two sittings Mrs Lloyd George was very pleased with progress. The Prime Minister returned to London and Walters to Llangyfelach, where Winifred joined him:

In Evan Walters small studio I saw the fine portrait of L.G. - in its early stage, but still 'him', and full of dignity and strength - fine in colour and feeling, in its restraint and balance. I am thrilled about it - In its present stage it represents less than an hour and a half's work, done in two sittings. Wrote to L.G. telling him my impressions of the picture and urging him to give Evan Walters a few more sittings. [5 January 1925]

Lloyd George consented and the next sitting took place at Churt, where after two days matters took an unexpected turn for the worse. Descending for Sunday breakfast his daughter, Megan, 'abused the picture, said it made L.G. look too old and like one of Parry's caricatures'. [24 January 1925] Clearly rattled by this domestic vote of no confidence, the former Prime Minister suspended the sittings and summoned Winifred to Churt for consultations. The Lloyd George ego had long been surprisingly fragile. The most spectacular consequence had been the suppression, at his insistence, of the epic film biography, *The Life Story of David Lloyd George*, made by Maurice Elvey in 1918.[87] In the case of the portrait, after talking to the sitter Winifred summed up the situation with the succinct observation that 'L.G. thinks it unflattering and consequently does not like it!!' [31 January 1925] The saga of the portrait continued until the end of July 1926, when it was finally delivered to her by Walters. Winifred rushed to London to buy a frame so that it could be installed for an impending visit

94

Evan Walters,
The Rt. Hon. David Lloyd George,
1926. Oil on canvas, 29×22
Photograph courtesy of City
and County of Swansea:
Glynn Vivian Art Gallery.

*long in a field of uncut hay gazing
at it. From that lovely home and those
surrounding mountains he was to go forth
to Pilkem Ridge and be made partaker of
Christ's death - as he is of his resurrection.
Haymakers were at work in the fields in
sunlight and peace. Coming back I got
out and walked as I always do to gaze on
his fine memorial statue - the vigorous
stride of young manhood, the clean cut
features. They shall grow not old as we
that are left grow old. Dear Cruff. We
returned by Festiniog and its lovely Vale,
beauty everywhere.* [13 July 1925]

of the sitter and his retinue to Cadoxton.

The resilience of Winifred's own ego was severely tested in the same year. The National Eisteddfod of 1925 was held at Pwllheli, and provided the opportunity for Winifred to take a holiday in Snowdonia in July and August:

Motored after lunch to Trawsfynydd and up the farm road leading to Hedd Wyn's home, a little farmstead in a clump of trees. I stood long and

On 23 July Winifred attended the opening of the art exhibition by Mrs Lloyd George, before resuming her expedition in a characteristically romantic frame of mind. 'Mountains not people is my need. I thinking of Ruskin much, and his noble storm tossed spirit, and his joy in beauty, and his sadness in life – and of Rosie, who could not understand.' Reality intervened on the Wednesday of the Eisteddfod in the person

Unknown photographer, *Winifred Coombe
Tennant with the Queen of Roumania,
at the National Eisteddfod at Pwllheli*, 1925
The National Library of Wales

*As Mistress of the Robes I robed the Queen on
her arriving at the Pavilion about 2 - a radiant
queenly woman who looked like a lovely snow
flake in her white chiffon dress and pearls as
she walked bareheaded onto the platform, I
immediately following her, after me Mrs Lloyd
George and the Mayoress. Elfed initiated her,
I handing him the Ribbon which he tied on her
arm. I then presented her with her Robes, making
a deep curtsy. Mrs Lloyd George put on the Robe
and I then did up all the hooks and buttons and
gave the Mayoress the hood to put on. I then
acted as lady in waiting standing immediately
behind the Queen through the ceremonies and
escorting her down to tea. She was very pleasant,
interested in my League of Nations meeting
of Roumanians at Geneva in 1922 etc. I was
photographed repeatedly with the Queen and
shall also be on the films - amusing for the
children. [6 August 1925]*

of her neighbour, Lady Mond, wife of Sir Alfred.
She noted that 'Lady Mond presided in afternoon
and made such a fool of herself trying to make a
long speech and finally being cut short by the
audience'. [5 August 1925] However, Winifred's
evident satisfaction at the discomfort of Lady
Mond proved a prelude to her own public
embarrassment on a rather larger stage. At
Pwllheli the Queen of Roumania was to be
installed as a member of the Gorsedd, an event
with which Winifred was involved because of
her responsibility for the robes:

Unfortunately for Winifred, her rather
ingratiating performance had been witnessed
by the Junior Member for Treorchy, the *Western
Mail's* anonymous satirist. On her return to
Cadoxton, Winifred found herself lampooned
at length in the Tory newspaper:

*Shortly afterwards I found myself face to face
with Mrs Coombe-Tennant - the Mother Hubbard
of the Welsh Liberal cupboard, as she delights to
be known. As soon as she caught sight of me she
rushed up in the most excitable fashion.*

96

'Ah, Treorky!' she exclaimed, with her characteristic gush, 'I can't tell you how delighted I am to see you, for I have a most important bit of information to give you. I confess to you that ever since I came to reside in Wales I have been obsessed with the presentiment that Providence had a special purpose in my coming amongst you as a people. And now, hey-ho! That presentiment of mine has been fulfilled. As you know the Queen of Roumania came down to Pwllheli to be enrolled as a member of the Gorsedd. As soon as the officials of the Eisteddfod heard that she was coming there was intense excitement among them. They were at an utter loss to know what to do for there was not among them even one who had any experience of receiving a Queen ... There was not a single Welshwoman who could adjust herself to the occasion with the necessary dignity and grace, and so I was called in to discharge the task of receiving the Royal visitor ...

'As you, no doubt, observed in the newspaper illustrations and in the cinema pictures, I was inseparable from her Majesty during the whole time she was at the Eisteddfod. And I don't mind telling you that I have sent scores of newspapers with the illustrations to my friends in England. When they see me in the chief place in the limelight on the Eisteddfod platform they will

Unknown photographer, *Meeting of the Commission for the Reform of the Gorsedd at Cadoxton Lodge*, 1926. Seated, left to right, Rev. J.O. Williams (Pedrog), Capt. Geoffrey Crawshay, Prof. Ernest Hughes, Rev. A.E. Jones (Cynan), W.S. Gwynn Williams; standing, D. Rhys Phillips. The National Library of Wales

Will Evans, *Stormy Down*, 1924
Oil on canvas, 19x25

see that I have not been just boasting when I
have told them that I am one of the leading
personages in the life of Wales ...

'It is true that I don't know a single Welsh
word and that I could not tell whether Ceiriog
was a man or a mountain, but I know how to
receive Royalty ...'[88]

Winifred reacted to the 'particularly horrid attack'
with a calm which, perhaps, was informed by
the experience of the nastiness of the election
campaign she had fought in the Forest of Dean
three years earlier: 'One ought not to mind this
sort of thing, it is all so meaningless, and yet it
stings ...' [29 August 1925] She was sustained by

the confidence displayed in her by the leading
figures of the Gorsedd. In February 1926, dressed
in National Costume, she played host at Cadoxton
to a commission for reform of the institution. 'I
believe this meeting will in future days become
historic as opening a new period in the history
of the Gorsedd', she reflected, at the end of the
day. [26 February 1926]

In parallel with the purchase of her French
pictures, Winifred's patronage of Welsh painters
expanded. Her first venture for some years beyond
the work of Evan Walters resulted from a visit to
the Swansea Art Society Exhibition in June 1925,
which, for the first time, was held at the Glynn

George Martin, *Speed*, 1926
Oil on board, 23×21

Vivian Art Gallery. The Society was undergoing something of a revival after a period of lethargy, and the exhibition included pictures by Walters, Grant Murray and Will Evans, whose work particularly attracted Winifred's attention. She immediately bought a landscape by Evans for the Tennant Collection and also became interested in the more unusual work of George Martin. Her belief that the painter was 'an odd, queer old man' was surely based on the reporting of Evan Walters since, in fact, Martin was a few years younger than she. [4 July 1925] Walters may also have been the source of her belief that Martin had studied in France. In fact he had been an electrical engineer before training in art at Swansea and then at the Slade School in London. The painter agreed to sell his *Sabbath in Canaan* to her, which depicted 'a typical Welsh village and people going or coming from Chapel'.[89]

These purchases occurred in a period of increasing excitement among the art community in Swansea, which was generated by the ambitious plans of the Art Committee for the 1926 National Eisteddfod. Under the guidance of Grant Murray, the Committee was planning the largest and most clearly envisaged art and craft section ever in an Eisteddfod. In the process of buying a second picture by George Martin, called *Speed*, shown at the Swansea Art Society Exhibition in April 1926, Winifred received a letter from the painter saying that he was 'looking forward to it very dearly', and expecting Evan Walters 'to carry off most of the prizes'.[90] Murray's active engagement with the

Eisteddfod went back at least as far as the Proclamation Ceremony of 2 July 1925, with which Winifred was also closely involved. It had been the occasion for the installation of Winifred's friend Geoffrey Crawshay, of Llanfair Court, near Abergavenny, as Herald Bard. His handsome mounted figure would become a feature of the Gorsedd for many years. He added much needed panache to the ceremonies, and his presence was also of especial personal significance for Winifred, since he had been a close friend of Christopher. Grant Murray produced a series of seven oil paintings of the proclamation ceremony, one of which depicted the procession with Winifred walking before the banner in her green robes.[91] The pictures were reproduced as a limited edition

William Grant Murray, *The Proclamation of the National Eisteddfod at Swansea: The Procession in Singleton Park*, 1925
Coloured lithograph 8x8
Private collection

series of lithographs. This was the first evidence that within his rather formal exterior Murray nurtured a flair for publicity. He was aided in his efforts to raise the profile of art and craft by the creation in late 1924 of a radio broadcasting station in Swansea which, though less productive than the British Broadcasting Company's earlier station at Cardiff, nevertheless was able to produce some programmes locally.[92] It had broadcast the proclamation ceremony, and in November 1925 T.J. Rees gave the first of three talks on the work of the Eisteddfod Art and Craft Committee, of which he was the Chair. With the co-operation of the art-loving John Davies Williams at the *Cambria Daily Leader*, from the spring of 1926 Murray fed the newspapers with a steady supply of stories so that for the only time in its history the Art and Craft Exhibitions provided the main focus for press interest in the National Eisteddfod.

In connection with the Eisteddfod Murray organised a large loan exhibition at the Glynn Vivian Gallery, and showed the competition works at the Patti Pavilion, although, in the event, the response was so great that an overflow venue (the secondary school) was also required. The competitions were open, and over 3,000 entries were sent from all over the world. George Clausen and Augustus John were appointed to adjudicate together in the painting competitions. Clearly, it was a combination that had been conceived with controversy as its intended outcome. Trouble duly began well before the day of the adjudication, when John, who it had been arranged would

Evan Walters,
Poster for the National Eisteddfod at Swansea,
1926 Lithograph, 40x25

EISTEDDFOD
GENEDLAETHOL
FRENHINOL   **CYMRU.**

travel from London with Clausen to stay at Cadoxton, changed his mind. Clausen arrived alone and was taken into Swansea the following morning by his host to begin work. Winifred later discovered that there he had been stood-up for a second time by John, who failed to appear until four o'clock in the afternoon, at which point the distinguished academician was, presumably, ready to retire to the metropolis, if he had not already done so.[93] To the delight of the local press the upshot was two separate and incompatible adjudications:

It is said that the explanation of the divided prizes at the National Eisteddfod art exhibition is the wide-as-the-pole difference in outlook between Mr George Clausen and Mr Augustus John. Mr Clausen to-day represents the academic school. Mr Augustus John, true to the Wilson tradition, belongs to tomorrow. And of course there was no place at which the two adjudicators could find contact. The result has been that the chief prizes have been divided, roughly speaking, between paintings of the academic and the to-morrow schools. And it goes almost without saying that the to-morrow school is represented by a Welsh artist, Mr Evan Walters ...[94]

Clausen had taught Walters at the Royal Academy Schools before the war. He had been his second notable Welsh student, following the more conservative Margaret Lindsay Williams. The night before the adjudication in 1926, at

Cadoxton, Clausen had 'greatly liked' the works by Walters on display, an opinion which, it would soon become clear, was expressed largely out of politeness to his host. The next day Clausen caustically observed that Walters' controversial poster for the Eisteddfod – 'the famous or notorious "celestial dragon"', as it was described in one newspaper – had at any rate served its purpose, which was to attract attention. The poster, with its conspicuous sexual innuendo, caused offence in some quarters, though it must have added to the sense of excitement about art in the Eisteddfod among adventurous spirits. Clausen's thoughts on the matter probably reflected his general feelings about the painter rather more accurately than the observations he had made at Cadoxton in the presence of his host.

Grant Murray's primary agenda at the Swansea Eisteddfod was to promote the development of new Welsh art and young Welsh artists, in the belief that the health of art was central to the health of society. Since the Eisteddfod aspired to be the most important public expression of the values and activities of Welsh society, art should take a central place there. The Catalogue of the Art Exhibitions was laced with pointed mottoes: 'There will be no living art in Wales until the artist can make a living wage'; 'Purchase your pictures from living artists, the old masters do not need your support'; 'Buy a drawing and burn your almanacs'; 'A purchase when the artist is alive means more to him than a wreath later on'. Unfortunately, these exhortations to buy could hardly have come at a worse moment, since the Eisteddfod took place against the background of the General Strike and the continuing coal strike. On 1 May Winifred had noted the impending start of the dispute with feminist foreboding:

General Strike to begin on Tuesday unless settlement reached. What does this mean ... it seems to me the possible beginning of a great and bitter struggle which will bring much misery. Men, men quarrelling and squabbling and fighting, and women helpless before their folly!
Wise One painting with great joy - I and Zanga wandering in the garden - all the tulips out and the fruit trees. That is peace and life, and for how few. The masses toil on, ill housed, unemployed, become unemployable, and so it goes on. Lord God of Hosts.

Newspaper reviews of the pictures in both the competitive and loan sections at Swansea were extensive and positive. Their general enthusiasm was shared by the procession of distinguished visitors led around the shows. Lloyd George informed reporters that 'If this is going to be the standard, in a very short time Wales will have established the same thing for art as she has thoroughly established for music'.[95] No doubt he had been well briefed beforehand by Winifred, since he was staying with his entourage at Cadoxton, guarded by a posse of local policemen. On the Saturday of the Eisteddfod Ramsay Macdonald was President, and Winifred

had a chance to meet one of Lloyd George's successors in office for the first time. She was not enamoured:

I had never heard him before. He got a tepid welcome, has no geniality or sense of humour; intellectual but cold. I received him among other Committee members at Art Section and was introduced to him. No gleam of warmth about the man - able but dour. [7 August 1926]

Among the artists and adjudicators, the press paid particular attention to the thoughts of Augustus John, by now well established as the most celebrated Welsh painter of his day. His main rival for attention was Evan Walters, though not simply because of his status as a local phenomenon. In the portrait section he was jointly awarded the prize for his *Welsh Collier*. The picture manifested a degree of contact with contemporary life in that time and place which set it apart from the work of any other painter:

The portrait was of a striking (or locked out) collier, for whose temperament the artist had considerable regard, and into whose eyes the circumstances of the time brought occasionally a certain fierceness. He sat two or three times, and in the week this picture was finished.[96]

In the loan exhibition Walters' painting *Bydd Myrdd o Ryfeddodau* also attracted attention but, at the same time, defied the comprehension of the critics.

The *Cambria Daily Leader* noted only that it had 'not a little horror in it', while another reviewer abdicated critical responsibility almost entirely, leaving it to 'readers to speculate for themselves about its meaning'.[97] Similarly, when she saw it in Walters' studio five months before the Eisteddfod, Winifred had sensed that it was a remarkable image but had little idea of how to read it:

Motored to Evan Walters' and saw a fine picture of a boy sitting on a bed listening to a watch, and a weird queer thing of a funeral group near a Welsh Chapel singing hymns whilst some naked boys (having stigmata à la S Francis) sprawl in the foreground. What I feel Evan Walters needs most is to get away from Llangyfelach to where he is surrounded by paintings by other men of his own age. [2 March 1926]

Later, Walters provided some guidance to Winifred about the image, and also an estimation of its importance to him:

I do not think many Welsh people will approve of this. I consider it to be about my best work, but my friends in Wales will hardly think so, I'm afraid. And yet it is quite true. Here you see the dark group in the hills; below, the grave, with its young white bodies. There is no sign of happiness or resurrection in the singing. All is hopeless, dreary, dark, and it rends the hearts of the spirits as they hear it, so melancholy and mournful are the sounds.

'Bydd Myrdd o Ryfeddodau' is an expression of my mind when looking at a group of people standing around a grave singing 'Bydd Myrdd', etc. That group of mourners is in the back ground in front of the little chapel. While the boys in the fore ground represent the expression of (and not an illustration) 'Pan ddelo plant y tonnau/Yn iach o'r cystudd mawr/Oll yn eu gynau gwynion/Ac ar eu newydd wedd/Yn debyg idd ein Harglwydd/ Yn dod i'r lan o'r bedd.'

The colour of the picture you will notice is rather in the minor key like the music in the hymn. The picture is an expression of the whole thing - the chapel - the graveyard - people and their voices - the tune and the words - all combined ...[98]

Evan Walters, *Bydd Myrdd o Ryfeddodau*, 1926. Oil on canvas, 42x52
The National Library of Wales

The boys who carry the stigmata were like 'our Lord' in his suffering as a human being, rather than in his glory as transcendent God. The picture was a meditation on the appropriate Christian response to the distressed state of society. This issue concerned many believers in the period and was much discussed in the pages of *The Welsh Outlook*, as well as in the denominational press, where it was generally known as 'the Question of the Kingdom'. Some regarded social distress and the tension which arose from it as an expression of God's will for man on earth, and as a consequence believed that the appropriate response was to wait with forbearance for the relief from suffering which would be granted the righteous in the next world. Others, and Winifred was prominent among them in her public life, believed that the state of society was a human perversion of God's will, which was for men and women to work towards his kingdom of justice and harmony on earth. The issue cost many Christians their faith in the period, notably the poet Gwenallt, who was both a contemporary of Walters and had been born only a few miles away from him. In a passage from *Credaf*, written later but reflecting on the period of Walters' remarkable picture, Gwenallt described the death of his father and his own rejection of Christianity:

Years later my father's body came home after he had been burnt to death by molten metal, and that unnecessarily. When, in the funeral sermon, the minister said that it was God's will, I cursed his sermon and his God with all the haulier's swear-words that I knew, and when they sang the hymn Bydd Myrdd o Ryfeddodau at the graveside, I sang in my heart the Red Flag.[99]

For Gwenallt, as for Walters, the hymn 'Bydd Myrdd o Ryfeddodau' was a potent focus for the crisis of faith which they experienced as the Question of the Kingdom. Walters was probably not singing 'The Red Flag' in his picture, but he was certainly asking the same question that was asked by Gwenallt and, indeed, by Winifred. However, Winifred understood visual art primarily as a medium for conveying God's vision, rather than the human perversion of it. God's vision she understood as beauty, and she found it at the Eisteddfod exhibition not in *Bydd Myrdd o Ryfeddodau* but in a small oil painting of Ogmore Castle which she bought. It was by a painter called John Cyrlas Williams, who was unknown to her:

To Arts and Crafts show. I like my little oil of Ogmore Castle more than ever and am interested to find it is by a young man living at Porthcawl who has studied in Paris, then had a nervous breakdown and been ill for 4 years though over worst and has just begun to paint again. [29 July 1926]

A few days later Winifred wrote to Williams for the first time about her 'delicious picture'. [16 August 1926] Over the next three years she would make considerable efforts to develop the career

J. Cyrlas Williams,
Ogmore Castle, 1926
Oil on board, 12×13

Unknown
photographer,
*John Aluned
Cyrlas Williams*,
c.1926

of a painter whom she believed had considerable talent – he was 'the real thing'.[100]

Williams lived at home with his parents, brother and sister at Porthcawl, a town with which Winifred was familiar from summer holidays spent there with her own children. She was soon in contact by letter with Williams' mother Gwladys. Since his family were well-off, John Cyrlas Williams had been able to study at the Newlyn artists' colony under Stanhope Forbes. As a part of his recovery from his nervous breakdown he had travelled to Australia. By the autumn of 1926 he was painting in Paris, at the ateliers of La Grande Chaumière in the morning and at

Collarossi in the afternoon. It was also in France, the following year, that Winifred eventually met Gwladys Williams, when both women attended the Gorsedd of the Breton Bards. At Pont Aven Winifred gained the impression that Williams was 'an example of the very best type of cultured Welsh woman'.[101] Winifred did not meet the painter himself until April 1928:

J. Cyrlas Williams,
The Dark Boats,
Martigues, 1927. Oil
on canvas, 18×21

*Motored with Wise One to Porthcawl to see
John Williams the young painter who painted
the Castle I bought at the National Eisteddfod
Exhibition 2 years ago - He had a number of
canvasses with him, and I bought 3 and a small
sketch. He shows great promise I think - painting
in a direct vivid style: I have commissioned him
to do a head of Wise One, an oil sketch at the
end of the month. The pictures I bought are
2 of boats and one of figures in an atelier.*
[15 April 1928]

Winifred immediately contacted Grant Murray
who invited the painter to exhibit with the
South Wales Art Society and proposed a one-
man exhibition the following year. Williams
visited Cadoxton and painted an oil sketch of
Henry which Winifred deemed a clever piece
of painting, if a less than satisfactory likeness.
However, when painter and patron met again
in the autumn, Winifred was 'dispirited to find
he has done no work all these months since he
painted Henry'. Williams had 'great talent but

he evidently is no worker'. She urged him to work hard for six months and then go up to London to see Evan Walters and Cedric Morris, whom she had recently met. She duly arranged the visits on his behalf. Subsequently Morris reported to Winifred that he had liked him well enough and thought him intelligent, but 'did not find him an arresting personality, like Evan'.[102] Williams' one-man show at the Glynn Vivian Gallery did not materialise. In 1931 Grant Murray was still inclined to wait before purchasing his work for the Glynn Vivian and gradually the promising young painter faded from Winifred's view.[103]

Unknown photographer, *The Visit of the South Wales Art Society to Cadoxton Lodge*, 1927. Centre front, Charles Coombe Tennant with Mrs Grant Murray and Isaac Williams to his right and Mrs Isaac Williams and F.J. Kerr to his left. Back row, left, William Grant Murray.

In the meantime, since his success at the Swansea Eisteddfod, Evan Walters' career had continued on its upward trajectory. Indeed, by the time he received Cyrlas Williams in his London studio he was at what would prove to be the peak of his celebrity at a British level. In 1927, as a result of his inability to meet an agreement to exhibit with the London gallery owner Dorothy Warren, Augustus John had recommended Walters as a substitute, having been so impressed by his work at the Swansea Eisteddfod. Warren agreed, and as the opening approached and Walters found himself an object of interest to the smart set in London, his excitement became intense. 'I was at Augustus John's party last Saturday evening!' he informed Winifred. 'I should think there were about 60 people there in his large studio. It was a very interesting evening – very artistic and amusing. I have so much to tell you – it would take me a whole day to write it …'[104] On 15 November Walters' first London exhibition opened to instant acclaim from the clearly well-primed English critics. The previous week, Winifred, who lent her portraits of Lloyd George and Gerald Balfour, had sensed the impending transformation of his life. Following a visit with him to the gallery in Maddox Street, prior

Evan Walters, *Self Portrait*, n.d.
Oil on board, 15×12

Evan Walters,
Llangyfelach,
c.1927. Oil on
canvas, 16×20

Below:
Evan Walters,
Courting, c.1927
Oil on canvas, 20×27

to the opening of the exhibition, she reflected that 'He will become famous now. In a sense I feel I am losing him – but he will not I think forget the help I gave him in his salad days'.[105] Winifred's assessment of Walters' loyalty would prove to be as accurate as her sense that the show would make him famous:

The Western Mail and South Wales News have huge headlines proclaiming Evan Walters' great success - fame achieved at one step. His 'one man show' has brought him into the very front rank of contemporary painters - as I foresaw it would. I rejoice to think of my share in his Career. He was a very raw timid boy when I first met him and he came here to paint the portraits of myself,

CCT and our big group, living here most of the summer. I was among his very earliest friends and he has always shown gratitude and friendliness to me, and loves the Emperors. I have little doubt he will go to the very top of the tree …

I feel like a hen who sees her swan breasting the waves after years in which many people kept yelling abuse at me for championing a one legged ugly ducking. [16 and 17 November 1927]

Winifred travelled to London to see Walters' exhibition at the end of November and, from among the few unsold works, bought the portrait *Elfyn* for 16 guineas – 'a big price for me to pay for it'. [30 November 1927]

Evan Walters had been introduced to Dorothy Warren, who was 'a strange, clever, exotic sort of person', in Winifred's opinion, at precisely the right moment. [30 November 1927] In the wake of the General Strike and the coal strike Walters' social origins appealed to many left-leaning London intellectuals, as well as to those still under the spell of the more deeply-rooted belief in the elevation of the working man. It is not surprising that, much to his irritation, Walters was reinvented by some of his new admirers as having been a collier, though whether Dorothy Warren herself was responsible for this useful piece of promotional mythology is unclear.

After the exhibition closed and very tired from

a weekend at Churt with Lloyd George and a visit to see Henry, who was now at Eton, Winifred ventured to Hampstead to talk to Walters for the first time in his Hampstead studio:

On reaching Paddington made myself go up to Hampstead to see Evan Walters' studio - by bus to Tottenham Court Road then by Tube to Hampstead Station. Found the studio easily and had a long talk, then looked at pictures come from the Warren Gallery show which had not been sold, only a few, but the two I most wanted were among

Evan Walters, *Elfyn*, c.1927
Oil on board, 16×12

them, and I bought them for much less than the catalogue price as E.W. had no commission to pay. I bought 'Llangyfelach' for £14 and Courting for £16 - the former a fine landscape had been greatly admired by Augustus John, and he had it photographed. 'Courting' is an odd picture with something noble and big about it. Evan Walters wrapped them up and carried them by Tube to Oxford Street whence I taxied to Paddington - just caught my train and so home ...

Unpacked the Evan Walters pictures and set them on the easel. Very joyful things they are. [7 and 8 December 1927]

Evan Walters' successful exhibition at the Warren Gallery in 1927 provided a focal point, albeit a transient one, for Welsh painters, patrons and the intellectual community in general. They coalesced around the event so that the notion of a Welsh art world seemed to crystallise again, out of the constituent parts that had dissolved with the decline of the national movement and the disruption of the Great War. Among the artists, the old guard of Christopher Williams and Goscombe John had things to say about Walters, and the current leading figure, Augustus John, was much quoted on the subject of a new genius arisen. A cluster of able young painters, either at or about to go to art school in London, were also drawn into the circle. Of the generation already making a reputation, which included David Jones, it was Cedric Morris who came most closely into contact with Walters.

Unknown photographer, *Cedric Morris and his Pet Rabbit*, 1928 The National Library of Wales

When Walters had visited Winifred in London during his exhibition he had brought Morris with him, and introduced him to his patron. Winifred did not approve:

In evening Evan Walters and Cedric Morris came. Had not seen the latter (a painter, belonging to the Swansea Morris of Sketty) and did not much like him. Look[ed] dissolute. Evan must of course meet and mix with all sorts - but can imagine the Art world of London having much jealousy and coarseness within its ranks.[106]

The social origins of Cedric Morris could hardly have been further removed from those of Walters. He was the descendant of the industrialist John Morris, who created the community of Morriston on the edge of Swansea. He had been educated at an English public school and then, exactly as Cyrlas Williams would do a few years later, had worked both at Newlyn and at the ateliers of La Grande Chaumière and Collarossi in Paris. He travelled widely in north Africa and continental Europe, though not always in the grand manner of his class, since sometimes he preferred to tramp. In 1927 he had moved to London, where he had a successful first exhibition at Tooth's a few months before that of Walters. From London, during the summer he returned to Wales to paint, and was much moved by the landscape. He was about to enter the period of his closest involvement with his own country and no doubt the appearance of Walters on the scene, late in the year, was a factor in drawing him back.

Despite her initial adverse reaction to Morris, Winifred resolved to pursue her acquaintance with him. Naturally, Evan Walters was a central topic of discussion. Notwithstanding the difference of only three or four years of age between them, Morris addressed himself to the matter of his contemporary with a patronising tone which expressed at one and the same time his sense of social superiority over Walters and equality with Winifred. Morris wrote to Winifred that he 'was both surprised and very delighted to find how good' a painter Walters was, 'and very proud to think that he is a compatriot':

I don't like the literature of several of them - but this has nothing to do with painting anyway. Now about him personally - I find him charming and I hope we shall become friends - there are one or two things I should like to talk to you about, to do with him - apropos of transplanting a simple and enthusiastic Welshman of his type into this damnable Town, so I hope we shall meet again soon.[107]

Morris invited Walters to his birthday party at his studio in Great Ormond Street, and duly reported to Winifred that the thirty-four-year-old innocent had enjoyed himself.[108]

It may be that this summary co-option of her protégé by Morris lay at the root of Winifred's distaste for him, and the uneasy relationship which developed and which persisted for some time. A few days after the birthday party Winifred visited Morris at his studio and left with even more hostile feelings than those she had experienced on their previous meeting. Winifred 'disliked him more than before, and equally the man who lives with him, and I disliked his paintings and didn't buy anything – which I think confused him'. [15 December 1927] However, both parties seem to have been drawn together by ties of social class, and in the Autumn of 1928 relations with Winifred improved:

Cedric Morris and his friend Haines came to spend the afternoon bringing a boy named Elton. Cedric is now a rising painter. I liked him much better than when I saw him at his studio in May - but I don't like his major domo Haines. They were all enthusiastic about the pictures here, the house etc. It was a day of lovely sunshine.[109]

During the summer Morris had painted extensively in Wales, and it may be that in their meeting he transmitted his excitement about the landscape to Winifred and revealed aspects of himself of which she was previously

Cedric Morris, *Seabirds (Pintail Duck and Tern)*,
c.1928-30. Oil on canvas, 21×27

unaware. Before Lett Haines joined him
from London, Morris wrote to him about the
landscape of Glamorgan in similar terms to
those often adopted by Winifred. The beauty of
the landscape was a vehicle for the expression of
a patriotic contrast with England, and it evoked
a deep sense of ancient history, albeit expressed
by Morris in less reverent terms than those
usually employed by Winifred:

*I always said that this was the most lovely country
in the world and it is - it's so beautiful that I
hardly dare look at it - and I realise now that
all my painting is the result of pure nostalgia
and nothing else - I thought I was homesick for
England but not at all - dirty grimy little market
garden - it was this I wanted ...*

*Cefn-y-Bryn - the highest point hereabouts is
just behind (not very high) - used to be a place of*

*great mystery to me with Arthur's Stone on the
top - you will have to climb up and pay your
respects to your namesake - he sat there when
he read out the laws - there are hundreds of
wild ponies still here - and there is a little
island belonging to this farm with only sheep
on it that we can go to when we like. There are
sand dunes and a great bay of sand ¼ mile off
and beyond that Worm's Head ...*[100]

Among the younger visitors to Walters'
exhibition at the Warren Gallery in
November 1927 was yet another painter from
Swansea, Archie Rhys
Griffiths. He was a face
worker at the Mountain
Colliery until the coal
strike of 1921 detached
him from the life of the
industrial worker. He had
always amused himself
by drawing. The strike

ROYAL COLLEGE OF ART, SOUTH KENSINGTON.
JULY, 1926.

Photo by Panora Ltd., 56 Eagle Street, London, W.C.

Unknown
photographer,
*Graduates of the
Royal College of Art*,
1926
Left, William
Rothenstein,
above, Archie
Rhys Griffiths.

provided him with more time to draw, and also
the opportunity to paint for his own pleasure.
He began to attend part-time classes at Swansea
School of Art under Grant Murray and, in 1922, he
took two first prizes at the Ammanford Eisteddfod.
As a consequence he won scholarships which
enabled him to continue his studies full-time at the
Art School. John Davies Williams commissioned
him to draw industrial subjects for the *Cambria
Daily Leader*. In 1924 he gained a scholarship
to study at the Royal College of Art and, again,

Williams publicised his progress in his newspaper. Griffiths' contemporary at the Royal College was Ceri Richards but, as in the mythologized case of Evan Walters, the spirit of the times demanded that the boy from the pit receive the encouragement. Richards was scarcely mentioned in the local papers during his career at the Royal College of Art, though he was a close enough friend of Griffiths to paint a portrait of him.[111]

Because of his heavy promotion by John Davies Williams and the exhibition of his pictures with the Swansea Art Society while he was training in London, Winifred must have been aware of the work of Griffiths by the mid-1920s. Grant Murray wrote to her to seek her involvement in the young man's career in November 1927. Griffiths had narrowly failed to win the Prix de Rome but had claimed the consolation prize of a travelling scholarship to France and Italy. Murray had met the painter in London shortly before his departure and discovered that he would be 'pennyless' on his return.[112] John Davies Williams also wrote to Winifred, asking her to invite the painter to Cadoxton on his return 'to brush him up and prepare him a little for his career in the world'. He had begun badly, in their view, by recently marrying his girlfriend, a model at the Royal College. She immediately became pregnant. In his reply to Winifred's invitation to paint at Cadoxton, Griffiths expressed the hope that his changed circumstances might not affect her attitude. In this respect, as in many others, Griffiths was no Augustus John:

After receiving your letter, I suffered a most anxious time, but now I am pleased to inform you that the anxiety is now over, as on Feb 28th my wife gave birth to a son - I am delighted to say that both are doing well.

Regarding your invitation for me to spend some time at Cadoxton Lodge to paint in peace, there is nothing I could have wished for better after returning from my travelling, than to receive such a wonderful opportunity and at such a correct time, again to be at Cadoxton Lodge, which is so near the material that I require for my future work - but being married makes it very difficult for me to answer your letter as I would like to -

Although the idealistic hill I have chosen is very steep, I want to avoid any deviations which circumstances might make compulsory. Your kind offer inspires with new enthusiasm, and coupled with my wife's sympathies towards Art would help me to climb with determination and confidence - but, now that I have revealed to you my present feelings and position, I feel conscious that your kind offer to me will assume a different aspect.[113]

Although she was concerned about the financial implications of Griffiths having a wife and child, Winifred did not withdraw her promise of support. She met the painter for the first time shortly after his return from Italy and on 1 September 1928 she was driven to his family home at Gorseinon to inspect his work:

He has a tiny studio in the garden behind his house. I saw some very fine drawings, and some good oils. He has great talent and he has character - and he is a fine draughtsman.

I commissioned him to do two heads in oil of Wise One and Zanga, to be done at Cadoxton, where he comes on Monday. [1 September 1928]

The intervening Sunday saw the visit of Cedric Morris and Lett Haines to Cadoxton, and on Monday Griffiths duly arrived to work. Winifred's impression was of 'a gentle and sensitive young man – earnest and unaffected. He has *character* and humility to add to his great gifts. He ought to give noble work to Wales':

Archie Griffiths painting in Music Room. He is a tragic figure. I find he has been too poor to buy paint freely 'I have not been able to use paint as I want to' he said, for this cause.

Thank God he will go away from here with £10-0-0 in his pocket - but the young wife and child in the background makes darkness near as far as his work as an artist is concerned. He can't at this stage sell enough to live on. [3 and 5 September 1928]

Griffiths' attempts at painting Winifred's children were failures, although she kept the 'rather prim little portrait' of Henry. Under Winifred's scrutiny, the painter's courage failed him. However, he did not lose his ability to image the things he knew, and while at

Cadoxton he made a confident drawing and an oil sketch of workers underground. At the end of what must have been a stressful as much as a stimulating week, Evan Walters was summoned to inspect progress:

Dear Evan arrived at 3. We talked tête à tête for an hour, had tea, then he saw Archie Griffiths' things. Told me privately they were 'rather bad' but what he most needed was to 'slap on paint

John Latimer Jones,
Archie Rhys Griffiths in his Studio in Gorseinon, c.1928

117

freely caring nothing for detail but putting down the strong facts of anything seen without a care of what the result was.' To learn to handle paint freely - that was the aim. As a result after he had left Archie Griffiths did a ¾ oil sketch of me (in my Welsh dress) quite terrible as a likeness but showing a big advance in the big handling of paint and massive and strong. He has given me this. The children doubled up with fits of laughter as they looked at it after Archie's departure. Poor fellow! But he has lived an age in this week and learnt much. [8 September 1928]

Griffiths left Cadoxton with Winifred's copy of Clive Bell's *Art*, which had been given to her by Evan Walters. Having seen both the young painters who were benefiting from Winifred's encouragement at the time, Walters was of the opinion that Cyrlas Williams was more promising than Griffiths. However, his opinion did not undermine Winifred's original assessment of Griffiths, and their relationship continued. She immediately dispatched to him a selection of frames, to enable him to present his work properly, and sought his help in getting George Martin to Cadoxton. Evan Walters had already failed in this mission and Griffiths efforts to pin him down were equally fruitless. When Martin did not appear as agreed one day in October 1928, Griffiths set off

Archie Rhys Griffiths,
Miners Underground, 1928
Oil on paper, 15x11

in pursuit and eventually found him at the Kardomah café, the haunt of Swansea painters and writers. Griffiths conveyed Winifred's invitation to him to work at Cadoxton, but Martin was non-committal. Having been stood up for a second time, the following week Griffiths wrote to Winifred admitting defeat.

Archie Rhys Griffiths,
Miner Underground, 1928
Chalk on paper, 15x11

Like Winifred, Grant Murray displayed undiminished confidence in Archie Griffiths. Although he found it difficult to see how the painter could support himself and his family (especially given the fact that Griffiths had told him that he hated teaching) he fulfilled his promise to give him an exhibition. It confirmed the feelings of both teacher and patron that Griffiths' work had a particular and powerful quality. Winifred peppered her copy of the catalogue with handwritten exclamations of 'very good'. Both she and Murray must have been sustained in their high opinion of Griffiths by the remarkable eulogy to him written by William Rothenstein, Principal of the Royal College of Art, and published in the catalogue:

Griffiths, coming to the College, soon showed unusual powers of drawing, but what appeared most striking was a passionate element of sincerity in his figure compositions. Again and again he tried to express in these, in a peculiarly imaginative way, a moving sympathy with toiling and sweating workers underground. The subjects showed an intimate knowledge of the miner's life; but objective though they were in treatment, one was always aware of an inner mystical spirit, which raised his designs far above mere illustration, however informative and interesting. As his grasp of constructive form developed, so did this imaginative insight grow. Finally Griffiths achieved work which combined a curiosity for form with a powerful imaginative vision, a

combination which has distinguished some of the rarest spirits in the history of the arts. For half a year Griffiths has been living alone in his own country of Wales. I have seen nothing of what he has been doing, but still in my mind I can see vividly those darkling scenes of labour underground, while in the womb of the austere green hills dwell the spirits of joy and of pain, chief, if invisible actors in the drama of human life. Gifts of great dramatic and lyrical promise, rare gifts these. It is to be hoped that Wales will not let such inspiring gifts go unused ...[114]

From the exhibition Winifred bought *Miners Returning from Work*, which she regarded as 'a rough strong thing of rough strong men'. [7 December 1928] The painter wrote to her about the genesis of the picture:

I feel greatly encouraged that the 'Miners Returning from Work' is to be included in your collection of paintings. I feel convinced that this painting is the best among my mining subjects - whilst painting it I just let myself go - and I feel that my impression has been conveyed more truly than in any of my previous work. It was painted the week following my stay at 'Cadoxton' and certainly the result of our talks.[115]

It is clear from *Miners Returning from Work* that among the subjects of discussion during Griffiths' stay at Cadoxton had been the work of the painter Eugène Laermans. Fourteen years earlier his picture

The Way of Rest had been
reproduced by Thomas Jones
in *The Welsh Outlook*, along
with an article presenting him,
as other Belgian Realists were
also presented, as models for
aspiring Welsh painters. Griffiths'
version of the subject was so
close to Laermans as to make it
unlikely that Winifred had not
shown him the reproduction.

Griffiths 1928 exhibition was
a success. Grant Murray reported
over 800 visitors on the first
Saturday and 'numerous sales'.
He would recommend three
works for purchase by the
Gallery. In thanks for her
support, Griffiths sent Winifred
the drawing for his picture *Tro
yn yr Yrfa*, a stark image of a
miner's funeral procession.[116]

Archie Rhys Griffiths,
*Miners Returning from
Work*, 1928. Oil on
canvas, 20×27

Eugène Laermans,
The Way of Rest.
The picture as reproduced in
The Welsh Outlook, 1928

Charles Coombe Tennant died on
5 November 1928. 'I suppose I am
now rich', Winifred observed in her diary,
'and somehow I don't care. I'm too tired,
and have seen too much of how little money
can give!' [24 November 1928] Although it
would take two years to resolve, the death of
Charles precipitated a fundamental change of
direction in Winifred's life. On 1 January 1929
she woke in Murren, Switzerland, to ' begin

a new year and a new existence' which, initially, involved a reinvestment of energy in Cadoxton. Before returning home she stayed in London and, most unusually, enjoyed herself there. Next, she visited her friend Walford Davies, now ensconced as Master of the King's Music at Windsor. On arriving finally at Cadoxton in early spring, Winifred resolved to 'go slowly and keep quietly on until I have got this house mastered. Then I want to sit down and enjoy it – paint, pray, read, and amuse myself'. [3 March 1929] She was visited by friends including George M.Ll. Davies – 'serene, simple, tenderly kind and charitable'. [27 March 1929] They discussed the 'Lost Land of beauty and aesthetic expression in Wales'.[117] However, Davies was as involved as ever in social projects which he presented to Winifred, perhaps not sensing her changed mood of retirement from public life. Davies was engaged with the Society of Friends in plans to relieve the increasing distress caused by the Depression. In December 1929 he reported to Winifred the early stages in the process which would lead to the establishment at Bryn-mawr in Monmouthshire of co-operative business ventures. The Quakers had 'got into the trust of the people' at Bryn-mawr. 'At the next village, Blaina, the Blue Pilgrims … are doing equally pioneering work. These women are mainly Anglicans from the Home Counties who have simply descended on Blaina like a flight of partridges. They have given relief through the existing channels, have lodged in the miners' houses and above all, have brought an indescribable courtesy and tenderness

to meet the spiritual hunger'.[118] In 1930 the Quakers facilitated the establishment of the Bryn-mawr furniture manufacturing business. Davies would become increasingly involved and in 1932 joined the sister settlement established by the Quakers at Maes-yr-haf in the Rhondda. Winifred was without doubt sympathetic to these ventures, rooted as they were in the belief of the Arts and Crafts movement that economic and spiritual development should proceed hand in hand. However, unlike her friend, she remained an outside observer.

In May 1929 Evan Walters arrived at Cadoxton. The purpose of his visit was to discuss a proposed portrait of Henry to be called 'The Eton Boy', for which he would sit in the formal clothes customarily worn for the Eton against Harrow cricket match, played at Lord's every year. At the end of May, Winifred remained full of positive thoughts about her home. Returning from a visit to the Royal Academy, where she saw a 'superb John' among 'many very dull pictures', Winifred perceived 'the peace of beloved Cadoxton – sweet scented air blowing in through the open windows, the trees in full leaf, chestnut and laburnum in blossom, quiet, out of the noise and dust of London – thank God.' [15 and 25 May 1929] A week later, in the company of Alexander, she visited the Glynn Vivian Art Gallery:

Had such a joyous break in my life! Went with Zanga to the Swansea Art Society's show at the Glynn Vivian Gallery and bought 2 joy-giving

Unknown
photographer,
*George M.Ll.
Davies at a Boys'
Camp*, c.1925
The National
Library of Wales

William Grant
Murray, *Swansea
from Richmond Hill*,
1929. Oil on
canvas, 33x33

*pictures - Swansea (under
snow) by Grant Murray and
a beach scene by Will Evans,
both full of light and life, with
in Grant Murray's a lyrical
quality. Oh! how my sad heart
leapt up with joy as I gazed at
these things. Alexander with
me and we spent such a happy
hour there, like old days of
Deedooge [Charles] and I
picture-rejoicing. There were
many poor pictures but in the
oils some I liked over and
above my two - a good Cyrlas
Williams. Some things of
Archie Griffiths I thought poor.
Some good etchings and water
colours. Oh! the smell of oil
paint - how my heart rose
and sang to it, crying out for
leisure, beauty and joy in self
expression. 'I am the dumb
musician ...' [1 June 1929]*

Winifred enthused about the show to John Davies Williams, with the result that he commissioned a review from her, which duly appeared in the *Cambria Daily Leader*. In it she praised Will Evans and Cyrlas Williams, but her greatest accolade was reserved for Grant Murray:

We all knew that he could paint with exquisite finish and delicacy, such as distinguished his set of small oil paintings illustrating the Gorsedd ceremonies at Singleton a few years ago (and any Continental city would have acquired these at sight for its municipal buildings - is it too late for Swansea to do likewise?) but this year he comes before us in a new light, as a master of the technique of the most modern school of painting. Consider the strength, the breadth, and the virile freedom of treatment in such things as No.12, 'Swansea from Richmond-road,' and No.8, 'Richmond-road, Winter Sunshine.' Allied

with these qualities is a rectitude of draughtsmanship and a sense of colour that is full of refinement and distinction. These pictures are strong and luminous, and show a mastery in the bold handling of the paint...

If a few of our townsfolk made it a regular practice to buy one picture from this annual show, they would in a few years find it an absorbing hobby - and art would be encouraged in our midst.[119]

Clearly moved by this public appreciation of his work, Murray presented to Winifred as a gift his landscape *Winter Sunshine, Richmond Road*.

On 1 August, Evan Walters returned to Cadoxton to begin work on *The Eton Boy*. Winifred recorded progress on the picture in detail. It was to be painted in the garden, with Henry attired in what Winifred regarded as his 'glorious raiment' of silk hat and grey waistcoat. The party wandered about, trying different backgrounds and lighting effects. Once the question was resolved, Walters made a small oil sketch, which he then squared up on the enormous canvas, which measured over 7'6" in height. Winifred had invested herself heavily in this image of her youngest son, and her anxious observations on its progress were marked by references to his 'aristocratic' bearing, to his 'extreme refinement and distinction'. Notwithstanding her anxiety that Walters succeed in conveying these qualities, she refrained from comment while he was at work,

Will Evans, *In the Bay*, 1929
Oil on board, 12×18

William Grant Murray,
Winter Sunshine,
Richmond Road,
Swansea, 1929
Oil on board, 18×12

and her relationship with him regained the ease which had been established eight years earlier. The painter was now thirty-five years old, 'a river of talk, a friend of Augustus John and of Ramsay Macdonald, much unspoiled and still very Welsh'.[120] They went together to see *Juno and the Paycock*, written by Walters' friend Sean O'Casey, who had been living in London for the past three years. Winifred found the play 'noble and poignant', written as it was from the point of view of a passionate Nationalist who deplored violence:

Ireland with its saviours and its faults … and Rachel mourning in a man-made world. Lord God of hosts how passionately my soul went out to thee on the words of the two mourning mothers of the play! [7 August 1929]

Evan Walters + Winefrae August 1929 – Painting of the full length Portrait on the Lawn at Cadoxton.

Walters worked ten days, broke off for a further ten days, and then returned to complete the portrait:

After lunch Evan Walters arrived and Wise One stood on the lawn for the final sitting, a long business, for with rests it went on to 5.30 pm. Thankful was I when at last I saw Evan Walters carrying the huge canvas across the lawn to the Music Room. Tea, and then he carried me off to look at it. It is a fine thing certainly, and has a great likeness to Wise One, but the lips are too thick which gives him a pout he has not got. Nothing had been said as to price and I had calculated at first £50, which was what I paid for the big group of myself and Emperors - but from things Evan Walters said at times I had made up my mind to £100, and was taken aback when he named £150 as his fee. I had to fair bon visage a mauvais jeu, but just now £150 is more than I wanted to spend on any picture. It is not that I think the price excessive - far from it.
[29 August 1929]

Left:
Unknown photographer,
Evan Walters and Henry Coombe Tennant on the Terrace at Cadoxton Lodge, 1929

Unknown photographer,
Evan Walters Painting 'The Eton Boy' at Cadoxton Lodge, 1929

Far left:
Evan Walters, *Sketch for the Portrait of Henry Coombe Tennant, 'The Eton Boy',* 1929. Oil on canvas, 22×9

Evan Walters, *Portrait of Henry Coombe Tennant, 'The Eton Boy',* 1929. Oil on canvas, 91×36

127

The Eton Boy was the most expensive work Winifred had ever commissioned. She was rewarded when it was well hung at the Royal Academy where, in the following June, she admired it in the stylish Bourlet frame she and Walters together had selected for it. She thought it a 'fine thing'. *Punch* was less charitable, satirising what it regarded as the pretensions of the patron. The magazine published a sketch of the portrait over the caption 'Why I am sending my son to Harrow'. Winifred kept a copy, but committed no comment upon it to her diary, though the cartoon may well have struck home. The commission was, indeed, a curious one, characteristic of Winifred only in the way in which it reveals her as a person who struggled to resolve conflicting ideas and feelings. Both in principle and in practice, she had severe reservations about public school education, and about Eton in particular. Henry's career there had been a troubled one, which revealed bullying and other unpleasant manifestations of the public school system. The departure of the boys from home for their respective schools always resulted in a resurgence of Winifred's guilt about her ambiguous attitude to motherhood. In 1926 she was sufficiently distressed to write a radical attack on public school education, which was published in a collection of essays under the title 'A Boy as Future Citizen'.[121] Nevertheless, Henry was not withdrawn from Eton and, over the years, she developed an attachment to the place, which met her need for the reassurance of deeply rooted historical continuity.

Unknown artist, *'Eton Boy; or, Why I am sending my son to Harrow'*, Cartoon from *Punch*, 14 May 1930 The National Library of Wales

During the painting of *The Eton Boy* in August 1929 it became clear to Winifred that her relationship with Cadoxton, and much of what flowed from it, had been irrevocably changed by the death of Charles. It was he who had brought her there and it seemed to Henry, in particular, that 'with the disappearance of CCT the raison d'être of Cadoxton is gone'. [4 November 1929] Henry would soon be away again at Eton and Alexander at Cambridge. Both had made it clear to her that they did not want to return to live in Wales when their formal education came to an end. Winifred feared a lonely future, and the practical difficulties of running a large house without the support of her husband weighed heavily upon her. In a wider context, she shared the anxiety, widespread among people of property, that the Labour government would impose unsustainable taxation. Although she rejoiced at the appointment by Ramsay Macdonald of the feminist Margaret Bandfield as Minister of

Labour, the first woman to hold a cabinet post, she came to 'regard this country as finished as far as the gentry are concerned'. [25 August 1929] As the summer of 1929 drew to a close, she began to 'long for life in a different *world*, and a different climate, and with some human companionship'. [31 August 1929] In particular, the memory of her happiness in France played on her mind. When she conversed with French sailors working on an onion boat docked at Swansea it was 'Like going home to be talking with them, there'. [1 September 1929] France had, indeed, been her home for a large part of her childhood: 'Ma jeunesse calls to me – all those happy places I loved as a girl draw me, call me …' [10 June 1930]

As the winter of 1930 closed in, the visible signs of economic depression in Wales oppressed her:

Into Neath paying bills, its dirty mean streets filled with ugly mean-looking people … I long for colour, light and warmth … Must I always live here? And yet I love Cadoxton itself and the memories which fill it of all the years - 34 now - that have passed since I first came here. [1 January 1930]

As in so many aspects of her life, Winifred was caught between conflicting emotions. She had no desire to live in England, and frequently felt a particular distaste for London. However, that city was likely to become the centre of the lives of her children, and from there she could travel easily to France, as she did in June 1930, on a visit which seems to have been crucial in making the decision to leave Wales. In Paris she spent her time visiting galleries and buying pictures: 'How lovely Paris is, how gay. I feel ten years younger, and sing to myself while out of sheer light-heartedness!' [20 June 1930] Her return to England was miserable – a 'dull, depressing, and drear country; where people do as little work as they can and grumble, whereas in France people work hard and are happy'. [24 June 1930] As her depression deepened, Swansea seemed even worse:

To Swansea early. Long day shopping - hideousness of industrial areas, mean streets, public houses, trams, slag heaps, litter, dirt.
Paris - Place de la Concorde, looking up to the Arc de Triumphe, across it from the Terrace of the Tuilleries gardens. I close my eyes and see it - and pray. [28 June 1930]

The comparison was hardly fair, but as a wealthy woman Winifred was in a position to make a choice between Wales in the Depression, where her work as a magistrate and a prison visitor brought her into frequent contact with the wreckage of a society under stress, and escape to what seemed to her the carefree French art world. In September 1930, she and Alexander took the decision to sell the estate and to close the house. It was 'a momentous day … the end of a chapter in family history – Cadoxton a thing of the past'.[122]

It was at this point also that Winifred decided formally to retain her French pictures, rather than to donate them as a collection to the National Museum. However, the decision had probably been a long time in the making, and was not essentially the consequence of leaving Cadoxton. It probably derived from a combination of the interest shown in the pictures by Alexander, and a lack of confidence in Isaac Williams, the Curator of Art. Her opinion of his judgement had never been high. In May 1930, for instance, on a visit to the Museum, Williams had shown her 'three historical portraits lately bought in terrible condition at low prices (one with a Welsh inscription) of 1500-1600'. Williams had taken photographs 'pre what he called "retrenching" – but when I saw the pictures it appeared to me he had entirely repainted them. They looked like oleo-lithographs'. Winifred spent some time in the Museum on this occasion and 'could have spent a day there with joy in solitude, but Isaac Williams' clacking tongue drove me away, as I could not get rid of him. Poor fellow, so kind and so utterly boring.'[123]

In contrast, Winifred's relationship with Grant Murray at the Glynn Vivian Gallery prospered. Increasingly it was through Murray that Winifred's engagement with young Welsh painters was maintained. By June 1929 she was acting as chair of the Art Gallery Committee which, among other things, made decisions about the purchase of new works. For many years to come she and Murray would co-operate closely on the development of the Glynn Vivian collection. She trusted his judgement and he hers, although Cedric Morris proved something of a difficulty. Murray felt that the gallery should buy a picture and an opportunity arose when the painter had an exhibition at Tooth's in March 1930. He selected *Llanmadoc Hill, Gower*, which was sent to the Glynn Vivian on approval. The picture was everything that Winifred might have been expected to like, given the qualities of vivid colour and freshness that she so often praised in the French works she bought. She inspected it and found it wanting, though the disagreement had little to do with the picture and much to do with Winifred's attitude to the person who painted it. On this occasion Murray prevailed, and the picture was bought for the gallery. On almost all other occasions Winifred and Murray were in accord. In June 1930, for instance, Evan Walters' *The Brothers* was bought immediately after Winifred had visited the painter's latest London exhibition and greatly liked the picture. A month later George Martin was to be the beneficiary of her enthusiasm, as Murray wrote to acknowledge:

I am delighted with your purchase of one of Martin's masterpieces for the Gallery, in time we shall get together one of the finest collections of modern works in the provincial Galleries. Regarding the cost the gallery can and must pay the full cost of £50. It is very kind of yourself and Mr. Chisman but we have close on £1000 for purchases in hand and it is time we used

*some of it, else it will be confiscated by
the Highways or Trams Committee.*[124]

Against the background of upheaval in
her private life, Winifred not only continued
to encourage established figures, but interested
herself in the current generation of students at
the Art School, several of whom would go on to
develop successful careers. She became aware of
Alfred Janes and Kenneth Hancock during 1929,
probably as a result of seeing the first pictures
which they had shown with the Swansea Art
Society in that year. She purchased a Janes drawing
and donated it to the Glynn Vivian, and the
following year bought a still life by Hancock for
herself. In a fawning letter of thanks, Hancock
described Winifred as 'the only patron of the Fine
Arts of Wales' and revealed that it was his first
ever sale.[125] The arrival of his picture at Cadoxton
demonstrates how much art remained, for her,
a vital refuge from the stress of public life. On
26 June 1930 she was required to serve on the
Grand Jury in Swansea. Later in the day she met
the 'intelligent and pleasant working man' who
was to be the next mayor of the town. He was a

*refreshing contrast to sundry 'County' magistrates
serving on good pay whose rudeness to myself and
the other woman juror was intense, especially
on our refusal to retire in a case of sex crime
in which a woman was the sufferer and wherein
were 3 women witnesses. It will 50 years hence
seem quite unbelievable that insolent hostility*

Alfred Janes,
Drawing of a Head, 1929
Pencil on paper, 7x5. City
and County of Swansea:
Glynn Vivian Art Gallery

131

Kenneth W. Hancock,
Still Life, 1930
Oil on board,
21x24

Ivor Thomas,
Miner Underground,
1929 Woodcut, 6x4

*should have been shown to women when
they first came on to Grand Juries!
 Brought out with me the still life by
Hancock which I had bought at the
Swansea Art show in May. Set it on the
drawing room easel - and felt comforted.
Beauty of colour, of design, deep feeling,
peace! 'Still Life'.* [26 June 1930]

The next week, she met the painter
for the first time:

132

To Swansea in afternoon, Grant Murray took me over to the Art School and introduced me to Hancock, a most likeable young fellow - also to Mr Hall, who showed me a fine bust of D. Davies of The Post which he is modelling. I also saw Ivor Thomas (George Davies sent me a woodcut by him in January last) who promises to be a fine draughtsman, and Alfred Janes, whose drawing of a head I gave to the Glynn Vivian last year.[126]

In August the 'three well mannered youths' took tea with Winifred at Cadoxton and inspected the pictures, in particular five new arrivals bought on her recent visit to Paris, which must have seemed to them exotic in the extreme. [26 August 1930] Nearly a year later, Grant Murray reported to Winifred that he was engaged in smoothing the young men's paths to London, where she would next meet them.[127]

In May 1931 Winifred undertook the 'lacerating task' of burning hundreds of the letters and documents which she had accumulated since her arrival at Cadoxton in 1895. With profound symbolic significance she also burned the relics of Christopher's life there, including his kit bag, 'stained with his blood, that was with him when he fell'. [6 May 1931] She then travelled to London to search for a flat, and eventually found what she wanted at 73 Portland Place, just north of Oxford Circus in the West End. In the middle of July the contents of Cadoxton were removed. On Saturday 5 September 1931 Winifred woke for the last time in the house, saw Alexander and Henry off, walked on the terrace in the sun, and then was driven away. That evening, at a hotel in London, she noted simply in her diary 'This day I left Cadoxton. Coeur sacré de Jesu je crois en votre amour pour moi!'

Chapter Three
THE VIEW FROM LONDON

At her flat in London, less than a month after leaving Cadoxton Lodge, Winifred Coombe Tennant received a letter from William Grant Murray, in which he asked her both to act as the official representative of the Glynn Vivian Art Gallery in London, and to interest herself in the wellbeing of a new generation of Welsh students at work in London colleges. The young artists, whom Grant Murray had sent on their way with 'fatherly talks on the temptations of City life', included Kenneth Hancock, Ivor Thomas, Glan Williams and Alfred Janes. Williams had just secured his first job as city cartoonist on the *Daily Express*; Hancock and Thomas were at the Royal College. Janes,

who before leaving for London had completed two still life paintings which Grant Murray regarded as 'the finest pieces of student work done during my 21 years in Swansea', was at the Royal Academy.[1] He felt that, alongside Archie Griffiths, Ceri Richards, S. Crowden Clement and Ken Chapman, they might form what he described as an 'Art Clique', with Walters as President and Winifred as general advisor.[2]

Opportunities to involve herself with young Welsh artists presented themselves soon after Winifred's arrival in London. On a dark Wednesday in February 1932 she fled the boredom of a meeting of the Magistrates Association, 'to the much more congenial atmosphere of the private view of a young Welsh painter named Morland Lewis of Carmarthen'. [24 February 1932] Lewis had been trained at Carmarthen School of Art and then at the Royal Academy schools, where he became closely associated with his teacher, Walter Sickert. The present exhibition, which Lewis shared with the English painter Robert Medley, was his second in London. Suitably impressed at the private view with both painter and paintings, the same day Winifred wrote an article about his work in a

Unknown photographer,
*Winifred Coombe Tennant in her flat
at 73 Portland Place, London, 1937*

nostalgic spirit which would soon become characteristic of her attitude to Wales. She sent it to John Davies Williams for publication:

Out of the noise and bustle of Bond Street, I stepped back today into the homely atmosphere of Wales. Climbing up a flight of stairs in the Cooling Galleries, I came to the exhibition of the work of a young Carmarthenshire painter - Morland Lewis, and all around the walls were lovely bits of West Wales looking at me ...[3]

Winifred also wrote immediately to Grant Murray to recommended a purchase. Deciding that he 'may as well be hung for a sheep as a lamb', the Principal settled upon the most expensive option offered by Winifred, and bought for twenty guineas *Distant View of Laugharne*.[4]

The purchase of *Distant View of Laugharne* for the Glynn Vivian marked a change of emphasis in Winifred's support for Welsh painters. From this point, she sought often to place works in the Glynn Vivian and other art galleries, and to introduce painters to private patrons, in addition to enriching her own collection of Welsh pictures. Among the first to feel the benefit of this approach was Archie Griffiths. Since their last meeting in 1928, Griffiths had struggled to support his wife, Winifred, and their children Rhys and Diana, in London. Transported into the Chelsea set through his friend, the novelist Geraint Goodwin, he drank heavily. As a consequence, Goodwin's role had too often been to help to load Griffiths' belongings and pictures on to a handcart and wheel them to yet another temporary home in rented rooms.[5] In 1931 Thomas Jones and others in the London Welsh community, and his former principal at the Royal College, William Rothenstein, came to his aid. Jones and Rothenstein co-operated to secure for him a commission to paint portraits for the Astor family.

Morland Lewis, *Distant View of Laugharne*, 1932. Oil on canvas, 20x30 City and County of Swansea: Glynn Vivian Art Gallery

In the same year Rothenstein arranged that he should paint a mural at the Camden Working Men's College, which had a strong tradition in visual culture, which extended back to John Ruskin and William Morris. According to John Davies Williams, Griffiths' mural, which was 14 feet across, suggested 'the whole course of life, from birth to death. Here is man, at his dawn, and at his setting. Here he is at play, at work at his best, at his worst. The Christ on the Cross looks down upon the human tragedy'.[6]

While working on the mural, Thomas Jones arranged for Griffiths to show his work at the Young Wales Association at Mecklenburg Square.[7] The exhibition was accompanied by extensive press publicity, most of it seeking to construct a mythology of Griffiths in terms of a perceived contrast between coal miner and mystic, which was most clearly expressed in a eulogy written by Geraint Goodwin, and published in *The Welsh Outlook*.[8] However, in his introduction to the catalogue, Thomas Jones was more concerned to make a wider point, directly pertinent to Winifred's activities and concerns:

It is a mistake for an artist to be born in the South Wales coalfield. There is material for art everywhere, but there is not everywhere sustenance for the artist. The private patron of native talent is rare in Wales and the effective demand for public art is feeble.

There is no living tradition in art as there is in religion, or music, or philanthropy. Our public authorities have no confidence in handling its problems. They will employ artists to teach Art in the schools but not to practice it on the walls of the classrooms. They trust the teacher, not the artist. They are nervous of the artist because they do not know how to judge him. Quite literally he is a person extra-ordinary. He is not part of the warp and woof of civilization as we know it in the coalfield. This is true whichever party is in power. Where art is concerned, there is a coalition agreed in regarding the promotion of beauty as a luxury and not practical politics. So our young artists come to London and seek appreciation and support from the enlightened Welsh community of the metropolis. That, as I see it, is the meaning of this Exhibition.[9]

The private view of Griffiths' exhibition was attended by friends, including Evan Walters, and by distinguished establishment figures, notably William Goscombe John, who had secured for the painter his first scholarship. Since Grant Murray was unable to travel to London, Winifred represented the Glynn Vivian Art Gallery. The gathering was addressed by William Rothenstein:

Here is someone who can put on the walls of the village halls or the city halls of Wales subjects which are common to all Welsh people. In these days we want to see what ordinary people are thinking about and what are the tragedies and comedies of their lives, and no-one can do that better than Mr Griffiths. It is no use just paying lip homage. Mr Griffiths has done an admirable decoration for the Working Men's college in England (Camden Town). Let us see that he does one for Wales.[10]

In Grant Murray's absence from Griffiths' private view, Winifred recommended the purchase of *Testing a Collier's Lamp* to the Swansea Art Galleries Committee. For herself she bought *Child Sleeping*, a portrait of the painter's baby daughter in her cradle, and also a linocut version of *On the Coal Tips*, a large oil painting owned by Geraint Goodwin. Presumably responding to the suggestion made by Rothenstein in his speech, which was reported by the press, Murray soon commissioned Griffiths to paint a decoration for one of the panels in the Glynn Vivian Art Gallery entrance hall.[11]

Archie Rhys Griffiths,
Child Sleeping (The Cradle), c.1932
Oil on canvas, 20×26

In his first letter to her in London, Grant Murray had suggested that Winifred make the acquaintance of William Rothenstein, in order to help keep an eye on the Welsh students in his care at the Royal College. The opening of Griffiths' exhibition presented Winifred with an appropriate opportunity. She had informed herself about his background by reading his memoirs, which she found fascinating, and she was not to be disappointed by the man himself. Two months later, for the first time she attended one of his weekly soirées:

Archie Rhys Griffiths,
On the Coal Tips, 1932
Lino cut, 12x8

Went to Sir William Rothenstein about 9 o'clock, and had a most enjoyable evening. He and Lady R. are at home every Sunday evening, in a longish house on Campden Hill. Met many interesting people, but none as interesting as Rothenstein himself, with whom I had a long tête à tête. [19 June 1932]

Winifred's relationship with the Rothensteins would flourish. She attended their smart parties, at which William, who was of small stature, gave her the impression of 'moving about like a friendly baboon'. [24 November 1932] In due course she stayed with the Rothensteins at their country house in the Cotswolds:

In afternoon to Oakridge to the Rothensteins, folk I love. Their Cotswold Cottage a place of peace and beauty. Morris hangings everywhere and simple waxed elm furniture, pleasant loggias in which to sit or sleep. Lady R. full of good talk and soon William (The Heavenly Dog) came in from a near-by field where he is painting a landscape - eager, small , friendly and a lovely human spirit. We sat under an apple tree laden with fruit and talked. 'I am a Yorkshire man and would have returned to Yorkshire after London and Paris but I was driven to be a parasite on London, as all we painters are - it's wrong. The impulse to leave one's natural place and see and study in London, in Paris, is sound, but one should return there, then one's best work would be

138

done. But an artist must live and Yorkshire has no livelihood for me.' [24 August 1934]

Evan Walters, who had helped Archie Griffiths hang his London show, also continued to receive Winifred's patronage. Soon after moving to London she visited his Hampstead studio and saw there several pictures which met with her approval, including 'a vast thing I thought very fine, though it will repel many, "Annunciation 2" – an airman in flying kit, all gold, a timid yet delighted girl clad all in blue'. [27 February 1932] She soon visited again, this time in the company of her old friend Geoffrey Crawshay. As well as being the Herald Bard of the Gorsedd, Crawshay was a connoisseur with a large collection of pictures. Some months later Walters was commissioned by Winifred to paint Alexander, as a partner to his younger brother's portrait, *The Eton Boy*, although the sitter was obliged by his mother to pay for himself the fee of £150.[12] Perhaps responding to Grant Murray's idea of creating a support system in London for young Welsh painters, in June Winifred invited Walters and a number of his youthful colleagues to supper at Portland Place:

Not out all day, but a pleasant Bohemian supper party - Evan Walters, and Morland Lewis the young painter from Carmarthen, and Hancock and Janes the Swansea Art students. They came at 7.00 and left at 11. Much very interesting talk. [26 June 1932]

Evan Walters,
Portrait of Alexander Coombe-Tennant, 1934
Oil on canvas, 91×36

Notwithstanding the success of the party, Winifred did not choose to repeat the experiment.[13] Over the subsequent three years she kept in touch with the progress of most of the younger Welsh painters as much through Grant Murray as by her direct contact with them. In March 1933, for instance, it was he who informed her of Mervyn Levy's presence at the Royal College. In the following January he forwarded to her an appeal from him for help, since he was 'in very difficult financial straits'. Levy had come up to London with his childhood friend Dylan Thomas, and they shared a flat with Alfred Janes. Similarly, Murray drew her attention to Paul Godfrey, a painter from Neath, who had briefly been a student at Swansea before studying at the Slade School of Art. Further encouraged by Godfrey's mother, Winifred bought an oil sketch by the young painter, whose career had begun well when he showed work with both the New English Art Club and with The Twenties Group at the Wertheim Gallery.[14] However, of all this generation, Winifred followed the career of Kenneth Hancock with most interest. In 1932, two years after their relationship began with the purchase of a still life, Hancock won a painting prize given by Winifred at the National Eisteddfod at Port Talbot. He wrote her a long description of the Arts and Crafts Exhibition, describing works by Archie Griffiths and Evan Walters and, perhaps most significantly, Ceri Richards, who was beginning to attract attention:

> *I am not sure whether you know the work of Ceri Richards, another of Murray's pupils. He was in the competitive section too. But again the recollection of the adjudicator explained the absence of any award in this direction. While thinking them good paintings, I thought them inferior to his work in the Loan Exhibition. There he had some fine work. I do not think I should be wrong in remarking a certain Matisse influence. But at least it was healthily digested, while remaining essentially Welsh painting.*[15]

Winifred had chosen not to return to Wales for the Eisteddfod at Port Talbot, and listened with sadness to broadcasts from the field on the wireless:

> *I have shed some tears this day, listening to the chairing ceremony at the Eisteddfod at Port Talbot, hearing L.G.'s Presidential address. Following the ceremony, far from it, stirred such memories in me and filled me with such long long thoughts. That was my world ... there I had a part, and much of the ceremonial I had worked hard to improve and develop ... Now it is all gone from me, and who there, in that vast throng, remembers that I ever existed! Oh Death in life, the bitterness of it.*
>
> *I love my new life, I look round this lovely and restful home, with its new interests and wider openings, but something is gone from my life for ever. Partir, c'est mourir un peu!*
> [4 and 5 August 1932]

Acute sadness for her lost world and her sense of loneliness in London often led to Winifred feeling that she existed there like a ghost. She travelled frequently, visiting Cambridge and Eton in particular. She stayed with her mother at Cheltenham, with Gerald Balfour at Fisher's Hill, and with Lloyd George at Churt. When at home, her domestic life troubled her, in particular her relationship with her son, Henry. Her depression was often expressed in the difficulty she experienced in the day to day management of her home and her small domestic staff. However, sometimes with bewildering rapidity her low spirits were transformed into bursts of energy, which were expressed in theatre going, visiting galleries, and collecting. In early

1934 she resumed her acquaintance with the plays of Sean O'Casey, to which she had been introduced six years earlier by the playwright's friend, Evan Walters. She attended three different performances in as many weeks, including the original production of *Within the Gates*. She visited art exhibitions of all kinds. Although her inclination remained towards the work of young artists, her taste was increasingly challenged by them. In 1932 she saw what she regarded as the 'hideous repulsive things of Epstein, drawings of the Old Testament subjects'. [29 February 1932] Before leaving Wales she had become interested

in collecting lace, and in the religious icons of the orthodox churches. In London, her collecting in these fields intensified.[16] As her public life receded into the past, her investment in icons expressed her increasing introspection, and the comfort she took from religious ritual. However, her greatest enthusiasm remained for French painting of the late nineteenth and early twentieth centuries. She showed her own French works at the Whitechapel Gallery, where they were augmented by works owned by Hugh Blaker, art advisor to the Davies sisters. At the end of 1931 she achieved her long-standing ambition to acquire

Unknown photographer, *Winifred Coombe Tennant and M. de Fleuriau, the French Ambassador, at the Whitechapel Art Gallery*, 1932

a picture by Maurice de Vlaminck, which she bought at a sale for 40 guineas, a third of the price at which she had seen equivalent works in Paris. Nevertheless, even her excitement at this acquisition was qualified by the intense ennui which characterised her life in 1930s London:

I saw on the easel the Vlaminck, and all the past of Paris days rushed over me - hot days of July when Deedooge [Charles] and I had wandered in the quays au bord de la Seine and strolled, hatless, after dinner in the Tuilleries Gardens, watching the lovely effects of light and the children playing near the round ponds; and

how we had tracked Vlamincks at every visit and discussed them and never found one within our prices which we could afford to pay, and how we admired them and now there is the Vlaminck and he is gone, and my youth is gone, and all those days of wanderings are gone, and I am dreadfully lonely and not well. I wept and laid my cheek on the canvas for comfort.[17]

For the first time since her move to London, Winifred returned to Wales in August 1934:

Preparing for my journey tomorrow. Strange and sad to be going home where no home now is. I think of the long years from 1895 when on a wet December day I arrived there as a bride and all the farmers drank our health in sherry from a round table ... [5 August 1934]

She found Cadoxton Lodge 'small but well kept, air heavy and much shut in by trees':

Motored out to Cadoxton and walked in the sunshine in the garden, alone, full of long long

Maurice de Vlaminck,
Paysage, n.d.
Oil on canvas, 24x29

Unknown photographer, *Winifred Coombe Tennant at the National Eisteddfod at Neath*, 1934 The National Library of Wales

'I presume,' I remarked, 'that although you do not know a word of Welsh, you are, nevertheless, a member of the Gorsedd.' 'That is so,' was the reply, 'and they gave me the bardic cognomen of Mam o Nedd, with the result that my English friends, with their congenital incapacity for pronouncing Welsh words, address me as Marmalade.'

thoughts, but I would not live there again. I went to the old Mulberry Tree in the North Garden and to the Acanthus near the music room, in full bloom, and round the 'African Path', and I looked up at the house - a house of memories. Birds were singing and the air was sweet with the scents.[18]

The National Eisteddfod at Neath proved to be a less agreeable experience. She thought the Arts and Crafts Exhibition 'a bad show' – a view which the press wholeheartedly endorsed. To make things worse, in the *Western Mail* the Junior Member for Treorchy chose the occasion to indulge, as of old, his remarkable animus against her. Reviving his familiar taunt that Winifred was 'a thorough-bred Saxon', the newspaper's satirist constructed another fictitious conversation with the object of his scorn:

Winifred affected to take this in good part, but was deeply hurt by a renewed attack only a month later. It was brought on by the expression in print of her belief that 'the Puritan revolution took away from Wales the religious rites which were an integral part of the daily life of the Welsh people'. This 'pontifical' view, contrary to the Nonconformist historical orthodoxy of the period, resulted in an angry counterblast from the newspaper, culminating in the dubious assertion that 'to the Puritans belongs the credit of arresting the steady process of the degeneration of the Welsh people'.[19]

Winifred's departure from the Eisteddfod took her into a more congenial, though no less problematic public arena. On her way to stay with her mother at Cheltenham, she travelled for the first time through Crickhowell. There she 'found an old handloom weaver and bought delicious stuffs, and had good talk. Such are dying out in Wales.' [11 August 1934] In her search for traditional textiles, Winifred had written to Charles Powell, the Crickhowell weaver, ten years earlier, at which time he had been unable to help her, giving as his reason pressure of work making shirtings for miners.[20] Meeting him in person stimulated Winifred to write her second newspaper article on the subject of the decline of rural crafts:

I knew that here there had lived the handloom weaver who had for many years spun fine tweeds for the Glanusk family from their own wool, and with whom I had corresponded some 20 years ago about patterns of the old Welsh weavers. Was he still alive?

Yes, here I had good luck! I was directed to a roadside cottage off the main road. An elderly woman answered my knock. Yes, the handloom was here; would I come in and see it?

Could I see the weaver? Yes, she would call him. He came in from the back of the house, a smallish man of rosy face, smiling and very cheerful, and he took me into the parlour and drew from a glass-fronted press rolls of tweed of his own weaving.

How beautiful they were, both in texture and colour - brown and blue and grey-green, and one of a very lovely light grey flecked with black and vivid red, as if the colour had been scattered from a pepper-pot with a sparing hand.

I had not said a word to him to give him a clue to my identity, but presently he said with a broad smile, 'I do know who you are, I seen your photo in the Western Mail. Mam o Nedd *you are' - and he went on to tell me something of his life's story.*

Like his father and his grandfather before him he had started to be a weaver at ten years

old, when he was set to wind the yarns, and a weaver he had been all his life. It was he who had set up the handloom now in the National Museum at Cardiff, 'the oldest I ever seen, all in black oak,' and I told him that once there had worked at it near Lampeter an old friend of mine who had made the bright-coloured 'carthen' for the great four-post beds at Cadoxton Lodge, each in different designs, things of beauty that will outlast any man living to-day.[21]

Like Lewis Jones, the Lampeter weaver, Charles Powell bemoaned the fact that young men, and in particular his own son, would not learn the craft. 'They don't seem to come to it today', he observed, 'they can't learn to set the loom, that is the difficult part'. In her article Winifred warned that unless this situation changed soon, it would be too late. 'If we could get a dozen boys of fourteen apprenticed at once the craft could yet be saved. If we don't get them, in 20 years it will scarcely survive.'

Ironically, even as handloom weaving was dying in rural Wales, there was a small revival in the industrial areas, brought about by the mass unemployment of the very miners whose demand for shirtings had sustained the craft in its last years. As a result of the publication of her article in the *Western Mail*, Winifred was made aware of a self-help group of weavers formed among unemployed men in the Margam area. The venture had been initiated by M. Ceri David, whose father, the Revd. David Hughes, had known Charles Powell and had bought cloth from him when a minister at Crickhowell, forty years earlier. She wrote to Winifred to describe the venture:

I can tell you now in this letter that the Margam Weavers are really unemployed boys who we are personally interested in and wishful to help. The whole scheme was started last January by Capt. and Mrs. Fletcher of Margam, my husband, Major Ll. David, and myself. We had been wondering for a very long time how we could help - our district had concentrated on Allotments which did not in any way solve the problem of the youths who had no trade and were not likely to have one.

At last we decided to try weaving - I had always loved it and knew just a very little about it, so I went to the Rhondda Weavers and got lessons and infinite help from them.[22] *Then my husband and I found a few old looms in Henllan and Hebron and bought them and the boys very sceptically put them up! I taught them first on hand frames and progressed to the looms. Today they are very keen and have progressed far beyond my knowledge.*

We gave them adequate stock and a small amount of capital and between us we have boosted our goods and found them a market. The rest they do themselves and I am quite sure that if pluck and determination and gradually increasing skill can win them a place in life - they will make a market and jobs for themselves.[23]

M. Ceri David's letter arrived while Winifred was staying in the Cotswolds, where again she took the opportunity to visit the Rothensteins at Oakridge. In the Morrisian atmosphere of their country home, the teaching of crafts to unemployed people in settlements such as Maes-yr-haf and Bryn-mawr no doubt came under discussion:

Lunched at Oakridge with the Rothensteins - he in fullness of glorious talk, reminiscences of John, Burne Jones and other painters, a vivid, vital talker. We had good herrings, a huge dish of very small baked apples and glorious fresh Gruyère cheese and perfect coffee - a meal fit for a King. After lunch, talk in the garden and then Lady Rothenstein and I started out for Chalford where one Waals, a Dane, makes beautiful furniture. On to Minchinhampton Common, saw the tower of the church in which I was Christened!! - and on to St Loos House ... to a show of craft work and pictures. A lovely old house and most pleasant people called Payne, who gave us tea. Saw lovely things under lovely conditions. Much talk with the son Robert on Welsh landscape. Then I took Lady Rothenstein back to Oakridge ... a delicious day. [30 August 1934]

Crossing back over the border to stay with Geoffrey Crawshay at Llanfair Court, Winifred resumed her pursuit of traditional textiles:

To Llanover and to a Flannel Mill in a deep valley, reached by narrow precipitous lanes.

On to Llanover Estate Office, where got patterns of hand woven tweeds made for Lord Treowen from undyed wool ... lovely stuff. On to Abergavenny where to the market - crammed - and saw some handwoven stuffs, not good. On to Crickhowell and had talk with Mr Powell the weaver and showed him Margam homespuns which he praised. He said my article on him had been copied in the Breconshire paper and had caused much talk. On then to Abergavenny again (all this in torrents of rain) and so to Monmouth.[24]

Early in April 1935, Winifred received a letter from Frances Byng-Stamper of Manorbier Castle in Pembrokeshire, informing her of an ambitious plan to hold an exhibition of contemporary Welsh art in the summer, and requesting a donation to assist the project. Having, for nearly twenty years, been accustomed to the idea that nothing of consequence in Welsh art happened without her knowledge, if not, indeed, her direct involvement, Winifred was clearly taken aback. No doubt her surprise and irritation were increased by learning that Cedric Morris was among those most closely associated with the plan. From the beginning, she had felt uneasy in her relationship with Morris, and their sporadic acquaintance had only recently been renewed after lying dormant for nearly three years. At a party given by Lady Astor she had a long talk with him 'about pictures and painters'. [7 December 1934]. Notwithstanding the length of the conversation, clearly Morris chose not to disclose his plans for

an exhibition if, indeed, he had formed them at that time, and did not do so as a consequence of the discussion with Winifred. He tended to treat Winifred with breezy familiarity, unlike most of her artistic associates, whose tone ranged from respectful to fawning. Their deference reinforced Winifred's need to feel indispensable in all aspects of life, so that the surprise of discovering, from Byng-Stamper's letter, that people in the Welsh art world talked to each other without necessarily informing her, was considerable. She immediately wrote to her confidants in Wales, only to find them as much in the dark as she. Grant Murray had got wind of the development only a week before Winifred, in the form of an enquiry from Morland Lewis about the addresses of some Swansea artists. He had then received a letter from Byng-Stamper requesting the use of the gallery to show the proposed exhibition. The gallery was booked until the following year but Murray was not inclined to be negative, since 'the more agencies for art development in the Principality the better'.[25] He advised Winifred to give the exhibition her blessing. At the National Museum, Isaac Williams had heard of the project from a different and even more galling source than Murray, in the form of a request from Llewelyn Davies of the National Library to advise and assist that institution in the hanging of the show in July. Byng-Stamper and her friends had identified the Gregynog Gallery at the Library as a more impressive space than the Museum from which to launch the project. Williams had consented, but nevertheless agreed with Winifred that 'the outlook of some of our "modern" Welsh artists is extraordinary':

> *They think that the whole world of art lies within the little circle that encompasses them in London and that they are building up a sort of New Jerusalem for the painter and the public. The conceit of it is comic - there is no other word for it. They don't seem to realise that novelty, in its crudest form, is not art; and so they go on living and working in a fool's paradise.*[26]

Clearly, Williams chose to identify the organisers with novel aesthetic tendencies of which he disapproved, a conclusion which was driven more by pique than by the facts, since Augustus John, whom he had been among the first in Wales to promote, was central to the enterprise. Her two potential allies having already capitulated, Winifred frostily offered Byng-Stamper her co-operation, on condition that she received satisfactory answers to a list of organisational questions, most importantly concerning how the works were to be selected. Simultaneously attempting to pre-empt the selection process, whatever it might turn out to be, she offered Evan Walters' recently completed huge portrait of Alexander as her contribution to the show. She requested a meeting with Byng-Stamper at Manorbier in late June, when she would be attending the Proclamation Ceremony at Fishguard.

Byng-Stamper replied that Augustus John was to be solely responsible for selecting the exhibition. This was not an entirely accurate answer, but one consistent with the policy of a committee which had realised that the best hope of success would be to present their exhibition to the public as John's own. His was the only household name amongst them. In fact, Cedric Morris was both the source of the idea and its driving force. Since at least January (perhaps, indeed, since his conversation with Winifred at Lady Astor's party) he had been gathering around him a loose association of expatriate supporters, the most notable of whom was Clough Williams-Ellis.[27] Their centre was London, and although the painters were certainly keen that their works should be seen in their own country, the exhibition came with strong undertones of the long-standing belief of the London Welsh that home-based artists and the Welsh general public stood in need of an enlightened art education, which they alone could provide. Indeed, in the catalogue, the writer Richard Hughes described the exhibition as 'a metropolis that moves from place to place'. Isaac Williams' response on first hearing of the project clearly indicates that such metropolitan parochialism was a familiar irritant to those involved in the promotion of art in Wales itself. The introduction to the catalogue of Archie Griffiths' London exhibition, written by Thomas Jones in 1932, had presented a particularly high-profile example.

In fact, although focussed on Wales, the views

of Jones reflected a wider British metropolitanism at a time when London was still perceived by many older people not only as the centre of Britain, but also the centre of the world. Many of Jones' criticisms of Wales were expressed by others about the visual culture of provincial England, and attempts were made to change perceived attitudes there also. Indeed, the British Institute for Adult Education sent out a travelling exhibition under the title 'Art for the People', at precisely the same moment and for some of the same reasons that stimulated Cedric Morris to bring his view of contemporary Welsh painting to Wales in 1935.[28] It sought to bring new painting to an audience in England which would not normally see such work. The following year's BIAE 'Art for the People' exhibition included Coleg Harlech among its venues, presumably at the request of Thomas Jones, who took the opportunity of a radio broadcast once again to air his views on the subject: '... in Wales we have good ears but no eyes. We are sensitive to the beauties of sound and blind to the beauties of sight. We are interested in music, we are not interested in art.'[29]

Nevertheless, for Cedric Morris the 1935 exhibition was not merely a reflection of a prevailing metropolitanism, but also a sincere expression of social conscience. As a Welsh person who, by virtue of his birth into the upper class, had not been sucked into the mire of mass unemployment, he felt driven to attempt to do something for the common people, whose

increasing suffering he had observed since his first return visit to Wales in 1927. More particularly, he seems to have felt personal guilt by association, since his own social status was based on the earlier success of the capitalism which now seemed to be in a state of collapse. His family name, enshrined in the industrial community of Morriston, was itself a constant reminder of the fact.[30]

Winifred's offer to loan Evan Walters' portrait of Alexander was declined on the grounds that it was too large, and matters proceeded without her involvement. When the Exhibition of Contemporary Welsh Art opened at the National Library in Aberystwyth she was not present, and it was not until the middle of August that she received any informed opinion of it. Her source was Evan Walters, a few small examples of whose work had been selected. However, Winifred's relationship of fifteen years' standing with Walters had suffered a severe setback immediately prior to the opening. The painter had recently married

Unknown photographer, *Evan Walters and Marjorie Davies after their marriage, with the portrait of Ramsay Macdonald*, 1935

148

Marjorie Davies, whom he had met when she was a student at Swansea in 1921. Just before Winifred left for Fishguard to attend the Eisteddfod proclamation ceremony at the end of June, Marjorie arrived unexpectedly at Portland Place:

Mrs Evan Walters to tea. Has been turned out of the house by Evan Walters who accused her of syphilis and other things of which she is totally innocent. From what she said I believe he has ill used her and that he is entirely to blame - a man of bad temper, and a bully, though a fine painter. He works little and is going to seed, as I suspected. I am so sorry. [23 June 1935]

For Winifred this incident broke the spell of Walters' genius. Coupled with the painter's adoption of a new style of painting, of which she did not approve, it resulted in a cooling of their relationship, which lasted for many years. In August, during the National Eisteddfod at Caernarfon, she spoke to him on the field, but only briefly. They agreed to meet at St Asaph, where Walters was painting the Bishop, but their interview at the palace was equally short.

The following week, perhaps seeking to mend fences, the painter wrote to Winifred at length. He was in peevish mood. Like Winifred, he had not been invited to the opening of the Exhibition of Contemporary Welsh Art at Aberystwyth. However, a request from the BBC to broadcast about the show had presented him with an opportunity to return the slight, with interest:

I am sure that a good number of people connected with this show, when they found they were not mentioned, are rather sore about it. I have been also invited to the Swansea opening and Cardiff. But I was completely ignored at Aberystwyth. So I shall not go to either. It appears a good number of people asked for me at Aberystwyth and then when I was chosen by the broadcasting people to give a talk in Welsh - none of the others could have given it - they have been wanting to rope me in on their good books.

There are about 150 exhibits with about 120 paintings, water colours and drawings. Augustus John and his family, and Cedric and his cousin (whom I had never heard of before) have about 70, leaving about 50 between the other 16 artists. Of these Innes, who is dead and is no longer a rival, has 23. Rivals have been either cut out or badly and sparsely represented. The first committee was John, Cedric and Cedric's two cousins. The rest of the committee is a sleeping one selected afterwards just to bluff the public. Now they want to rope you in. Augustus John himself has 31 things, most undignified.

You must tell everyone you meet that the Art Show is not nearly representative of Welsh artists.[31]

Though reacting to what he regarded as a conspiracy against him, Walters' accusation that the show was not representative of the state of Welsh painting was correct. Furthermore, its selectivity was certainly the result of cronyism, rather than of philosophical or aesthetic considerations. The figurative painters, Archie Griffiths and Vincent Evans, were not represented but, equally, neither was the most aesthetically radical of the Welsh painters of the period, Ceri Richards. Among the others who did not exhibit, the most indignant response came from Timothy Evans although, in fact, he had not been passed over:

I received an invitation to send work to the Exhibition of work by Welsh painters, which was initiated by A. John. I refused the invitation. I have a number of reasons for this, which perhaps I will publish later. Of this I am certain, it is not for a group of half-English snobs like Clough Williams Ellis and his mates to chatter about art in Wales. All that rubbish like this want is to be in the limelight and show off. I know the effort will quickly fail. And then I will express my opinion in public. Keep this a secret please.[32]

Notwithstanding ruffled feathers within the art world, there was considerable public interest in the exhibition at Aberystwyth, where Cedric Morris reported that there were two thousand visitors in the first week. The success was repeated subsequently at Swansea and Cardiff.[33] Byng-Stamper took care to inform Winifred of the fact, and invited her to tea with Morris at Manorbier. The meeting did not take place. Nevertheless, in terms of its impact on the condition of the people, Morris soon became disillusioned, feeling that 'a few pictures can't

Unknown photographer,
Hanging some pictures by Cedric Morris in the Exhibition of Contemporary Welsh Art at the Deffett Francis Gallery in Swansea,
1935 The National Library of Wales

do it'. When the experiment was repeated, the following year, his involvement seems to have been minimal. He would soon redirect his energy into creating the opportunity for people to participate in making pictures and sculpture.[34]

In October 1935 Winifred travelled to Swansea to open an exhibition of works by former students of the School of Art:

Got to the Glynn Vivian Art Gallery by 10 o'c and had an hour's talk with Grant Murray - nice man, such brains, character and manners. Saw the show I'm opening tomorrow. Janes and Hancock very good and Evan Walters, but a better show could and should have been got together I think. [10 October 1935]

The exhibition was part of Swansea's programme of events to mark the centenary of the Municipal Corporations Act. The local authority was proud

Unknown photographer, *Cedric Morris*
with his picture Llanrhidian Mill, Gower,
at his exhibition in London, 1935
The National Library of Wales

of the fact that the town had been one of the
first two in Wales to establish an art school, under
government legislation, in 1853. Grant Murray saw
the exhibition not merely as a local celebration
but as evidence of Swansea's contribution to the
founding of a 'National Art'. Like Winifred, he
continued to have faith in that concept, although
it was beginning to be questioned. The Exhibition
of Contemporary Welsh Art had provided a focus
for the more radical among the younger generation
to challenge pre-war Nationalist orthodoxy.
D. Kighley Baxandall had written that, by
including the words 'Welsh Art', the official title
of the exhibition had been misleading, 'because
there is, of course, no such thing as Welsh painting

and sculpture today, although there is a great deal
of truly important contemporary painting by
Welsh artists'.[35] Baxandall's remark, appropriately
published in the second number of the magazine
Tir Newydd ('New Ground'), marked the
emergence of what was to become, for most of
the twentieth century, the dominant philosophy
of Contributionism in Welsh art – the belief that
the role of the Welsh artist was to contribute to
the mainstream of international Modernism. Evan
Walters, rooted in the same pre-war notions as
Grant Murray and Winifred, took a cynical view
of this aspiration, describing the work in the
Contemporary Exhibition simply as 'English
art by Welsh artists':

> *Welsh art would express the ideals and soul*
> *of Wales - just as 'Bydd Myrdd o Ryfeddodau',*
> *'Calon Lân', and 'Yn y Dyfroedd' are expressions*
> *of the very soul of Wales.*[36]

Grant Murray believed that the realisation
of a National Art need not be far off. However,
internationalist Modernism infiltrated his own
exhibition, in the form of works shown by Ceri
Richards, who would ultimately become by far
the most celebrated of his pupils. Even the work
of Evan Walters would soon reflect Modernist
tendencies. From 1936 until the end of his life,
formal experimentation would dominate
content in his work.[37]

The opening of the exhibition was a happy
occasion for Winifred:

Unknown photographer, *The opening of the 'Exhibition of Works by Past Students of the School of Art and Crafts'*, 1935. Caradoc Evans, centre, in light-coloured suit; Winifred, front row, second from left, Grant Murray, back row, right.

Lunched, changed, and got to the Art Gallery at 3.15. Tremendous ceremony, and, thank God, I made a very good speech. Once on my feet the art of speaking came back to me. Caradoc Evans, the writer, who was there greatly praised me - a man not given to praise. The Mayor was there, W.A. Jenkins, and so many I knew. Grant Murray gave me a lovely picture of his, which I was unwilling to take but had to accept - figures on a beach ... I took Caradoc to see Evan Walters' picture of Zanga [Alexander], over which he was enthusiastic. It all went off wonderfully well and I enjoyed it.[38]

The event resounded with expressions of self-satisfaction and mutual congratulation. Councillor Jenkins, Chairman of the Arts and Crafts Committee, effusively praised the contribution of John Davies Williams to the development of art in Swansea and, in her speech,

Winifred described Grant Murray as 'the chief inspiration, guide and friend to all students'. She then returned to the theme upon which all three of them had pronounced so often, the development of patronage for artists. She proposed that 'a contemporary art society' be established, supported by subscriptions, to buy pictures each year.[39] Her proposal is of particular interest given the experience of the organisers of the exhibitions of contemporary Welsh art in 1935 and 1936. The following year they decided to redirect their efforts, and established the Contemporary Art Society for Wales, with the intention of purchasing works by living Welsh artists and placing them in public collections. Winifred's friend, Geoffrey Crawshay, became its Honorary Treasurer, and she soon became a member.

For Winifred, the most promising of the young painters on show at Swansea in 1935 remained Kenneth Hancock and Alfred Janes. She had

Unknown photographer, *Vincent Evans*, c.1935 The National Library of Wales

152

visited Janes on the morning of the exhibition opening and took tea with him in the afternoon, when she commissioned him to paint a head for her.[40] She was also interested in buying a picture exhibited by Vincent Evans although, strangely, she seems to have been previously unaware of his work. Evans was well-known to John Davies Williams who, in the *Cambria Daily Leader*, had publicised his early success in gaining a scholarship to the Royal College of Art and having his work exhibited at the Royal Academy. However, on leaving the Royal College he had emigrated to New Zealand and had not returned until 1933. That summer, he showed his work, which had always been concerned mainly with mining subjects, at the Cooling Gallery in London, where it was seen by Rothenstein. He wrote to the painter expressing the wish that 'some of the people interested in Welsh art could go and see your things', yet seems not to have informed Winifred.[41] Less surprising was Winifred's failure to note Evans' work at the chaotic art exhibition at the National Eisteddfod at Neath in the following year.

As well as by exhibiting his work, Evans sought to raise his public profile on his return from New Zealand by entering the debate about the state of art in Wales:

It is my considered opinion that we as a nation should identify ourselves with our artists. It is not enough that Welsh artists succeed outside Wales. We need our own representative patrons,

committees and institutions ... I suggest that a committee be set up to canvass for patrons, and to arrange for an annual art exhibition of a national character.[42]

The timing of this proposal, immediately prior to the Exhibition of Contemporary Welsh Art, suggests that it was motivated, at least in part, by his exclusion from that show.

Having at last noted the work of Vincent Evans in the former students exhibition, Winifred expressed her interest to Grant Murray, who put the painter in touch with her. At the end of the year she visited him at his studio in Chelsea. The occasion was not a success:

Called to see paintings by Vincent Evans, a Welshman of 39, vain, little gifted and loquacious. He wanted me to buy a picture, and one I liked, 'The Columns', [I had] seen at the Swansea Exhibition. But I didn't like the impression his accumulated work made on me, and refused it for a nominal sum. [31 December 1935]

Evans had missed the peak of the fashion for 'miner painters' in the late 20s, when he was in New Zealand. The correspondence of William Rothenstein, Grant Murray, and Winifred reveals that his paintings, in particular, were not to the taste of any of them. Both Grant Murray and Rothenstein thought his black and white work superior. Similarly, Isaac Williams at the National Museum was unimpressed, despite Evans' continued success in having pictures exhibited at the Royal Academy. Like Winifred, the National Museum cited what it regarded as personal arrogance and over-pricing on the part of the painter as an excuse not to buy either of the two pictures exhibited by Evans at the Academy in 1936. However, when he reduced the price to fifteen guineas, Murray was willing to purchase *A Snack*, which had been shown at the Swansea exhibition, but there considered too expensive.[43]

Notwithstanding her exclusion from involvement with the Exhibition of Contemporary Welsh Art, and her residence in London, in 1935 Winifred remained closely involved with affairs in Wales. Following the National Eisteddfod at Caernarfon, a stay in Snowdonia of over a month's duration aroused in her the same intense feelings for Welsh landscape that she had felt on her first visit in 1921. It was a refreshment of the first principles

Vincent Evans, *A Snack*, 1935
Oil on canvas, 12x16. City and County
of Swansea: Glynn Vivian Art Gallery

of national identity in the tradition of Tom Ellis and O.M. Edwards, still represented for her by Lloyd George, with whom she stayed for part of the time:

> *L.G. took us to a lovely spot among the mountains for a picnic lunch - Cwm Penant, immortalised by a Lyric written I believe by Eifion Wyn: 'Lord why didst though make Cwm Penant so beautiful, and the life of the Shepherd so short'. Elfed, Crwys and the Chaired Bard joined us. The narrow road was rough - the gateposts barely let us pass in the Sunbeam, in which I and Mrs L.G. were. L.G. and Megan in the Rolls Royce following. By the side of a stream near a little wooden bridge we ate lunch, all talk in Welsh and much laughter. L.G. in teasing spirits, his white hair blowing in the wind, the mountains rising above us, all so beautiful.[44]*

Invigorated by this experience, later the same day Winifred set off for the birthplace of T.E. Lawrence at Tremadog:

> *At Tremadog I went in pilgrimage and prayer to see the house in which Lawrence of Arabia was born. A house set by the roadside, near a pleasant looking old chapel. Miss Bryant, who now lives there, took me up to the room where he was born ... I stood in silence, longed to be alone that I might have knelt down and kissed the floor. I prayed for that glorious spirit - and to it - and wondered at the nearness of grandeur to dust. From this house went forth a King among men.[45]*

Two days later Winifred's stay was interrupted by the death of her mother at Cheltenham.[46] On returning to the Royal Hotel at Capel Curig, having dealt with her mother's affairs, she recalled that the first part of her stay there had been 'certainly the happiest I remember for years, and all the spring in me, body and spirit, had returned'. [30 August 1935] She wondered 'Will it be so again?', and although the following day she was able to answer in the affirmative, in the longer term Winifred's stay in Snowdonia in 1935 marked the beginning of a gradual withdrawal from Welsh affairs in the years leading to the outbreak of the Second World War. Although she returned to Snowdonia in 1936, and continued to attend the Eisteddfod until 1938 and the Proclamation until 1939, the decreasing frequency in her diary of reflections upon the visual culture and upon Welsh affairs in general suggests that Wales became less important in Winifred's inner life. Nevertheless, she continued to be engaged with practical matters, honouring commitments, including that to represent the Glynn Vivian Gallery in London. She also maintained her interest in the Gorsedd, though in 1937, while staying with the poet Cynan in Anglesey, she offered to resign from her role in charge of the robes.[47] Clearly mindful of the persistent jibes of the Junior Member for Treorchy in the *Western Mail*, she acknowledged that as 'an English-speaking woman now living in London' she might have become an embarrassment, but 'Cynan would not hear of it – said my status and authority

Unknown
photographer,
*John Williams Davies
and friends on a hill
walk*, early 1930s
The National
Library of Wales

The people associated with her life in Wales
continued to tie Winifred firmly to the country.
Relations with Evan Walters slowly improved,
and she met socially with him from time to time.
In 1936 they went together to watch the dancer
Pearle Argyle, for instance, though the painter's
fascination with formal problems in his work
left them intellectually estranged. 'He is avidly
off on the tack of double vision, and what the
result on his painting I cannot imagine!' [15
January 1939] On the other hand, her faith in
Thomas Jones remained unshaken. She met him
both at Cymmrodorion events and privately:

*Dined with the Rothensteins, Tom Jones the
only other guest. Marvellous talk - Pilgrim
Trust, travel, politics, people, art, literature,
ethics and oh so much fun! I drove Tom Jones
back. How much I like and admire him.*[50]

were vital'. [20 July 1937] Notwithstanding the
experience of lunch with the future Archdruid,
Crwys, 'an insincere man and a great windbag',
Winifred's enthusiasm for the Gorsedd remained
strong.[48] The Eisteddfod of 1937 provided a poor
Arts and Crafts Exhibition, but the meeting as
a whole was salvaged for her by 'one of those
unforgettable moments of life':

Occasionally Winifred received visitors from Wales,
including George M.Ll. Davies, who she felt (as
she had done on their first meeting in 1920) was
'a man full of the beauty of holiness and the light
of God'. [13 February 1936] Davies told her of
his work with the settlement movement in the
Valleys. At the end of the summer came news of
a less welcome kind. John Davies Williams, 'my
dear friend of Swansea days – saint and dreamer
and poet!', had been killed while climbing in
Snowdonia. [3 August 1937] The newspaper with
which he was most closely associated, the *Cambria
Daily Leader*, had ceased publication in 1930,

*In the robing Room I came to take leave of Elvet
Lewis - old, nearly blind, the light of God shining
through him. 'Give me your blessing', I said, 'I
always ask for that'. He took my hand between
his, and after a moment's silence said, 'It is
with you now, and will be with you to the end.'
I could not speak for emotion and the tears
rushed to my eyes. There was solemnity and
holiness in his mien.*[49]

but as editor of the *Evening Post* Williams had continued to promote local painters. His death marked the end of the era, already on the wane as a result of Winifred's departure from Wales. At the height of their activity, Winifred, Williams and Grant Murray together had given Welsh visual culture a higher public profile and provided it with a better support system than it had ever before enjoyed.[51]

While in Wales for the National Eisteddfod at Cardiff in 1938, Winifred took the opportunity to refresh her friendship with the poet Huw Menai. They had met in 1926 at Trefforest, where Winifred heard him read his work. He was 'a tall lean figure, a bush of hair above a long face, a dreamer, seer, visionary. I felt I might have been in Blake's presence. He recited many beautiful things.' [25 March 1926] He revealed to her his longstanding interest in psychical matters and she sent him a copy of *Christopher*. An extensive correspondence ensued, which was maintained until the end of Winifred's life. She was able to help him in practical ways. For much of the Depression he was unemployed, and by 1931 was in debt and unable to sustain his large family. When bailiffs removed the furniture from his house, Winifred sent beds, tables and chairs from Cadoxton Lodge. However, they met only occasionally, and it was not until the Eisteddfod at Cardiff that Winifred was able to visit the poet at his home in the Rhondda for the first time:

To Penygraig where I found Huw Menai in a clean comfortable little house. Such good talk - philosophy, religion, books (I took him 8 or 9 as a present) and days gone by. He is a remarkable man - a visionary and a true poet, though the man is far greater than his work.[52]

It seems that during this conversation Huw Menai told Winifred about an untutored painter named James, living in Pontypridd:

Doubled back to Pontypridd and in an unemployed man's little house saw paintings of animals of quite remarkable quality. He has never shown and never sold and no one has ever seen his work. I gave advice and commissions and am to have things up in October with a view to getting them sold for him. How gifted the Welsh are and how few of the well to do will lift a hand to help native genius![53]

Although her interest in Huw Menai's painter friend can in part be attributed to Winifred's undoubted sense of *noblesse oblige*, her admiration for the poet himself had its origins in a different aspect of her complex and often contradictory psychology. Winifred was particularly attracted to working-class Welsh radicals, especially when (as in the cases of Evan Walters and Archie Griffiths, as well as Huw Menai himself) she identified in them a mystical spirit. In the early 1920s, when her political activities were at their most intense, she often manifested an equal and opposite distaste for privilege and for the gentry. However, within the subtle gradations of class to which her social sensibility alerted her, the aristocracy occupied a somewhat different position. As she grew older, and the world around her more disturbed, Winifred expressed with increasing frequency a fascination for the aristocracy and a longing for the continuity which she felt they represented. For instance, on a visit to Beaumaris in 1936, Winifred visited Lady Magdalen Bulkeley at Pen-y-parc:

Lady Magdalen has been a beauty and still has distinction and a lovely smile - old, hushed, deaf, but so noble looking and with noble manners, very tall and handsome. There is for me a charm about ancient family aristocrats of their type - simple, exquisitely bred ... In a world where all is being levelled down to the lowest common denominator I know that I am a patrician and love the beauty of the older ways ... [30 August 1936]

By the time of the Second World War Winifred's social attitudes had coalesced around these opposite poles of empathy with the working class and the aristocracy, leaving between the two a distaste for the gentry and, increasingly, for the 'noisy, insensitive, illbred' English middle class. [21 August 1939] With them she associated much of the ugliness and banality which she experienced in the modern world:

Ghastly squalid hideosity of Kingston By-pass road appalled me - a higgledepiggledi of ill-designed sham 'Tudor' and other sort of yesterday-houses (Oh! Corbusier, where art thou!) scattered along it in a welter of advertisement hoardings, petrol stations and suchlike. [12 August 1937]

Although also deeply offended in Wales by the ugliness she perceived in the industrial landscape, Winifred regarded the common people as the victims rather than the perpetrators of the abuse of beauty. In general her aesthetic revulsion was not accompanied by hostility towards them, but rather by a compensatory longing for the 'colour, light and warmth' which she associated with the Italy and France of her childhood.[54] In the late 1930s, removed from Wales and experiencing a sense of alienation in England, Winifred attempted to satisfy her longing by travelling extensively. She visited France both independently and, on one occasion, with a group organised by the Anglo-French Art Society with which she had become involved.[55] She bought further pictures there for her collection. However, her journey to Scandinavia, Russia and Germany in 1936 was more important in terms of its immediate effect on her thinking. The Great War had left Winifred with an intense dislike of what she regarded as the innate characteristics of the German mentality. Her observation in 1934 that 'the Germans are, and remain, the criminality of Europe and until their philosophy is destroyed none can sleep in their beds in peace', was characteristic of her attitude. [26 August 1934] As a person with a deep interest and a practical experience of foreign affairs, she observed with alarm the rise of Fascism from its earliest manifestations. Her distaste for the movement in Italy and in Germany was informed by personal acquaintance with Sir Oswald Mosley, leader of the British Union of Fascists. Winifred worked with Lady Cynthia Mosley, whom she liked, on a committee of the English Speaking Union, and they also met socially at parties and exhibitions.[56] However, Winifred's admiration for the 'very handsome' Cynthia did not extend to her husband. Shortly before Cynthia's sudden death in 1933, Winifred listened to a speech by Mosley and noted that 'in my bones I dislike that creed'. [22 March 1933] On her tour in 1936, in Oslo, Danzig and Lübeck, Winifred experienced at first hand the 'idolatry of Hitler':

Ghastly crowd of Huns from a German excursion in boat who greeted me with outstretched arms and cries of Heil Hitler. I having wandered away from our crowd. I stared uncomprehendingly at them ... [29 June 1936]

Her visit to St Petersburg was undertaken with a more open mind. However, she was profoundly shocked by what she observed there:

Landed at 10.30 and saw this once noble city now falling into ruins. houses unrepaired and unpainted. roads unmended and hoards of grim people who never smile. never speak to each other. but hurry along in silence like hunted animals - ghastly to behold. I saw the desecrated churches. with statue of that vile little dwarf Lenin set up with face towards the high altar of St Isaac's Cathedral as if in challenge. I saw the Winter Palace now a Museum of the Revolution ...

Our Lady of Kazan,
Oil on panel, 18×12.
An icon from the collection of
Winifred Coombe Tennant.

*Holy Russia has been destroyed and a savage
rule of fear and hatred replaces it. I landed
yesterday more favourable to the Bolsheviks, but
after hearing the flood of trash propaganda and
seeing the cowed and miserable look of the people,
ill clad, ill fed, neglected, wild, I realised it was
a world from which all human values and all
spiritual values have been removed and a
mechanical maniacal tyranny of violence
and slavery set up.*[57]

Winifred found her most deeply sustaining
beliefs affronted in the disruption of Orthodox
tradition and the desecration of the beauty of
the churches of Russia. She was able to buy a
number of icons, displaced by the new order,
to add to her collection.

In 1937 Winifred again left England, on this
occasion to visit Sri Lanka and Egypt over a period
of three months. She interested herself both in
historical sightseeing and in the arts and crafts

Unknown photographer, *Winifred
Coombe Tennant in the Drawing Room
at 18 Cottesmore Gardens*, 1937

of the places she visited. At Luxor, in Egypt, she
visited the grave of the illustrator E. Harold Jones,
who was of Welsh ancestry. Jones had been
employed to record mural decorations in tombs
excavated in 1911.[58]

On her return to England, in May 1937
Winifred decided to leave her flat at Portland Place
and search for a house which would provide more
space both for her and for Alexander, and a
garden. She very soon found what she required
at 18 Cottesmore Gardens, not far from her flat.
The outbreak of the Second World War in the
following year would disrupt the process of her
settling there, but, eventually, it would become
her home for the rest of her life.

While expressing her anger and exasperation
at the appeasement policies pursued by
the government of Neville Chamberlain, through
1937 and 1938 the succession of crises resulting
from Italian and German expansionism drove
Winifred increasingly inwards. Her withdrawal
from Wales in these years was, in many ways,
no more than an aspect of her withdrawal
from a wider world which she felt was in a
state of imminent collapse. The compensatory
intensification of her inner life was expressed
in attendance at Roman Catholic and Russian
Orthodox churches when in London, but much
of 1938 was spent out of the city, visiting and
staying with friends in the east of England. In
Norfolk, she discovered the shrine of Our Lady
of Walsingham. The shrine had been among the

most important of English medieval pilgrimage sites because of visions seen there of the House of the Annunciation in Nazareth. Expressing much the same revival of faith as had been expressed in the reconstruction of the shrine of the patron saint at St. David's (which Winifred had visited ten years earlier), in 1922 a statue of the Virgin had been installed in the parish church. Nine years later the statue was relocated in a new pilgrimage church where, in August 1938, Winifred prayed to Our Lady of Walsingham for the first time. Her longstanding devotion to the Madonna found intense expression there. During the course of the next year she returned on many occasions and commissioned the making of a silver votive light.

At the same time as her discovery of Walsingham, Winifred found a further aid to contemplation in the practical work of weaving:

To Elsing Hall ... Here live 2 sisters, Mrs Thackery, a widow, and Miss Clarendon Hyde, having turned their house into school of weaving on small portable hand looms. Easy to learn and lovely things made - scarves, bags, tweed materials, rugs and I know not what. One pupil at work. Made me long to go and learn and have a small (folding up) loom to work on. [27 July 1938]

Winifred duly acquired a loom and was comforted by working with it as she retired further into herself. She felt that she had 'outlived this world, except the beauty of nature, the treasures of Art and Literature, and the Beloved who are yet in this stage of things.' [7 October 1938] She was appalled by the prospect of imminent war. Henry was already in the Welsh Guards, and Alexander was also of an age to fight. When the war finally came, he sought to join the navy, but was prevented by his poor eyesight, and entered the Ministry of Economic Warfare. Together, he and Winifred decided to close their new home in Cottesmore Gardens for the duration and, in December 1939, Winifred went to live at Didlington Hall in Norfolk, as she described to Grant Murray:

When war broke out I was staying some 15 miles east of here, and have been on a round of visits to friends in Norfolk ever since. Now I have come here to be with distant kinsmen of mine, indefinitely, in one of the loveliest of the great houses of Norfolk.

I am thankful to be here, and my work is now confined to running family affairs and finances, plus hand weaving war comforts for the Welsh Guards.[59]

Her correspondence with Grant Murray continued into the first year of the war. The Principal was engaged in the establishment of a school of printing, which Winifred supported strongly, in part because of what she perceived to be the failure of Gregynog to have an impact on the quality of book production for ordinary people in Wales. It was 'a rich man's toy':

I have pleaded for the production of books priced for all which are well printed ... and have begged for a branch within reach of population where commercial printers could be trained ... What is the Press actually doing to encourage fine printing, good type and such-like in Wales, and what has it done?

People have hurled themselves at me when I have dared to say all this - except Tom Jones (C.H.), who I believe has some sympathy with my views, but the Llandinam (which includes Gregynog) prestige and ascendancy suffers criticism badly ...[60]

As ever, Winifred was able to maintain a show of business-like normality while, inside, she was oppressed by the prospect of Henry's departure for the Continent, as Christopher had departed in 1917. Henry sailed for Boulogne with his regiment in May 1940, and within three months was reported missing. It seemed that the experience of the loss of Christopher was to be repeated. In June, still tortured by having received no news as to his fate, Winifred returned to Wales, to live with friends who had rented Triley Court, near Abergavenny. However, at the end of the month came word that Henry was a prisoner of war in a camp at Laufen, in Germany, and was uninjured. She received her first letter from him in September, and on the same day drove with Alexander and friends to Llanthony Abbey:

Noble ruin in a heavenly valley, the Priory Church in desolation but full of beauty. Prayed in silence the old Latin prayers to comfort those who had loved it in its richness, and to invoke their aid. Drove on to Father Ignatious in monastery at Capel y Ffin in the heart of the mountains, its tall church falling into ruins, the monastery secularised. A lovely crucifix memorial to its founder. Tea high up on a slope to the left of the monastic buildings and then, blessedly alone, I went to pray beside the Crucifix 'Peace to the Wayfarer', and so to the monastery where Eric Gill's daughter lives (Mrs Williams). Walked alone in the tiny cloister till she came. We spoke of Moorfields - she knew her father's bas relief. Lovely watercolours of David Jones in the refectory. A deserted chapel of the brothers, peace and decay. She has some paying guests, and is far from sound of war. I entered into Peace there, and for a moment the burden of life fell from my shoulders. [6 September 1940]

In September 1941 Winifred moved again, though only as far as Llanover Court, where she lived until April 1942. There she was engaged fully with matters relating to the care of prisoners of war, lobbying government and attempting to influence the agreements which affected their conditions in Germany through the medium of the Red Cross. Her knowledge of Henry's whereabouts and occasional reassuring letters provided her with some respite until she received the news that, along with some thirty others, he had escaped from the camp where he was held. She heard nothing further until November 1942, when she was informed that he was one of only three of the escapees to reach Gibraltar, with the aid of the resistance in Holland and France.[61]

By the time the news reached Winifred, she had left Wales to live at Windsor Castle, in a grace and favour apartment in the Cloisters. There she remained until after the war's end, calmed by the atmosphere of St George's Chapel and the devotions which she attended, but disturbed by a fractious relationship with the authorities who controlled her temporary home. Among her neighbours was her old friend Margaret, wife of Walford Davies, but a widow since 1941. Less agreeably, the painter Alfred Munnings, 'an odious insincere hustler' was in residence, 'the King and Queen trying in vain to dislodge him'.[62]

In addition to her war work, at Windsor Winifred made a discovery which would engage her for some years:

Cross Neath, carved and painted boss in roof of Ambulatory, north side, outside the Lincoln Chapel in St George's Chapel! An unforgettable 2 hours being taken over the Chapel by Canon Ollard in company with Governor of Military Knights Cavanagh. Was shown above boss, and Canon casually remarked 'that is Edward IV and Richard Beauchamp, Bishop of Salisbury, kneeling beside Cross Neath, which was a cross brought from Neath in Wales and the chiefest treasure of the Chapel.' I was staggered.

I found out a little about it and mean to research all I can. Here is the exquisite carving of a Celtic Cross from Neath - and who in Wales knows of it! [24 September 1942]

*Roof Boss depicting the Croes Naid,
St George's Chapel, Windsor, c.1480-1
Dean and Canons of Windsor*

Winifred rapidly discovered that the Canon's 'Cross Neath' was a garbled version of 'Croes Naid', and that the relic depicted had no connection with the town of Neath. However, the knowledge that the cross represented on the boss (and in two other places in St George's Chapel) was the bejewelled fragment of the True Cross, which had belonged to the princes of Gwynedd until taken by Edward I in 1283, fired her imagination. She set about gathering all the known references to the cross from contemporary documents and first published them in 1943 in the Report of the Friends of St George's Chapel, Windsor. After the war she presented the documents themselves in transcripts and facsimiles to The National Library of Wales, and published in the Library's *Journal* what remains the fullest account of the Cross Naid.[63]

The anxieties of the war were far from over for Winifred when she was reunited with Henry in November 1942. Alexander was posted abroad, to serve in Greece and Egypt, and at the time of the invasion of the Continent Henry returned to active service, initially parachuted behind German lines and out of contact with his mother for a month, before he met his advancing regiment. Nevertheless, both Alexander and Henry survived the war, to be reunited with their mother in 1945.

Jenkin Evans,
Self Portrait, 1949

Notwithstanding the difficulties of living at Windsor, Winifred was slow to emerge from her wartime retreat. As a first step she took a flat in London with Alexander, but they did not return to live at Cottesmore Gardens until May 1947.[64] Her first post-war visit to Wales was for the National Eisteddfod at Mountain Ash in August 1946. All the complexities of her social and political attitudes, with their aesthetic corollaries, were immediately apparent. The Eisteddfod, in the heart of the Valleys, was to be the occasion for the investiture of Princess Elizabeth into the Gorsedd:

Left London by the 11.55, received like Royalty at Paddington as 'in waiting' tomorrow on Princess Elizabeth. A carriage to myself and Station Master and in Inspector escorting me thereto. Oh! The joy of watching the countryside as we sped through it - fields of golden corn, green, green fields, woods, the Berkshire Downs, the Chiltern Hills, the Thames, cows in fields - all denied so long to my eyes. The Severn Tunnel, Newport and finally Cardiff, where again Inspector awaiting me. A lovely car and up I sped, past the Town Hall and Law Courts, all once part of my life. On to the Valleys, rounded hills rising from them, mining huddle of ugly houses, and at last miners, my heart gave such a leap. Oh how my heart went out to them. For years they were part of my life, in happier days. Drove up to this strange house inhabited by a coal bigwig and determined vociferous wife evidently hating Wales and all things Welsh - in fact the atmosphere which explains the psychology of the miner. Thank God for the Nationalisation of the Mines! [4 August 1946]

During her investiture the next day Winifred was in close attendance on the Princess, whose conversation did not hugely impress her. She found Elizabeth 'an amiable girl lacking vitality and animation'. [5 August 1946] Her Gorsedd responsibilities largely dispatched, Winifred turned her attention to the Arts and Crafts exhibition where she was met by the organiser, Iorwerth Peate, whose sense of the centrality of

folk tradition in the crafts it was designed to express. Winifred observed the 'lovely weaving, wood turning, wrought iron work, quilting' which Peate had displayed, along with the craftspeople themselves, who demonstrated their skills for the public. In the painting and sculpture sections Winifred noted in particular the work of Jenkin Evans of Ystalyfera, who had exhibited a bust of Danny Jenkins, a miner who worked at the Pwllbach colliery. After the Eisteddfod she wrote to him, asking for details of his training. She was certainly unaware that Jenkin was the younger brother of the painter Vincent Evans, to whom she had taken a dislike when she met him in 1935, and it was for this reason, no doubt, that in his reply to her letter Jenkin omitted to mention him. Jenkin himself was a dentist, and had begun to make sculpture in his spare time in the 1930s. He had won the sculpture prize at the Cardiff Eisteddfod of 1938, following which the adjudicator, Goscombe John, had troubled to write to him to encourage him to continue. Jenkin had no professional training in art, but his dentistry had given him the means to feed a lifelong interest in it by travel on the Continent and to the United States. By the time of the Mountain Ash Eisteddfod, he was attending the life class at the Swansea School of Art.

In Norfolk, early in the war, Winifred had met a sculptor called Zeitler, who she commissioned to make a bust of Henry. 'I feel like getting something done for Wales', she observed to Grant Murray in 1940, and conceived the idea of having made a

Unknown photographer, *Jenkin Evans and Huw Menai*, 1946

portrait bust of Huw Menai.[65] Nothing came of the project at the time, but following the Eisteddfod at Mountain Ash she proposed to Jenkin Evans that he carry out the work. She was unable to pay him the £100 which, generally, he asked for a portrait commission, and so he agreed to do the work gratis.[66] Provided with a letter of introduction to the sitter, written by Winifred, Evans proceeded to the Rhondda:

I visited Huw Menai at Pen-y-graig on Sunday and found him to be all that you said, also an 'Ideal' study. I sincerely hope I shall be able to do justice in Sculpture to such a fine head.

I had remembered that he is not at all well in health so suggested to him that he could be my 'Guest' for a fortnight in order that it might improve his health, also that I can work on the Bust, in my own 'homely studio'.[67] With this arrangement he was well pleased, so am fetching him in my car next week end.

The bust of Huw Menai was complete by the end of the year and, on the way to the bronze foundry in London, Jenkin took it to Winifred at Cottesmore Gardens:

We dined first and unpacked it later. For a long evening I re-entered very Wales of very Wales. Jenkin Evans knew many of our haunts in

Cadoxton days. Cwm Gridd and the lovely valley branching off to the left after passing Craig y Nos, where the circle of standing stones is, hidden in heather, and Llyn Fawr above Hirwain. By profession a dentist, a burly figure with a strong Welsh accent. In his fifties, full of good talk, with the imagination and fire and intellectual zest which marks the Welshman and makes so many of the southern English appear to me so dull. We unpacked the bust and set it on a table: it is a very fine piece of work and has Hugh Menai's tragic and noble grace and all his psychology embodied in it. It is to be cast in bronze and sent in to the Academy, a venture we both agreed, doubtful of success. [7 January 1947]

Notwithstanding their pessimism, the bust was accepted at the Royal Academy, as was a painting by Jenkin's brother Vincent, *At the Coal Face*. Winifred approached the National Museum, through Iorwerth Peate, to purchase the bust with the aid of a substantial donation from herself. As a result of her dealings with Jenkin, Winifred became acquainted with his wife, Bessie. The relationship became the most intimate of Winifred's later years. The two women corresponded often and met on Bessie Evans' frequent visits to London. Sometimes she stayed for as long as a week at Cottesmore Gardens. Nevertheless, it was not until 1950 that Winifred became aware of the close family relationship with Vincent Evans. Following the private view of an exhibition of the work of Evan Walters at which

Evans and Winifred were both guests, the painter wrote to her, seeking her patronage. Winifred was mystified, until Walters supplied the information that Vincent was Jenkin's elder brother.[68] As in 1935, she did not care to buy his work.

Once she had returned to Cottesmore Gardens, the institutional art world of Wales soon re-established contact with Winifred. Her longstanding acquaintance, Isaac Williams, the first Keeper of Art at the National Museum, had died in 1939. In November 1947 John Steegman, the current Keeper, visited Winifred at his own suggestion, to inspect the Welsh Collection. The new Keeper began badly by presumptuously, and unsuccessfully, soliciting Evan Walters' *Courting* as a gift to the Museum. Winifred's relationship with Isaac Williams had not been an outstanding success but that with the new occupant of the post would prove to be worse.

Winifred did not note other details of her first talk with Steegman, but it is likely to have included discussion of the new arrangements for the public funding of the arts through the Arts Council of Great Britain, which had been created the previous year. Although internally it had changed little since the death of Isaac Williams, eight years later the presence of the Arts Council had transformed the art infrastructure into which the National Museum fitted. The origins of the new institution lay in the institutional response to the distress of the Depression of the 1930s, with which Winifred's old friend Thomas Jones had been much involved as Secretary of the Pilgrim

Trust. In the context of increasing government direction of all aspects of life, the public-funded Council for the Encouragement of Music and the Arts, known as CEMA, was founded early in the war. Under its chairman, John Maynard Keynes, it presided over a remarkable increase in the popularity of art galleries, concert-going, publishing and many other arts activities, which seems to have expressed a widespread sense that the war was being fought for civilisation against barbarism. In the field of visual culture its modus operandi was to bring high art to the people in the form of exhibitions, which were shown not only at public buildings but also at educational settlements and places of employment. In this sense it persisted with the philosophy which Thomas Jones had promoted all his life, and which had occasionally been realised with the support of the Davies sisters. In the emphasis it placed on contemporary practice, CEMA's exhibitions policy was also close to that pioneered by Winifred with her French collection. Among the exhibitions toured by CEMA was one of the work of Cedric Morris – a curious choice, given the painter's apparent rejection in 1936 of the top-down model of working-class acculturation.

Both through his network of powerful friends and his position at the head of the Pilgrim Trust, Thomas Jones' influence on the development of CEMA was felt at the end of the war in the evolution of the Arts Council. The experience of Wales was in no small measure responsible for one of the more radical aspects of the design of the new institution. A decentralised structure of 'regional' committees, including those for Wales and Scotland, facilitated the taking of some small steps away from the metropolitanism which had characterised the patronage and practice of art in Britain throughout the modern period. The regional committees distributed their own funds and would soon demonstrate a potential to develop their own policies. David Bell, the son of Sir Idris Bell, a longstanding acquaintance of Winifred in Cymmrodorion circles in London, was appointed art officer of the Welsh Committee.

Although it took some time for the full implications of the creation of the Arts Council to become clear, the general direction of change was quickly apparent. As early as June 1946 the young painter and teacher, Esther Grainger, saw that it undermined the purpose of a federation of music and arts clubs which she was seeking to develop with the support of Cedric Morris. The clubs had emerged with the voluntary settlement movement in the 1930s. She saw that the professionals of the Arts Council would soon take on the responsibility.[69]

Unknown photographer, *David Bell*, c.1945

Equally, if rather higher up the social ladder, Lord Ivor Churchill, with whom Winifred had been involved in organising the Anglo-French Art Society before the war, told her that 'I have renounced all my Anglo-French activities and, in any case, the present does not conduce to private initiative in such fields of activity.'[70]

At the time of John Steegman's first conversation with Winifred in 1947, the practical implications of the creation of the new institution were the subject of intense debate. Shortly before their meeting he had participated in a discussion on the wireless about the future of art in Wales, along with Cedric Morris, A.G. Tennant-Moon, Josef Herman and Ivor Williams. Though couched in the most gentlemanly terms, the script did not seek to hide considerable differences of opinion between Steegman and his painter colleagues.[71] The question of whether the 'ordinary people' – defined by Williams as 'miners, dock workers and so on' – could be interested in art was central to the debate. Steegman's view was unwaveringly elitist. Since 'an artist is different from other people' he did not believe that 'the community in England or Wales will ever be interested in art'. Like Winifred, Morris had more ambivalent feelings about that matter. In a letter to Tennant-Moon, who was to co-ordinate the writing of the script, he had initially suggested that 'someone a bit younger and with less experience of the complete indifference and ignorance of the Welsh people towards the visual arts would be more suitable' as a participant in the debate.[72]

However, he agreed to take part, and in the broadcast itself, when pressed on the subject of Welsh visual ignorance, he firmly placed the blame on the influence of English bad taste, defending what he regarded as indigenous Welsh traditions in craft and architecture: 'The English point of view has been forced on Wales – that is why there is no art in the country'.

In the broadcast debate, Josef Herman had suggested that there was a need for an exhibition of contemporary painting, to establish the credentials of a new generation of Welsh artists. His idea had been brought to fruition by David Bell, through the Arts Council. The 'Exhibition of Welsh Art', at the Mansard Gallery of Heal's department store in London was opened by Idris Bell, who spoke on the subject of art and nationality. Winifred took the chair. The opening gave her a first sight of the post-war generation of Welsh painters. She was not impressed, and compared the pictures unfavourably with 'the vivid beautiful oils I bought in France after World War I for sums under 25 pounds, many of them!!' [7 February 1948] Nonetheless, the exhibition liberated a flow of energy which she would direct into Welsh art affairs for the remaining few years of her life. In letters written to Grant Murray and in her diary, Winifred's reportage of the tittle-tattle of the private view at Heal's, and many subsequent social occasions, reveals something of the workings of the institutional power structure as it settled down to the new order. 'What an odd little man Ralph Edwards is', she wrote to Grant Murray in February, for instance, 'and why do he and Steegman belabour Iorwerth Peate – who has always been so extremely kind and welcoming to me!!'[73] Winifred had known Edwards before the war. He was a specialist in the history of English furniture at the Victoria and Albert Museum, where she had occasionally gone to seek his advice.[74] His views about art were elitist, which tended to bring him into alliance with Steegman but in opposition to Peate, who was energetically promoting a revival of Welsh visual culture across a broader range than high art, in which folk traditions would be the source for new work. The Welsh Folk Museum at St. Fagans was about to open, after years of development by Cyril Fox, the Director of the National Museum. Peate would be its first Keeper. He visualised St. Fagans as a living museum, with craftspeople at work, and with the aspiration to stimulate a revival

of design comparable to that which was making Scandinavian work famous throughout the world. The conflict of philosophy between Peate and the high art elitists – Bell, Steegman and Edwards – would find its public expression in a debate about the nature of Welsh visual tradition for which the exhibitions at the National Eisteddfodau of the late 1940s and early 1950s provided the focus.[75] In a letter to Grant Murray, Winifred mildly mocked the transparent pretensions of Edwards and Steegman:

What an odd couple Ralph Edwards and Steegman are, so grand and 'Over Edom will I cast out my shoe', both it seems desirous of my friendship - Ralph Edwards because he aims to succeed Cyril Fox and Steegman because he wants me to give an early Evan Walters to the National Museum collection!![76]

At the opening of the Heal's exhibition Winifred renewed her relationship with several old acquaintances. Foremost amongst them was Cedric Morris. She found him less dominated than before the war by what she regarded as the bad influence of his partner, Lett Haines. Morris visited her at Cottesmore Gardens two days after the opening:

Cedric Morris, now Bart, spent an hour here - came to ask me to enlist Geoffrey Crawshay's influence with Steegman of the National Museum to get the exhibition of Welsh pictures transferred

Geoff Charles, *Iorwerth Peate opening the Art and Craft Exhibition of the National Eisteddfod at Mountain Ash*, August 1946 The National Library of Wales

to Cardiff and shown in the Museum. We had a great talk on Welsh affairs and personalities. Cedric is now an ageing man and enormously improved from the rather audacious man I knew circa 1932. He runs a school of art in Suffolk. I do not much care for his own work as a painter, but he loves Wales and knows many interesting people in it. [17 January 1948]

Morris failed to persuade Steegman to show the exhibition at the National Museum, though it did travel to Cardiff, where it was presented at the David Morgan department store.

At the Exhibition of Welsh Art at Heal's, Winifred had been impressed in principle by the number of young women artists shown. However, she was not disposed on grounds of gender to admire what they produced. In particular she disliked the pictures shown by Lynette Roberts, a feeling which extended to personal animosity on their first meeting. In December, Roberts and her husband, Keidrych Rhys, visited Cottesmore Gardens:

Keidrych Rhys of 'Wales' and his wife here for coffee after supper. An ill-assorted pair, he a literary peasant, she an intelligentsia, [a] pretentious woman of higher class ... Paints badly and writes atrocious so called poetry. Very patronising ...[77]

Winifred felt more comfortable with the pictures shown by Esther Grainger, who worked at the Pontypridd Settlement and more widely in the Valleys as a peripatetic teacher. She was one of three young painters shown at Heal's who had become closely associated with Cedric Morris as a result of his interest in the settlement movement. With Glyn Morgan, who hailed from Pontypridd, Grainger often visited him at his art school at Benton End, and became much enamoured both of his personality and his ideas. The third member of the group, Heinz Koppel, who was a Jewish refugee from Germany, had taken over the teaching of the art classes initiated by Morris at the Dowlais Settlement.[78]

The Exhibition of Welsh Art was also the first occasion on which Winifred saw the work of Kyffin Williams. Again, she was not impressed, but was soon made aware by Ralph Edwards of the high esteem in which he and several other connoisseurs held the young painter. Edwards regarded Williams as his 'particular protégé'. The Heal's exhibition had coincided with his first one-person show:

I was the means of getting him his show at Colnaghi - I bought one of the pictures for the Welsh Contemporary Art Society some years ago. He will have a good send off as I have bought three pictures for friends and a small one for myself before the opening. His work is not in the least like Augustus John but I think highly of his talent all the same and expect him to become well-known in time. However, he is an extremely nice young man, though his appearance does not suggest that he is long for this world.[79]

Kyffin Williams, *Deposition from the Cross*, 1948. Oil on board, 9×13 City and County of Swansea: Glynn Vivian Art Gallery

his Cross, a group of women and 2 Roman soldiers in scarlet cloaks: the two other crosses stand out across an angry sky. Colnaghi reduced the landscape from 20 to 15 Guineas and the Pietà from 25 to 20 Guineas. I have written to Grant Murray to say, if [Swansea] does not want to keep the Deposition, I will gladly have it myself. [5 March 1948]

Having received this communication on the headed paper of the Victoria and Albert Museum, and a request from Grant Murray, who had also been alerted to the talent of Williams, Winifred hastened to Colnaghi and rapidly changed her opinion of the new painter:

Determined to get to Kyffin Williams show at Colnaghi, where Grant Murray had asked me to buy a picture for the Gallery in Swansea. Was glad I had made the effort, going and coming in a taxi. Kyffin, a very considerable painter. My only regret was that much had already been sold. The National Museum, Cardiff, Arts Council of Great Britain, Ralph Edwards of the V & A, had all bought: 15 out of the 31 pictures had been sold, counting the 2 I bought. A beautiful landscape of Welsh mountains and a small noble, deeply moving, Deposition - Christ lying dead, beneath

Winifred soon came to regret sending *The Deposition* to the Glynn Vivian, rather than buying it for herself. Over the next seven years she bought five other oil paintings and a group of six watercolour drawings by Kyffin Williams, and so became one of his most important early patrons. Nevertheless, although they both lived in London and corresponded, they did not meet until December 1950. They became friends, but were not close. The matter-of-fact confidence of Williams, exemplified in the enormous flowing hand of his letters, did not encourage Winifred to proffer motherly advice. On the other hand, Williams' courtesy and obvious ability did not suggest arrogance, against which Winifred always reacted strongly. Although they met occasionally, their relationship was maintained mostly at a respectful distance. Shortly before their first meeting Williams wrote to thank her for her purchase of *The Wave*:

Kyffin Williams,
The Wave, 1950
Oil on canvas, 18x24

*I was very pleased to hear that you
had bought my picture of a wave -
I only hope it wears well. I painted
it about a year ago, and like all my
seascapes, was painted in London.
Having lived by the sea nearly all my
life I find it much easier to paint it from
memory. It is of no special place, but my
other seascapes are of the St. David's area.*[80]

The sombre picture precisely suited her mood. From the time of her childhood stays at Langland Bay, Winifred had always enjoyed the sea, and in old age she found increasing comfort in the contemplation of its 'life-giving' quality. Shortly before buying *The Wave*, she had stayed alone in a hotel at Porthcawl:

*I came here two days ago, on Wednesday,
travelled to Bridgend, where a car met me and
bought me to the sea ... I unpacked just before
dinner, having gone out the moment after tea to
look at the great waves rolling in and hearing
again the thunder of the surge. To breathe in sea
scent and to know that nothing will ever dim my
passionate love for the sea. For its wild tumult, its
great expanse, its freedom, its untamed beauty.
Far across the water lay the Devon and Somerset
coast and, to the West, Cefn Bryn and Gower*

*and Wixen sands, on which as a child I heard
the bell tolling. And I thought of the days when
Cruff was here, long ago, and later Alexander
and Henry and Gaggi and Dedooge and G.W.
B[alfour]. I look back and long for vanished
faces, loved as ever.* [30 June 1950]

Notwithstanding her admiration for Kyffin Williams, Winifred's great enthusiasm in the last years of her life was for John Elwyn Davies, with whom she developed a relationship comparable only to that she had made with Evan Walters in the early 1920s. As the son of a hand loom weaver at Newcastle Emlyn, John Elwyn attracted Winifred not only for himself, but for the tradition that she felt he embodied. The single painting exhibited by him at the Heal's Exhibition of Welsh Art had been the only work to make a favourable impression on her:

My heart warms towards this young man. I've written to him to stay in Wales for a year working at his mill - painting what he sees and what he likes, giving time of an evening to his drawing, avoiding the withering atmosphere of London studio life, where his individual talent may easily be extinguished, and the deadly grind of teaching. He is the only young painter whose work (and that, of course, only in one painting) I have seen in the 1925-48 years that I have felt 'this is the real thing'.

Clearly the discovery of John Elwyn reminded Winifred of the promise of the young Evan Walters, but she was also mindful of what she regarded as that painter's subsequent decline. She concluded her initial description of John Elwyn to Grant Murray by acknowledging the need for more than ability in a painter:

John Elwyn, *Approach to a Welsh Village – Pontrhydyfen*, 1949 Oil on board, 12x8

It is what he might become that I think of. Now is the time of promise. It looks to me as if he has the right sort of character to carry talent - and for lack of that how many fall by the way.[81]

Winifred introduced herself to John Elwyn by writing a long letter, in which she encouraged him and explained her long-standing interest in young painters. At the same time, she recommended to Grant Murray the purchase of *In the Valleys* for the Glynn Vivian. Murray duly obliged, describing the picture as 'a little gem' and making an interesting association with the work of Breughel. Winifred's initial assessment of John Elwyn was confirmed by the work he showed at the National Eisteddfod at Bridgend in August 1948, which she thought 'magnificent'. In 1949, at the Paul Alexander Gallery in Notting Hill, he was given his first large exhibition. Though it was shared with another painter, he was able to present twenty-four pictures of life in Cardiganshire. Winifred was overwhelmed with enthusiasm.

Went to John Elwyn's show at the Paul Alexander Gallery and was amazed at what I saw. Over 20 pictures, small oils, figures in landscape, Cardigan countryside, scenes of Welsh country life, wonderful colouring and composition. I felt thrilled, for I have been his friend and guide, all these he painted in or near Newcastle Emlyn last year, when I said to him, 'paint out of doors, paint in Wales, the life you know, paint small pictures, figures in landscapes, paint Wales', and there is something of both Daumier and Innes in these pictures. I bought number 18, a lovely scene of field and mountains, with figures in a cart, or trap in the foreground. 'Approach to a Welsh Village', 13 Guineas. I will keep it for myself, unless the

Glynn Vivian wants it. The rush of joy these pictures have given me. Here is the making of a fine painter. Something individual, not deviating, fresh, native and real. [29 June 1949]

Winifred's 'lovely landscape', depicting 'the road leading down to Pontrhydyfen, beyond Cimla among the hills opposite Cadoxton', was soon joined by two more, bought by Alexander with her encouragement. She then set about spreading the word, by dispatching numerous letters and catalogues. When she met the painter for the first time, his exhibition was already a success, which he generously attributed solely to Winifred, saying that 'he did not know how he could ever show his gratitude'. [17 July 1949] Winifred had been directly responsible for a further purchase by Iorwerth Hughes Jones and, crucially, for introducing the work to Steegman and Bell:

By 11am I was at John Elwyn's exhibition, went around with him, more impressed than ever. Then David Bell, Assistant Director for the Arts Council of Great Britain in Wales, arrived, whole-heartedly praised his work, and thanked me warmly for having let him know about the show. The Contemporary Art Society for Wales has bought the largest picture, 'Funeral at a Welsh Farm'. A fine thing with many figures, this sets the seal on Elwyn's work and will be an enormous help to him. David Bell said he was himself the buyer for the Tredegar public gallery and would record a purchase of one of Elwyn's pictures. So now Elwyn is launched, discovered by me in 1947, coached as to subjects and size, publicised by my hard work since the show opened. How glad I am and how it takes me back to the days at Cadoxton and young painters there.[82]

John Elwyn,
Palm Sunday, 1949
Oil on board,
12×19

In their construction and colour John Elwyn's pictures of 1948-9 seemed to be a perfect manifestation of Winifred's taste. The painter's openness and humility encouraged her to seek to keep him in line. In the many letters she wrote to him her criticism of his pictures became detailed to the point of intrusiveness, as if the painter was her visual amanuensis. At the deepest level she perceived in his work a cultural rootedness which confirmed the beliefs she had formed in the intellectual atmosphere of the Wales of the late nineteenth century, but which seemed no longer to reflect reality in art or society as a whole. She wanted from him 'something in the rough with an immediacy of vision and emotion born of contact with the earth and racial inheritance':[83]

Keep close to Wales and within remain a man of the Welsh countryside, of one of the most truly Welsh counties ... Today is full of influences tending to blur the outline of nationality. Radio, cinema, press, politics, sport are all anti-Scottish or Welsh atmosphere and 'feel', but it is within such atmosphere that a man's most individual work is produced.[84]

A young painter's work reflects the development of his relation to life, his fellow creatures. There is a 'deep' in him from which his finest work springs, begotten of inspiration fed from inner springs.

In a rare moment of self deprecation, which suggests the unusual level of empathy she felt with John Elwyn, Winifred acknowledged that

Unknown photographer, *John Elwyn painting 'The Wool Dyers'*, January 1950
Private collection

'All this may seem bosh to you, because I can't put it into words'.

After thirty years of hope and expectation for Welsh art it seemed to her that, at last, the country had produced its quintessential painter.[85] When he proposed to paint workers dyeing wool in Cardiganshire she responded with enthusiasm. She described her long-standing interest in the craft of hand loom weaving and recent attempts she had made to find a weaver for Iorwerth Peate. Her 'ancient weaver' at Crickhowell, Charles Powell, was now too old to work, but she was able to have white wool from John Emlyn's family mill woven into a rug and presented to St. Fagans.

There can be little doubt that Winifred's enthusiasm for John Elwyn was given a keen edge by her awareness of the growing number of painters, of whom the most prominent Welsh example was Ceri Richards, who were attracted to abstraction or to entirely non-figurative painting. In this art she sensed a manifestation of the

John Elwyn,
Easter Communion,
1949
Oil on board,
9×12

erosion of cultural identities which distressed her deeply. She saw John Elwyn as a bastion against the trend. For her, representational painting was the true path – 'the visual arts *must be* that ... Do not be put off by the artists whose work will not be looked at in 20 years', she advised him.[86] One such was Wyndham Lewis. At the height of her enthusiasm for John Elwyn, Grant Murray asked Winifred to visit an exhibition of his work at the Redfern Gallery, with a view to making a purchase on behalf of the gallery:

The oils, and especially the larger ones, I thought hideous, but I am no judge of painters, hailed by critics as serious artists, who portray the human frame as if made out of scrap iron or geometrical designs. I am most anti-Munnings but my eyes are hooded where a certain sort of surrealist-cum-cubist work is concerned. I just can't see in them either meaning, strength or beauty - it is my limitation, must be, since scores of the Wyndham Lewis pictures of that type were lent by the Manchester and Birmingham public galleries.[87]

Curiously, Winifred later acquired a Wyndham Lewis drawing for her collection, but the new proponents of the abstraction which he had practised before the war excited only her indignation. She reported to Grant Murray that the news of the appointment of Ceri Richards among the selectors for the Art and Craft Exhibition at the National Eisteddfod at Caerffili in 1950 'made my hair stand bolt upright on my head!!'[88] She had recently seen his work, apparently for the first time, at the Redfern Gallery. 'I was horrified', she wrote to John Elwyn:

*The most hideous jumbles of cubist stuff -
'abstract' and 'non-representational'. For God's
sake don't go after that form of madness. Every
picture was grotesque - hideous, horrible in
colour. I never saw such nightmares.*[89]

Winifred's distaste for Richard's work and her
support for Kyffin Williams and John Elwyn was
not simply a rearguard action against new styles
of painting. Indeed, the pictures by Williams
which she so much admired were somewhat
unconventional in the way the paint was applied
and in the degree of simplification which the
painter imposed upon what he observed. As her
distaste for Munnings indicates, she was not
wedded to a superficial realism, but rather to
what she felt was a deeper realism – a painting
which confirmed the reality of God, as revealed
in his earthly creation. It was the rejection of
spirituality and the celebration of the mechanistic
materialism of man (indeed, primarily of men),
that disturbed her. The reconstruction of God's
creation in terms of the rigid, inorganic forms of
human manufacture, was not only a travesty of
the truth but a blasphemy.

The National Eisteddfod of 1950 at
Caerffili brought to a head the debate about
democratisation in the arts, and in particular
the tension between cultural particularity and
internationalism with which it was bound up
in Wales. The Chairperson of the Arts and Crafts
Committee was Iorwerth Peate, and the Eisteddfod
proved to be the Waterloo of his campaign to
establish the precedence of craft tradition over
high art. Peate felt that if any truly Welsh painting
was to emerge, it must do so from within a deep
familiarity with craft tradition – the tradition
of the common people, as he saw it. He had
signified his intentions at the start by habitually
changing the conventional word order of the title
of his section to 'the Craft and Art Department'.
However, the enemy was already well established
within the camp. In the late 1940s David Bell had
organised a series of selected exhibitions of new
art which were shown at the Eisteddfod, side by
side with the traditional competitive exhibitions,
in an attempt to raise what he considered to be
low standards. In the *Welsh Review* in 1947 he had
condemned the work thrown up by competitions
as not likely to find a place 'in many village art
societies'. Three years later Bell's alternative
proposal for an exclusively selected exhibition
was implemented. The art committee appointed
Ceri Richards, Cedric Morris and George Mayer-
Morton to select the work. In effect, this meant
choosing artists rather than works, and resulted
in a strong emphasis being placed on young
professional painters. It was a considerable irony
that this step was taken under the chairmanship
of Peate, for whom the competitive principle
was fundamental to the Eisteddfod tradition.
In his public pronouncements on the matter
he emphasised that the new principle was an
experiment, and his tone made it clear that he
thought it a dangerous one. The criticism of the

178

Percy Wyndham Lewis,
Woman with a Bowl, 1923
Pencil on paper, 26x18

August 1923.

Alexander Coombe-Tennant, *Winifred Coombe Tennant at 18 Cottesmore Gardens*, 1949

competitive principle had come from 'snobbish critics', he alleged, plainly referring to Bell.[90] However, the exhibition was hailed by most people as an outstanding success. Notwithstanding the involvement of Ceri Richards, Winifred shared in the general enthusiasm, and felt that the art exhibition was by 'far the best National Eisteddfod show of pictures I ever saw'.[91] Steeped as she was in the tradition of Ruskin and Morris, she did not experience the tension between art and craft in the same way as the younger intellectuals around her. Peate retired from the fray to the bastion of St. Fagans, remarking, with something less than good grace, that 'Welsh artists should not become too complacent just because they have enjoyed a successful exhibition at Caerphilly. If we in Wales are to see a school of Welsh artists, the artist must familiarise himself with the whole background

of Welsh material life'.[92] It was precisely on these grounds that Winifred celebrated the arrival of John Elwyn and Kyffin Williams, both of whom were selected for Caerffili. She remained bullish on the matter. 'Of course there is a distinctly Welsh school of painting', she observed. 'You look at a John or a Kyffin or a John Elwyn or an Evan Walters, and you know no Englishman could have painted their pictures'.[93] However, Peate sensed that whatever the qualities of these particular painters, their work did not reflect the mood of the times in the art world. To the indignation of Winifred, evidence was soon at hand of the accuracy of Peate's estimation of the prevailing mood, and of the increasing marginality of her views (and his) in the art world. Shortly after the Eisteddfod she wrote to Augustus John:

The Festival of Britain has commissioned work - one picture - from three 'Welsh' artists out of a number of whose names came before their selection committee. They have chosen 1) Ceri Richards! 2) Merlyn Evans (to me his pictures represent men and the visible world in terms of ironmongery!) 3) A Pole now living at Ystradgynlais ... Herman or some such name! Are these three cranks to go out to the world as representatives of Art in Wales!!! What has David Bell got to say about this![94]

Ceri Richards, Merlin Evans, and Joseph Herman came to represent a devilish trinity in Winifred's mind. Her antipathy to Richards and to Evans was unsurprising, given her distaste for abstraction in general. Her response to Herman's pictures might have been expected to be more nuanced, to reflect her strong sympathy with the mining community and the number of images of miners which she owned. However, like many other people at the time, she took offence at the depersonalisation of the miner which she sensed in Herman's representations. His exhibition, 'Miners at Ystradgynlais', shown at the Glynn Vivian Gallery in 1948, had aroused strong feelings in some visitors:

Probably my appreciation of modern art is not developed but the impression left on me after spending some time looking at [these] monstrosities was of deep depression ... The miners and the women look like blotted, misshapen prehistoric beings emerging from the primeval swamps of the carboniferous age, and the pictures are ghastly travesties of the present-day miner and his womenfolk.[95]

The exhibition had been organised by David Bell. He had a high opinion of Herman and saw him as a crucial part of the revival of Welsh painting, which he felt was underway. Herman cut an exotic figure in the minds of some Welsh and English intellectuals – a Jewish émigré who brought 'in his suitcase', as Bell put it, a vaunted tradition of central European expressionism. Winifred found him 'heavy and dull, and a poor draughtsman'. In his many conversations with Winifred, no doubt

Bell took care to avoid the subject of Herman, in the interests of maintaining cordial relations. He is scarcely mentioned in their correspondence.[96]

Winifred's re-engagement with Welsh art as a consequence of the Heal's exhibition extended to a resumption of her relationship with Evan Walters, whom she had not seen since 1939. To her great relief, in February 1948 Walters wrote to say that his latest commission, to paint the Archbishop of Wales, would be 'just straightforward painting', 'not in his later and to me, mad manner'.[97] At a St. David's Day function an opportunity arose to catch up on Walters' life through the eyes of a third party:

Dragged myself by car to a Welsh gathering, where met a woman I have long wanted to, Mrs Caradoc Evans. We sat next to each other at Princess Marie Louise's table, and had a long long talk - Evan Walters and his history of recent years. She had never forgotten the Eton Boy, Henry, and Evan painted Caradoc. She touched Caradoc's lonely embittered life and it has flowered under her touch. [1 March 1948]

Caradoc Evans had married the novelist Marguerite Hélène in 1933, two years before Winifred first met them at the opening of the Exhibition of the work of former students at the Glynn Vivian Gallery. Marguerite and Caradoc stayed in contact with Walters (who painted them both) during the remainder of the 1930s and then through the war.

Caradoc died in 1945 but Winifred's interest in Marguerite did not represent a vicarious curiosity about her husband. She was a woman of great style, a quality which always attracted Winifred and, furthermore, she held unusual and eclectic views on religion and life after death. The Evans' home near Aberystwyth had been 'full of Marguerite's antiques and religious bric-à-brac… Madonnas and Buddhas on tables and shelves'.[98] A week after her discussion with Marguerite, Winifred was able to assess Walters' present state for herself, when the painter came to visit her at Cottesmore Gardens:

Evan Walters came and spent 2 hours here, absolutely normal and full of excellent talk. Described his portrait of the Archbishop of Wales, Prosser, which is to be hung in Llandovery College. Evan told me he intended to do what he called plain, straightforward painting, as well as his double vision painting. I know that if I had money to give him commissions I could draw him back

to painting the great pictures he has it in him to paint. Discussed with him whether I could … get Monty to sit for him, the picture to be given to the National Museum of Wales. I will have a try. I explained that I could not pay any reasonable fee for it and Evan said he

Unknown photographer, *Evan Walters*, c.1940-50

would paint it, for me, for nothing. We had much talk of old days at Cadoxton, and of Henry, and of the intervening years of war. Evan, quite unchanged and all the rumours of him having become queer, absolute rubbish! [7 March 1948]

Although she got as far as an appointment with Montgomery's ADC, her plan for the portrait, like that she had conceived the previous year to persuade her wartime hero to sit for a bust to Jenkin Evans, came to naught. Nevertheless, she was able to assist Walters by interesting David Bell in his work. In the company of Winifred and Henry, Bell visited the house where Walters had stored his paintings during the war.[99] Among the pictures they inspected was the portrait of Ramsay Macdonald, which Winifred coveted, and the infamous portrait of Caradoc Evans. Walters' portrait of Evans had experienced a difficult life, though only because of the strong feelings aroused in some people by the opinions of the sitter. The National Museum and the Glynn Vivian had both refused it in 1931, amidst considerable controversy, and it received the ultimate accolade of the anti-icon when it was slashed by an indignant patriot at the opening of a revival of the sitter's play *Taffy*, at the Grafton Theatre in 1938.[100]

In May 1950 Walters had a one-person exhibition at the Alpine Gallery in London. Winifred was shown the work by Walters himself, 'grown very heavy, greying and with a small white imperial'. [6 May 1950] She liked a few pictures, but many of them depressed and bored her, and overall she felt saddened by the experience. She took a still life of apples, which had appealed to Henry, but more importantly she was moved to commission Walters once again to paint her portrait. The idea had arisen as a result of comments made to her by Augustus John. After years of admiration and sporadic correspondence, eventually she met the painter in December 1949, when he called for tea at Cottesmore Gardens. It was one of the highpoints of her later life:

Soon after 5pm Augustus John arrived. Large, heavy with white dishevelled hair! Clear in brain and wonderful company. Talk of pictures and painters and people, T.E. Lawrence, Munnings!, the Sitwells, ... of Wales and Pembrokeshire 'which tugs at me. I want to live at Slebech'.
[8 December 1949]

Later in the week, Winifred recounted their 'grand racy wonderful talk' in a letter to Grant Murray, and expanded, in particular, on John's memories of Evan Walters:

On Thursday Augustus John spent an hour with me, full of life and energy and zest, and good talk. He is ageing, dishevelled white hair ... Examined closely the two portraits by Evan Walters of my husband and myself. Of mine he said, 'It is beautifully painted. I did not know that Evan could paint like that. After the First War I told him he should go abroad - to the south, Provence or south of Spain, and steep himself in

colour and paint it there, where he had it under his eyes. He didn't go, and since has wandered off the track to all sorts of wilfulness' ...

His conversation was brilliant - artists, pictures, his own work, his early days in Paris, where he had known Picasso well ...[101]

Mindful of Grant Murray's high regard for modesty, Winifred reserved for her diary the compliment paid her by John, which concluded their discussion of Walters:

He looked at the Evan Walters portraits, thought mine a fine painting, then wheeled and said 'but you have much improved since then'! (I had my lace cap on!) He stayed near on two hours and when we parted I said to him 'Ah, did you once see Shelley plain ...', quoting the whole verse, which I feel pleased him. He spoke of Ingres, Matisse and Will Rothenstein, and of his life in Paris when young. A great man.[102]

Evan Walters,
The Apples, c.1950
Oil on board, 16x20

Clearly, Winifred chose to understand John's remark as gallant, rather than as a vacuous appeal to her vanity, and she confided it to Walters. 'I shall paint you again', he said, to which Winifred agreed on condition that there was 'no nonsense about double vision. It must be straight painting'.[103] She sat in the lace cap, which had become her habitual headgear in the house, but the painter's first attempt was not encouraging. After three hours, instead of the 'small quietly painted head, against a dark background', which she envisioned, he produced the head 'of a pink and white woman who looks as if she has just escaped from a music hall. Oh dear!' [16 June 1950]

After a break of a couple of months, Walters began again. Although it felt to Winifred like old times to have him in the house, she did not sense that the portrait would be a good likeness, 'all this double vision manner' having 'put his eye out'. However, he pulled the picture together and finished after a month of occasional sittings:

Evan Walters finished my portrait in my lace cap. It was a good likeness and a fine piece of painting and I am well satisfied with it. I am to pay him £50 for it. I have had about 7 sittings, of about 1½ hours, here in the Library. He signed it and high upon the left side of the canvas wrote Mam o Nedd, 1950. It is exactly 30 years since the sedate squiress was painted by him at Cadoxton, a fine portrait of me as I then was in 1920. [12 September 1950]

Evan Walters,
Winifred Coombe Tennant, 1950
Oil on canvas,
12×10

Evan Walters,
Sketch for the portrait of Winifred Coombe Tennant, 1950
Oil on canvas,
12×10

Notwithstanding Winifred's reticence when writing to Grant Murray, in due course the story of Augustus John's compliment to her and its outcome in her portrait by Evan Walters emerged from the privacy of her diary to became a favourite anecdote. She believed that John was 'the greatest artist we have, and perhaps of any country'. [17 January 1953] Alongside her support for Kyffin Williams and John Elwyn, much of her engagement with Welsh painting after the war was taken up with the acquisition of his work, along with that of his sister, Gwen, and his friend J.D. Innes. Initially, Winifred's interest was manifested on behalf of the Glynn Vivian Gallery, which had no example of the work of Augustus, who was now in his seventies. 'Oh! haste, haste, to secure one of his pictures', she urged Murray, 'he is in poor health and once he dies his pictures, I am told, will rocket up in prices. Do you want a landscape or figures? His early pictures of Dorelia are glorious things'. Winifred suggested Murray write directly to John, 'not forgetting his O.M., R.A., about which I hear he is very sensitive'.[104] The Director was pessimistic, having been badgering the artist to no avail since the late 1930s to paint a landscape for the Civic Centre.[105] Winifred therefore turned for assistance to Peter Harris, who owned several works by John (including two portraits of Dorelia), and was on good terms with him. Harris had been a friend of Winifred's since 1916, when he and Christopher had met as subalterns before going to the trenches. He informed her that John was 'unapproachable and living on brandy', but that the Leicester Gallery had an appropriate work for sale. [4 March 1948] Winifred immediately inspected the picture and reported her favourable impressions to Grant Murray, but her negotiations were forestalled by the generosity of Richard J. Strick, who had also been in pursuit of a John for the gallery for some

time. In March 1948 he succeeded in buying *The Tutor*, and donated it forthwith. Nevertheless, Winifred persisted with her enquiries, soon locating another picture, *Irish Landscape*, at the Leicester Galleries. Taking advantage of a sudden fall in the market for pictures, brought on by the Berlin crisis and general post-war austerity, the Glynn Vivian bought the second picture at a good price.[106]

The gallery was also without a work by Gwen John, a situation which presented a greater challenge. Notwithstanding the generally depressed state of the art market, the reputation of Gwen John was rising rapidly, with a consequent rise in prices. Winifred shared the critical admiration for Gwen, which had been fuelled by the memorial exhibition at the Matthiesen Gallery in 1946:

Went to see the exhibition of Gwen John's exquisite pictures at a Gallery in Bond Street. The work of such a remote, withdrawn spirit. A few lines, Et Tout Est Dit, a few strokes of the brush, and mysteries are revealed. She was Augustus John's sister and I have met her in days gone by, a rare artist. [5 October 1946]

The meeting may have taken place before 1909, since Winifred made no record of the event in her subsequent diaries. 'I knew her long ago', she reported, only a little more specifically, to Grant Murray. She was 'a remarkably ugly woman, as I remember her!'[107]

Augustus John was enlisted to assist in the search for a good picture, but surprised

Augustus John, *Irish Landscape*, c.1912 Oil on board, 20x23
City and County of Swansea: Glynn Vivian Art Gallery

both Winifred and Murray by remarking that 'Sometimes I have thought that a number of her drawings – in colour or otherwise – would illustrate her gifts as well as a simple picture – or perhaps better'. Winifred begged to differ with the great man – 'there's arrogance! It is her oils that are her – the finality of them – the moon-beam range of her palette.'[108] The problem of finding a picture was resolved with unexpected speed when Winifred was informed by Peter Harris that Edwin John, the artist's nephew, was disposing of his collection through a London gallery. Winifred immediately went to see what was available and wrote an excited letter to Grant Murray:

186

*This afternoon I had a wonderful experience!
I found a fine collection of Gwen John's work
that belongs to nephew Edwin John and which
Matthiesen of Bond Street is selling on commission.
I knew her work fairly well and went twice to the
Memorial Exhibition of her work. These paintings
at Matthiesen are the real thing, and the 31 picked
out among the finest specimens of her work. This
sounds conceited but I spent an hour there with the
senior partner of the firm showing me the collection,
and he remarked before I left that I had picked
out what he himself regarded as the finest.*[109]

In the lengthy report on the pictures, which
she attached to the letter, Winifred was in no
doubt that the pick of the bunch was *The Nun*, 'a
glorious thing' and 'a quintessential Gwen John'.
The picture, with two others, was sent on approval
to Swansea. In the meantime, an opportunity arose
at an opening at the Tate Gallery for Winifred to
make some comparisons between *The Nun* and
other pictures by Gwen John. She was taken to
the event by her old friend Lady Rothenstein:

*I had some talk with John, her son, the Director,
standing in front of a Gwen John, 'Girl with a
Black Cat' - a small picture, and the same model
and dress as the two I had seen at Matthiesen.
He said to me that her pictures were now very
expensive but that they would, he was sure, rise
in value and that 50 years hence she would be
classed among the best painters of her time. The
first picture bought from her for the Tate was
bought on his father's urgent representations. He
took me to look at it - figure of a girl in a striped
dress. I said nothing to him about my having seen
any Gwen Johns, or Swansea wanting one. The
Tate as now hung is a glorious treasure house.
I saw fine Innes, Augustus John, Sickert, Wilson
Steer, Serjeant and many others. One ultra
modern room had some mighty strange stuff
presented by the Contemporary Arts Society -
Piper, Spencer. By the way, nowhere did I see
a Tonks, and I like his work so much. I saw to
me a very ugly Ceri Richards. Cripps in opening
ceremony was brief and good. A crowd present...*[110]

Gwen John, *The Nun*, 1915-21
Oil on canvas, 22x14 City and County
of Swansea: Glynn Vivian Art Gallery

Winifred had negotiated with Matthiesen to pay £250 for *The Nun*, considerably less than the price at which it had been offered three years earlier in the Memorial Exhibition. 'Your letter warms my heart', she wrote to Grant Murray on receiving the news of the Gallery Committee's approval of the purchase:

> *How glad I am the Gwen John has been secured for the Gallery and that you thought so highly of it. It was certainly far and away the finest example of her work that I saw, and far and away finer than anything the Tate has. You mustn't think of buying any more pictures now for a long time - but 'The Nun' was one of those undoubted treasures to snap up whilst still available.*[111]

The acquisition for the Glynn Vivian of a Welsh landscape painted in oils by Innes proved more difficult than finding works by either Augustus or Gwen John. Winifred had been aware of Innes probably since his London exhibitions before the Great War, which showed both French and Welsh landscapes. Shortly after the war she had greatly admired a painting of Arennig by Innes bought from the Chenil Gallery exhibition of 1912 by the Stepney family of Cilymaenllwyd, Llanelli. Winifred, who was a friend of Marged Howard Stepney, was promised by her mother that if she ever sold the picture, she should have the first refusal. In 1932 she hoped that she had bought an example of his work cheaply at auction, but the picture proved to be by an American painter of the same name. An exhibition at the Redfern Gallery in 1939 further deepened her admiration for his work:

> *With Zanga to marvellous show at Redfern Gallery of John and Innes and Derwent Lees. Some of the early Johns a wonder - some of Innes so sincere, rich and strange. Much of N. Wales. At 27 he died - what a painter, utterly unknown in his lifetime. We linger long rejoicing in the pictures.* [25 February 1939]

J.D. Innes, *View in Wales*, 1911
Oil on board, 9×12 City and County
of Swansea: Glynn Vivian Art Gallery

Ten years later Winifred sought the help of Peter Harris and Augustus John in her search for an Innes oil painting for Swansea. John supplied her with information about the descendants of Horace de Vere Cole, close friend both of himself and Innes, who had pictures. He also suggested she try Euphemia Lamb, 'to whom Innes was devoted', and who might be in need of money and so willing to dispose of some her pictures. Winifred knew of Euphemia from Harris, in some of whose Innes pictures she appeared, painted when they walked through France together. John, whose early admiration for Innes had not diminished with the passing years, was enthusiastic about acquiring a work, but felt that 'The Glynn Vivian must wait a bit for a typical Welsh Innes, which I am sure can be found. Innes was with me in France before his final illness. Tell Grant Murray to hold that money till we find a beautiful thing for Swansea'.[112]

Eventually, in September 1950, Winifred was informed that the Roland, Browse and Delbanco gallery in Cork Street had just acquired two oils by Innes, one of which was a small Welsh picture, painted on panel. She hastened to the gallery and wrote immediately to Grant Murray to recommend its purchase.

At the end of the war, since Grant Murray had retired from the School of Art, Winifred was initially less aware than she had been in the 1920s and 30s of young students emerging at Swansea. She was able to assist Brian Rees, whose mother had worked for her as a typist in the 1920s, and

who wrote appealing for her support in 1945. She encouraged him for some years as he trained at Swansea and Camberwell, and Alexander commissioned a picture from him.[113] However, when the generation of young painters whose career at art school had been delayed by service in the forces began to emerge, Murray again called on Winifred for her help. In July 1950 he reported to her on an exhibition of student work which had been held at the Glynn Vivian, commending pictures by Rees and three painters who were unknown to Winifred, Ogwyn Davies, Archie Williams and Norman Tudgay. Murray sent a selection of their pictures on approval to Winifred, and she bought examples by all three. *The Bar of the Victoria Arms*, by Ogwyn Davies, impressed her particularly. The pub in question was at Pontardawe and was among the favoured haunts of the young painters then at the School of Art. Among them, Davies and Rees were particularly close, though Davies was older by some years, having served in the Royal Air Force during the war. His arrival as a student at Swansea had been somewhat unusual, but characteristic of the sense of liberation and potential that was in the air among the young at the time. His intention had been to use the grant available to all ex-service personnel to study Chemistry at the University, and he was duly granted an interview. Finding himself with an hour to spare before catching his bus to the campus, he decided to visit the Glynn Vivian, having a long-standing interest in painting. On the way he met an acquaintance, Ceri Davies,

Ogwyn Davies,
The Bar of the Victoria Arms,
1950 Oil on board, 8×12

who was a student at the School of Art. Diverted into the School, he was much taken with the bohemian atmosphere, as he perceived it – though the Principal, Kenneth Hancock, to whom he was introduced, seemed to him more 'the officer type'. Davies skipped his interview in the Chemistry Department and enrolled in the School of Art the following week.

Winifred seems to have been little aware of students who attended Cardiff School of Art. It was on the recommendation of Cedric Morris that she met Glyn Morgan, who had studied there until 1944 under Ceri Richards. Notwithstanding this unfortunate aspect of his pedigree, Winifred was impressed by Morgan when he visited her in 1950:

Glyn Morgan of Pontypridd came to see me. Brilliant young painter sent by Cedric Morris - some lovely drawings. Dressed in corduroy trousers and a loose coat, bearded, very handsome, dark haired, came at 5 and left at 7.30pm. All that time talking art, painting, painters, himself, my collection, etc. A wonderful refreshment. [28 September 1950]

Morgan was enthused by the Rhondda as a subject, which he toured on his motorcycle:

Really, the mountains are so beautiful that they take one's breath away. How can one mortal painter hope to put down all that mystery and dignity? They can keep Switzerland. I should like to have a large studio on wheels, thousands of canvasses, and two lifetimes to paint the Rhondda Valley.

Nevertheless, 'after that, Paris – that is, if the Russians don't get there first'.

Morgan informed Winifred of a scheme which would have important consequences for Welsh painting. He had been speaking to students at Cardiff, who were 'all rather tired of art school proceedure, all full of energy and vitality, and they want to get together (about 20 of them) with Janes, Esther Grainger, myself and possibly Cedric, and have an exhibition some time next year'.[114] The painters included Charles Burton and Ernest Zobole, who, with their contemporaries, would soon become celebrated as the Rhondda Group. Sadly, Winifred seems not to have made contact with them, and a single, brief, expression of approval of Charles Burton's *Back from the Club*, awarded the gold medal at the National Eisteddfod at Ystradgynlais in 1954, appears to define the extent of her awareness of their work. Neither would Glyn Morgan be counted among them, though his work of the period was painted in much the same spirit. Winifred hoped he would paint Huw Menai and, indeed, he visited the poet with an introduction from her, but in 1951 he succumbed to the attractions of Paris.

By no means all of Winifred's interventions in the lives of young painters brought forth the enthusiasm which she showed for Ogwyn Davies and Glyn Morgan. The precedent set by her personal dislike of both Vincent Evans and Lynette Roberts was followed in the summer of 1950 when she met Elvet Thomas, a painter originally from Aberdare, who had recently trained at the Slade School of Art. On their first meeting he appeared to Winifred to be 'pontifical' and 'obsessed by Cubism, Surrealism, mad on Paul Klee' – not a combination likely to endear him to his potential patron. [3 August 1950] Notwithstanding this inauspicious beginning, the following year Winifred had Henry drive her to his home near Northolt to inspect his work. There she 'saw the most revolting and hideous paintings I have ever seen':

Glyn Morgan, *Tonypandy*, 1951
Oil on canvas, 21x27 Private collection

A woman's head with a corkscrew in place of a nose and such like horrors. [The] painter said [they] were 'beyond abstract'. God help us if such things debauch the eye and mind. Came back along a hideous road hiving with shoppers. I said to Henry, 'This is West Ealing', and he replied, 'It may be West Ealing, but for me it is Hell'. I agreed.[115]

Winifred's unfamiliarity with the Cardiff students was due largely to the fact that Grant Murray remained her most important source of information about events in Wales. He had little contact with Cardiff. Indeed, it was Winifred who drew his attention to the work of

Glyn Morgan. Nevertheless, as Murray was still engaged with the Glynn Vivian Gallery, he was as anxious as ever to learn about new talent, from wherever it emerged, and in a letter dated 13 October 1950 expressed to Winifred his desire to meet Morgan. However, in the same letter he revealed to her that, for the first time since it opened in 1911, he had been unable to attend a committee meeting at the gallery. He wrote from his bed at home, where he had been ill for some weeks. His condition worsened and he was taken into hospital, but his stay there was brief. It was decided that nothing could be done for him and he died at his home in Richmond Terrace, Swansea, on 17 November. Winifred had maintained an unbroken relationship with him since they were introduced by Evan Walters thirty years before, and hers would be among the most authoritative of the many tributes paid to him:

It is not art alone but life that is impoverished by the death of this rare and noble man ... He honoured me with his friendship for more than thirty years, he taught me much, I was proud to work for and with him, and to the end we remained in close touch ...

He was indeed a man of outstanding qualities - generous and warm-hearted, with the exquisite breeding of the Highlander and a broad humanity and wide sympathy that endeared him to all. He had an inner rectitude that never wavered, a goodness and a personal kindness that never failed. He was full of wisdom and of charm, with

a delicious sense of humour that often brought a merry gleam to his eye. He was completely disinterested, un-selfseeking, and withal shrewd and sternly just. Above all he had that rare quality - distinction: distinction of mind, of diction, of appearance and bearing ...

There is no sadness of farewell when such an one puts out on the sea of Eternity. Rather, in the words written by John Donne more than three hundred years ago, let us 'sing the progress of a deathless soule'.[116]

Notwithstanding the brave face which her religious beliefs required she show the world, the death of her friend Grant Murray left a void in Winifred's life. In private she expressed with increasing intensity her sense of isolation, of being

Unknown photographer, *William Grant Murray*, c.1930 Private collection

192

left behind. Early in 1951, the death of Murray was followed by that of Evan Walters. Rather to her surprise, while painting her portrait the previous year, Walters had told her 'that if anything happened to him, he relied on me to help with his affairs and that I was to choose about 10 or 12 pictures from his studio that I liked'. [12 September 1950]. He was not apparently in bad health, but on 14 March 1951 she received a telephone call from Erma Meinel, Walters' partner of many years, to say that he had died of a heart attack at half past two that morning:

He had complained of 'indigestion' on Saturday - felt unwell on Monday and Tuesday, did not suspect he was ill, and died suddenly when Miss Meinel was in the kitchen getting him

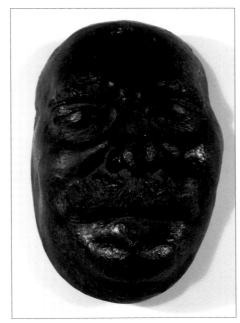

The Death Mask of Evan Walters, 1951
City and County
of Swansea: Glynn
Vivian Art Gallery

some sugar dissolved in hot water ...

It was a great shock to me - he was 58 and had been at intervals part of our family life since I first saw him when he was under 20. He painted at Cadoxton, and as his life drew to its close he painted the beautiful portrait of me in old age wearing my lace cap last year ... I shall miss him in my life for he was linked with its earlier happier years and with Cadoxton and my beloved Wales.

Miss Meinel asked me to find someone who would take a death mask of him - rang up Rothenstein at the Tate and he sent me on to Professor Dobson, head of the Sculpture School at the Royal College of Art. I was able to make all the arrangements. Miss Meinel rang me up again at 2.30. The funeral will be at Hendon Park Cemetery on Monday. Hail and Farewell! [14 March 1951]

In fact, Walters body was taken to Llangyfelach for burial. Winifred ordered a sheaf of spring branches and pussy willows, with daffodils clustered at the base and tied with emerald green ribbon. Her card read, simply, 'With love from Mam o Nedd'.

Even though the two women had yet to meet, Erma Meinel was in daily contact with Winifred in the week following the death of Walters, who had suggested to his partner that she could rely on her for support:

Miss Meinel rang me up about various matters concerning Evan Walters. She is the sole executor of his will and told me briefly its contents - all his

193

Evan Walters,
Primavera, 1951
Oil on canvas
National Museum
of Wales

pictures left to the National Museum of Wales.

    She told me things I had not known of Evan's feeling for me - how I was his inspiration, his ideal, and that all through his life from the early days when he painted me in 1920 I had represented something to him which influenced him, that was his standard of values as it were, something infinitely precious and unchanging.

    As I think of this I weep!

    Lying in the dark alone I heard Brahms requiem on the Home Service, a perfect tribute to him. Full too of the memories of the war days at Windsor, when in chapel I often heard 'How lovely is Thy dwelling place'. God's love sustain us![117]

Evan Walters,
*Blue China and
White Jug*, n.d.
Watercolour
on paper, 10x14

On the 23 March Winifred met Erma Meinel for the first time:

Miss Meinel, Evan Walters' friend, came to see me - our first meeting. She had met him when a student at the Polytechnic evening classes, when she was in her twenties. That must have been twenty years ago. Very intelligent, cultured and unglamorous ... I expect has been his mistress for years, no matter. I liked her very much and feel she must have brought peace and kindness to Evan's life. Tomorrow I go up to her house to see his studio and his last picture, Primavera, which he had just finished. I showed her a number of my Evan Walters pictures. We spoke much of him. She is a link with him. [23 March 1951]

When Walters was painting his portrait of Winifred in the summer of 1950 she had proposed to him that the time was ripe for a retrospective exhibition at the Glynn Vivian. Grant Murray had taken the idea forward, meeting with the painter to discuss how it might be done as a part of the town's Festival of Britain celebration in the following August. In the event, in the spring of 1951 the gallery would be occupied by Murray's own memorial exhibition, and with the agreement of the new curator, David Bell, the Walters retrospective would be transformed into a second memorial, delayed until May 1952. In the meantime, the more pressing issue was the disposal of Walters' pictures, left to the National Museum. On a visit to the house in Hampstead where he

and Meinel had lived together Winifred 'saw his palettes, brushes, paints, and many unframed pictures – not all double vision – his chair, easel, my heart rushing out to the memories of days gone by, and in a long black wooden box which Miss Meinel unlocked were his papers. Some bundles of letters from me. One envelope of mine I saw 1920 and postmarked Mumbles – it was all poignant and tremendously moving'. [24 March 1951] After some weeks Meinel completed an inventory, and Winifred returned to the house, in the company of Henry, to look at the surviving pictures:

We were there a long time, and what a feast to the eye and the imagination. His work was practically unknown. He had no understanding of publicity or of handling dealers. I was amazed at the number and magnificence of the work I saw, some of it dating back to 1915, and much dating from 1949 and 1950 - superb landscapes, still life, figures. If I had seen these things in his lifetime I would have picked out a hundred and made them known.

His [exhibition] last May in the Alpine Gallery gave no idea of what he had to show. Henry was filled with admiration, and I so sorrowful that Evan Walters had died practically unknown. The Memorial Exhibition at the Glynn Vivian ... will be an astonishment to many.[118]

At the National Museum, John Steegman was not of the same mind. In May Winifred wrote to David Bell:

Miss Meinel is in Swansea this week and seeing the National Museum people. I saw a letter written to her by Steegman of what I considered a very off-hand and chilly nature saying that he expected to be in London the day she came to the Museum, i.e. today, but if that were so Mr Charles would see her. I saw that she was rather hurt by the tone of this letter, but I explained to her that the writer of it was like that to everybody.[119]

Four months later came confirmation of the Museum's luke-warm response to Walters' bequest:

Miss Meinel came to dine with me. Much talk of Evan Walters. The Keeper of the Art Department National Museum Cardiff has written to her lawyers to say he expects to keep very few of the pictures sent down, worded in a very surly manner.

I hate rudeness, which is more common today than in times past. Discussed what course should be done with work rejected by the Museum. Poor soul, she is very sad, and with Evan's death the light has gone out of her life.[120]

Shortly afterwards the main reason for Steegman's indifference became known to the public. In early October Winifred read in *The Times* that Gwendoline Davies of Gregynog, who had died recently, had left her collection of pictures to the Museum. In comparison to works by Monet, Renoir and Van Gogh, pictures by Evan Walters seemed to Steegman and his friends to be of no consequence. Walter's bequest 'included a vast

quantity of the sweepings of his studio', as Ralph Edwards put it in a letter to Winifred, with singular disregard for her feelings. The letter was written ostensibly to thank her for sending a catalogue of the Memorial Exhibition.[121]

Winifred travelled to Swansea for the Memorial Exhibition in May 1952. She stayed at Ystalyfera with Bessie and Jenkin Evans, who drove her into town:

Saw the devastated area still in ruins as the vile Huns left it. Met David Bell at the Glynn Vivian Gallery - strange to walk into that familiar building and find no Grant Murray to greet me. Up to D.B.'s room, where was a dark and to me unattractive Sickert about which he was enthusiastic - hoped the Committee would buy it ... Saw the collection of Evan Walters' work. Some very fine works - the singing boy, the boy blowing a feather, and the boy listening to a watch especially outstanding. Hanging on a wall seen through an archway was the large picture of myself, Alexander and Henry, sitting on the floor of the Music Room at Cadoxton playing dominoes - figures excellent but I do not like the garish pink carpet, and never did ... Hanging in another room and directly opposite this large picture is the small portrait of Mam o Nedd - a most interesting contrast - also beautifully painted. What a tragedy it is that Evan did not remain on the lines on which he painted his best pictures. Restless, obstinate and full of turmoil within, he charged wildly now this way and now that, hurting himself, hurting his work, producing tired and ugly pictures. Born in different circumstances and in a different world he might have become one of the great painters of his day. [9 May 1952]

The following afternoon Winifred returned to open the exhibition:

A great and wondrous day for me ... Reached the Glynn Vivian shortly before 3, in driving rain. Rested in what was beloved Grant Murray's own room, until David Bell led me to where, at a table, sat the Chairman of the Art Gallery Committee, the Deputy Mayor, and Sir William Jenkins and other Big Wigs. Two spoke before me, introducing me with eulogies composed, I suspect, by David Bell. Then I rose. My speech went well, closely following the lines of my script. I had a most attentive audience and great applause at the end. More speeches, one most inappropriate, vulgar and jaunty by Sir William Jenkins, a typical provincial industrial vulgarian. Then much shaking of hands and greeting in the market place ...

After leaving the Gallery we drove up to high ground to the west of Swansea to the home of Dr Iorwerth Jones - a charming house with heavenly sea air blowing past it. Most kind and intelligent people, and with some fine pictures. Janes the painter was there, very self-assured and didactic.

Well, this has been a great day in my life.
[10 May 1952]

Winifred stayed on with the Evans family, touring in Jenkin's new car to see landscapes which stirred loving memories in her heart. Nevertheless, her interest in the present remained equally keen. Having heard that Ogwyn Davies was in Ystalyfera, staying with his fiancée, Beryl, she let it be known that she would like to meet him. The news was conveyed to Davies by Beryl's father, a postman:

I remember him saying, 'Hey, you've got to go up and see Madam' (Madam they called her!) in Jenkin Evans' place, so I went. I was sort of ushered in and, you know, I always remember the similarity of when I was a boy and when the doctor came and my mother used to say 'Galw Doctor arno fe'. This is the way respect is created. Well I had the same feeling when I went in, plenty of respect. She was propped up in bed, quite a high bed, but all beautifully turned out, you know the sort of wear they wear in bed. Mrs Evans was hovering about - I had to be made aware that I was entering on royalty - and the chat was about painting really, yes, talking about some of those other people, Evan Walters, and I think she mentioned John Elwyn, too, and Kyffin ...[122]

Winifred recorded her rather different perception of the meeting in her diary:

In evening Ogwyn Davies, the young painter, came. I had bought 'The Bar of the Victoria Arms' from him in '50 or '51, chosen for me by Grant Murray as the best picture in the Art Students'

Exhibition. A most likeable 28 year old man, living in Ystalyfera. He brought me some of his work to see and I bought a lovely small oil study, 'The Mangel Field', very Millet in feeling - peasants working in a field, farmer in background, mountains beyond. He was so pleased and I was so pleased! [13 May 1952]

It would appear that Davies did not disabuse Winifred of her romantic notion of 'peasants working in the field'. The peasants had included himself and two art student friends from Swansea, working in their holidays to earn a little spare cash. Nevertheless, Winifred's sense that the picture owed much to Millet was correct. Davies and his contemporaries at Swansea were much in awe of Millet, Courbet and the Barbizon *plein air* painters of mid-nineteenth-century France.

On her return to London, Winifred experienced a less agreeable aspect of such youthful enthusiasm for a career in art. The *News Chronicle* had recently published a description of her Welsh collection, in which she drew attention to the work of John Cyrlas Williams, one of the young painters whom she and Grant Murray had encouraged in Swansea in the 1920s. She had heard nothing of him for over twenty years, but the article came to the attention of Williams' mother, who wrote to say that, much to her regret, her son no longer painted.[123] Soon afterwards, he called on Winifred at Cottesmore Gardens:

Ogwyn Davies,
The Mangel Field, 1952
Oil on board, 11x16

Cyrlas Williams, the artist, came. I showed him his five pictures bought in the twenties. He was amazed. I think he is in some state of mental confusion, and I ask myself, will he ever paint again? I doubt it. He is on the Board of Trade, been living in London all this time ... I felt an ailing mind. He was surprised at the warmth of my welcome. He had it in him to be a very considerable painter ... [25 May 1952]

Three days later, Winifred was again taken back to her life in the 1920s. Her contribution to a programme about Evan Walters was her first experience of speaking on the wireless, but the producer was impressed. As a consequence, Winifred began a late career giving the talks which were part of the staple diet of what was still, for much of the time, a distinctly sober medium. Her first script, 'Escape to Wales', was broadcast live one morning in July. She returned to Cottesmore Gardens to enthusiastic wires and telephone calls from friends. Over the next two years she made several more such evocative broadcasts for the BBC Home Service, including 'The Story of Craig y Ddinas':

'Once upon a time I lived in a white-washed Manor House in the Vale of Neath, a very happy young woman ...' So begins this talk, a mixture of memories and legend, which have as their focal point that 'great rock from which one looked out over a glorious view of the Vale and the winding river Nedd below ... and beyond it is spread a tableland covered with turf and dotted with old thorn trees and mossy hollows, where rushes and tall foxgloves grow.'[124]

After the death of Evan Walters and Grant Murray, Winifred became increasingly fascinated by the personalities of the art world of her youth. Through J.D. Innes, Augustus and Gwen John, the two countries she most loved, France and Wales, were united. The anecdotes of her friend William Rothenstein, who had known John well in London and in France, brought her a further perspective on that world. She read and reread his book, *Men and Memories*, and her knowledge of the period was deepened by the biography of the painter Charles Condor, another of the group, written by Rothenstein's son, John. Having found works by Innes, Augustus and Gwen John for the Glynn Vivian, she longed to acquire pictures by them for herself, but had been unable to do so because of the high prices which galleries were now asking. The painting by Innes that she had been promised by the Stepney family after the Great War eluded her for precisely that reason, and under particularly trying circumstances. On the death of Marged Howard Stepney, in 1953 the picture was offered to her, and it was agreed that David Bell should estimate its value. His figure of £250 was well in excess of what Winifred had expected or could afford, with the result that it was sold to the Glynn Vivian Gallery.[125] However, by this time Winifred had already secured her first pictures by

Innes. On a chance visit to the Leicester Galleries in the summer of 1951 she found that Oliver Brown, the senior partner, had bought two Innes watercolours just a few days earlier:

They were not on show but knowing of my interest in the work of Innes and my search for an Innes for the Glynn Vivian ... he had them brought up from the cellars for me to see. One he said was from Lord Howard de Walden's collection and had a label on the back showing that it had been in the possession of Horace de Vere Cole ... they asked 75 guineas for it. The other was a smaller picture of a rocky peak 'Welsh Mountains', a slighter work of exquisite quality - I could not make out whether it was the Arennig Mountain or one of the mountains seen in the picture of Bala Lake in Lilian Browse's small book. It was signed and dated 1911. They asked 30 guineas for it - a low price compared to other water colours by Innes seen elsewhere.

J.D. Innes,
Mountains, North Wales, n.d.
Watercolour and pencil on
paper, 12×17

I gazed long at these superb and characteristic examples of Innes' work done in his best period - Innes in North Wales. For years I have been longing to have an Innes to live with - here were two noble examples and I asked myself could I afford to buy the small one if I went without something in my own personal expenses ...

I slept on the problem and wrote next day offering £100 for the two, a reduction of 10 guineas - but I had little expectation of it being accepted ...[126]

Three days after she had seen the pictures, she received an answer from the gallery:

Oh joy beyond belief! About 11a.m. I was rung up by the Leicester Galleries to say my offer was accepted - the two Innes are mine. I can scarce realise it. All day I have gone about as in a dream - 'I have two Inneses! I have two Inneses!' Tomorrow they are being sent here. I shall live with them. I shall see them every day. Innes has drawn near to me and I to him. Praised be God! [7 September 1951]

When the pictures arrived, her opinion of them was confirmed. She found them 'intoxicating ... superb and glorious', and longed to show them to Augustus John, to discover whether he had been present when they were painted. [8 September 1951]

In October Winifred was fortunate to find, once again, a picture of the period she loved

200

at a price she could afford. On this occasion
the painter was Charles Condor. At the Wilton
Gallery she saw 'lovely things at give-away prices':

*I bought a chalk drawing by Charles Condor
with an inscription 'A Blanche. Souvenir de
Charles Condor Dec 3rd 1901', and on the left
of the drawing 'Voyage de Plaisir à Dieppe'. The
figure of a woman and 3 men. and to me most
precious from the many references to Condor and
Blanche in 'Men and Memories' by Rothenstein.
This is one of my Jewels.* [10 October 1951]

Like Innes, Condor had died when still young,
a fact which increased his appeal to Winifred's
romantic imagination. 'He ruined himself by
drink and dissipation, but, what a loveable
character, what a mind, what a painter.'[127] Her
run of good luck in the galleries continued until
the end of 1951. At the Beaux Arts Gallery, where
something of a clearance sale was in progress
following the death of the owner, she found a
drawing of the head of a woman by Augustus
John, priced at 30 guineas:

*For past 3 years have been trying to get one. but
nothing under 60 to 125gns. Found a catalogue
lying on the table of the summer show at Beaux
Arts and mention of an Innes. After hunting
Mrs Lesson produced it. Had been in Lord Ivor
Churchill's collection and sold in May 1950 at
Sotheby. It is a poorish water colour in poorish
condition - but at 25gns a real find. Made an*

Charles Condor, *Voyage de Plaisir à Dieppe*, 1901
Pencil heightened with pastel, 8×10

*offer of 25gns for the John and 20gns for the
Innes. and bought them both. Especially do I
rejoice in having a fine John drawing in our
Welsh Collection. The Innes is a landscape
at La Ciotat. a coast scene ... This is a great
day in the history of the Welsh Collection.*
[17 December 1951]

Winifred went on to acquire a total of nine
works by Innes. She became acutely sensitive to
his reputation. When a note on Augustus John,
written by the art critic of *The Times*, remarked
that Innes had been a 'very minor artist', she
responded not only with an indignant letter of
her own, but an appeal to John to refute the slur.
He was little moved. 'If I start correcting all the
bloomers perpetrated by Art Critics, I should have
little time left for my own work', he wrote to her.
'Of course the *Times* man was completely wrong

201

J.D. Innes,
Lady at the Piano, n.d.
Ink and watercolour
on paper, 8×7

Augustus John,
Head of a Woman,
n.d. Pencil on paper,
12×8

about Innes and I shall show him up in good time and in my own way. Innes was never "a very minor artist", nor did he "turn me into a painter", though I hope I learnt something from him. If I weren't somewhat sick of publicity I would send the letter you suggest. Perhaps I will yet.'[128]

In this late burst of picture-buying Winifred acquired further works by Condor, and three small drawings by Gwen John, two of them probably made in the zoological gardens in Paris. In 1953, to these she added both a watercolour and an oil painting by Derwent Lees, who had occasionally accompanied Innes and John in Wales and in France, and adopted their fresh, open manner of painting. As in the cases of Innes and Condor, the story of Lees matched Winifred's sense of all that a painter should be. Mental illness cut short both his career and his life.

Winifred became interested in the women who were close to these young men, and in particular Euphemia Lamb, intimate friend of Innes. In 1949 both Augustus John and Peter Harris had spoken to Winifred about Euphemia, who now lived near Andover in a house 'stacked with Innes drawings and paintings from floor to ceiling. Twenty-three dogs and many cats live in it with her, her golden hair now bleached artificially, her blue eyes unchanged'. [25 November 1951] In 1952 Winifred lent her first two Innes watercolours to an exhibition of his work, shown with that of Kyffin Williams, at the

Leicester Galleries. Euphemia was among the other lenders. After the exhibition, with the assistance of a friend, Morton Sands, who acted as intermediary, she was persuaded to sell the Innes watercolour *Cloud over Arennig* to Winifred. 'A most wonderful thing has happened today', she recorded. 'The Innes I longed for, prayed for, came! Morton Sands brought it up from Euphemia's house in Hampshire – he came here, carrying it. "I have got your picture", he said … "How, How", I said, "did you do this miracle?" "By persuasion", he replied … "It is very fine" …' A week later, Morton Sands brought Euphemia herself to Cottesmore Gardens:

Gwen John,
Two Women, n.d.
Pencil on paper, 8×6

Derwent Lees,
Russian Peasants, n.d.
Oil on canvas, 24×16

I was resting in bed about 3.30pm … when the parlourmaid came in and said 'Mrs Grove and Mr Morton Sands have called to see you'. I rushed into a dressing gown and my lace cap of the Portrait, and found them in the Library. Euphemia, Innes's Euphemia, who walked in France with him - a tall, slender woman with a shock of golden hair, a pale complexion and lovely features. I could have fallen at her feet! I said to her, after a joyful greeting, that when I beheld her the words came to me 'Ah, did you once see Shelley plain'. She was warmly friendly to me, and begged me to come and see her. I showed her my large Innes of 'Mountains in North Wales' and she exclaimed 'It once belonged to me. I sold it to Lord Howard de Walden'. I told her I knew it had once been in his collection and that it was from him the Leicester Galleries bought it. She greatly admired the John drawing, 'Head of a Woman', and the Condor drawing 'Voyage de Plaisir à Dieppe'. Liked the Kyffin Williams and the Evan Walters - Morton Sands beaming with the success of our rencontre.[129]

Winifred remained in touch with Euphemia Lamb. Through their friendship, and also through her earlier friendships with Augustus John and William Rothenstein, it was as if she sought to relocate her own youth in theirs. For Winifred, *fin de siècle* France had been the abode of genius, a place inhabited by painters especially gifted by God. She too had been of that period and often in that place, and yet it seemed as if by some mysterious oversight she had not been of their company. Her fascination with the period brought forth one of the most revealing observations about herself that she would make in her old age:

> *Did a lot of work, and rejoiced exceedingly in the material I am gathering for my note on Condor. That mine of interest, fun and happiness, 'Men and Memories' (Rothenstein), has a lovely description of the party gathered in 1900 at Vattetot - John, Orpen, Sickert, Condor, Rothenstein and his wife, Mrs Walter Crane, and Rothenstein's sister-in-law. He described how they all bathed at night in a little cove near Vaucottes, the womenfolk undressing and dressing in a cave under the cliffs, 'and returning, the women would hang glow worms in their hair'.*
>
> *That is the sort of world I was meant to live in, with men far cleverer than myself - vital, creative, not in the world of Martha Martha in which so much of my life has been passed. Beare it deare heart![130]*

Throughout the second half of her life Winifred had compensated for the misplacement of her own youth by the encouragement of the new youth of succeeding generations. The energy of young painters energised her. Their works brought

her the joy or the certainty she needed to resist the depression which daily threatened to engulf her. She had begun with the erratic excitement of observing Evan Walters at work. She ended with the exultation of Kyffin Williams' deiform mountains and the calm reassurance of John Elwyn's legends of a living past. Together, these two restated the ideal of Wales, land and community, which she had absorbed in the imagined country of Tom Ellis and Cymry Fydd in the years after her arrival at Cadoxton in 1896. Winifred followed these young painters until the end of her life, writing to them and reading their letters to her, looking at their pictures whenever possible, persuading others to look at them and to buy them and, increasingly, as her health failed, receiving reports of their progress from her friends.[131] From the National Eisteddfod at Llanrwst in 1951, for instance, Bessie Evans reported that she and Jenkin had spent hours in the exhibition, which was 'delightfully set out'. For the first time since 1876 the Arts and Crafts Committee at Llanrwst had provided a special pavilion on the field to show the work, and had instituted the Gold Medal for Painting, won by Brenda Chamberlain.[132] In the way of Eisteddfod art exhibitions, the following year Bessie Evans reported the general disappointment felt at Aberystwyth. Bessie's letters to Winifred, whom she addressed with greater familiarity than any other correspondent as 'My darling Mam o Nedd', reflected the trust and warmth of feeling between the two women:

Dear Bessie Jenkin Evans arrived from Ystalyfera, laden with gifts - so warm hearted and so Welsh [and], after these chilly English, like a Ray of Sunshine. We had peaceful hours of talk - her life, my life, Welsh news. Oh! how encouraging and healing it is to be with someone who cares, who loves one, to whom one can say anything, who is in tune as one is oneself in tune with the other. I went to bed warmed and comforted! [26 April 1951]

Winifred's relationship with Bessie Evans was among the most intimate she made, although it was formed so late in her life. It seemed to Winifred that Bessie succeeded in fulfilling a role as a female home-maker without sacrificing her intellect. She believed that Bessie lived a life of 'serenity and faith and courage'. The sudden death of her friend in August 1953 was a cause of great sadness:

I have been blessed with many friendships during the course of a long life, but few that brought me such richness and tenderness and fun as that which grew up between Bessie Evans and myself during the past seven years ...

Above: J.D. Innes,
Cloud over Arenig, c.1911
Watercolour on paper, 10×14

Right: J.D. Innes,
Landscape with a Pine Tree, 1909
Pen and watercolour, 11×8

Kyffin Williams, *Skye from Harris*,
1954, Oil on canvas, 18x22

*Hers was indeed a rare spirit - she was full
of vitality and imagination, with a power of
sympathy possessed by few. She was 'very
Wales of very Wales', racy, of the soil - loving
and giving. She had a lively intelligence and
fine judgement of people and things ... She was
one who lit many fires in cold rooms ...* [133]

Winifred's world contracted further in 1955,
with the death of Thomas Jones. Their friendship
had begun before the Great War, when they worked
together in the campaign for woman's suffrage:

*Read last night in the evening paper of the death
of my beloved T.J., aged 84. How I envy him, gone
home after a long and wonderful life, for years
my close friend and advisor. Irreplaceable, the
greatest Welshman alive these many years, born
in a workman's house in a Welsh valley and*

*rising to the Zenith of power and distinction
as under secretary to the Cabinet. Under four
Prime Ministers a man of glorious integrity,
vivid sympathies, wit, friendliness, judgement.*

*His death leaves my world emptier than ever.
God Bless him, God speed and joy I wish you,
your Mam o Nedd.*

*Dear T.J., what a fount of wisdom, unselfishness
and clear sighted helpfulness you were to me, over
so many years. Few can have been loved by so
many. I miss the feeling of his presence in this
world, it is emptier and sadder. He was a great
man and a rare personality. Please God I shall
see him again some day. He has gone to his
beloved child Elphin. There is none in Wales
who could replace him.* [16 October 1955
and 3 November 1955]

Winifred also wished to be gone, to join her own
children, Daphne and Christopher, and her many
departed friends. 'I am poorly and downhearted',
she wrote to John Elwyn in October, 1955. 'I just
long to change my world – like my beloved T.J.,
who died just now …' Yet, in the fatigue and
ill-health of the last two years of her life, she
continued to invest what energy she could spare
in the encouragement of John Elwyn, Kyffin
Williams, and other young painters. She looked
forward on their behalf. 'Some day I should like
you to meet Ogwyn Davies of Ystalyfera, just
appointed art master at the grammar school at
Tregaron, a place I know and love', she wrote to
John Elwyn.[134] A few months earlier, she had

enjoyed the company of Kyffin Williams, for what would turn out to be the last time. He brought her *Skye from Harris*, 'a lovely picture I saw at his private view. Rocks, islands, sea, mountains; just throw open [the] window and let my spirit escape into a world of beauty and colour, the sound of waves and the uplifted beauty of mountains'. [28 January 1955] For Winifred there was no contradiction between longing to be gone and investing in the future – feelings which had, in fact, coexisted in her personality for over forty years. Her unshakeable faith in the continuity of the individual after death led her to understand earthly life as the prelude in a greater whole. Given the depression with which she was afflicted, it was, perhaps, a necessary faith, and the only possible resolution of her condition.

John Elwyn,
Manor Deifi Church, 1955,
Oil on board 11×14

The sense both of cultural and spiritual continuity which she found in the pictures of John Elwyn, in particular, closely matched her needs towards the end of her life. On her last trip to Wales, in August 1954, she visited the Glynn Vivian Gallery and saw there several of his paintings. 'Oh! I just cannot live without something as near as may be to the small painting you gave David Bell – *Village of Llechryd*. Of all your paintings it is the one I think most perfect, after my early *Approach to a Welsh Village*.'[135] Over a year later, John Elwyn sent as a gift the last picture that Winifred would add to her collection:

Received from John Elwyn a lovely picture, [an] oil painting of Manordeifi Church ... Label at the back - 'To Mam o Nedd, with gratitude, and thanks for her help and encouragement, August 1955, John Elwyn. Manordeifi Church, near Llechryd'. A lovely pink washed cottage, beside a white washed church. It brings all Wales into my room and rejoices my heart. A few graves in the little church yard and a white marble cross, some trees and a blue sky with clouds in it.

How kind. Wrote to him of the joy it gives me. [20 September 1955]

A little less than a year later, on 1 September 1956, Winifred Coombe Tennant died at her home in Cottesmore Gardens.

FOOTNOTES

Chapter One

1 Winifred's father was involved in the sugar industry in Bristol. On a visit to Stroud in 1932 she mused that 'I left it before memory begins in a child. Gaggi [Winifred's pet-name for her mother] says it stood alone in fields … I found it surrounded by largish houses set in gardens … confined itself to little ground … I looked at it and it meant nothing to me, nothing at all, this house where I first saw light …' Diary, 2 September 1932.

2 The National Library of Wales holds many of Parker's drawings.

3 Hebe Spaull, *Women Peace-Makers* (London, 1924), p. 92. The essay on Winifred in this volume, entitled 'A Mother's Work for Peace', is clearly based on an interview, and as such is a useful source of information. Nevertheless Winifred did not have a high opinion of it: '*Women Peace Makers* arrived. I read the Chapter on myself – the whole book is rather sugary and inane but the chapter on me is perhaps rather better than the one on D.D.' Diary, 19 July 1924. The identity of 'D.D.' is obscure – none of the women discussed in the book has these initials.

4 'Memoir of George Edward Serocold Pearce-Serocold' (1906). The document is held in a private archive but a substantial extract was published in Winifred Coombe Tennant, 'Slavery and the League', *The Welsh Outlook* (June, 1927), 150-3.

5 For the Tennant Canal, see Keith Tucker, *Scratch in Glamorganshire: George the Founder (1765-1832): A study of the life of George Tennant* … (Cilfrew Historical Projects, 1998).

6 'She remained a vivid and arresting human being, full of individual traits, and joining, as it were, in her own person two different epochs of European history – for she had danced as a child in Paris at the Court of Charles X (1824-1830), and she lived to see the three great battles of Ypres in the present war (1914-17).' Winifred Coombe Tennant, 'Memoir', in Oliver Lodge, *Christopher: A Study in Human Personality* (London, 1918), p. 93.

7 Mrs H.M. Stanley, *London Street Arabs* (London, 1890), introduction. The Welsh painter B.S. Marks, working in London in the same period, seems to have been more directly aligned with the social reform movement. See Peter Lord, *The Visual Culture of Wales: Industrial Society* (Cardiff, 1998), pp. 158-9.

8 Lord, *The Visual Culture of Wales: Industrial Society*, pp. 140-57.

9 Quoted in Bernard Lloyd, 'The Talented Tennants of Cadoxton Lodge', *Country Quest*, 31, no. 8 (1991), 40-1. Dorothy Tennant was a close friend of Millais, and she modelled for both *Cherry Ripe* and *Yes or No*. Unidentified press obituary of Charles Coombe Tennant by the Vicar of Aberpergwm, preserved in the Diary of Winifred Coombe Tennant for 1929. She was 'reputed' to be his love-child. Diary, 5 November 1951. The work of Dorothy Tennant was not included in the canon which Welsh writers on art in the early twentieth century sought to establish, presumably because she was born in London, and that remained her primary home. Furthermore, until Winifred's son, Christopher, members of the Tennant family did not publicly identify themselves as Welsh. In fact, her credentials – a Welsh father and a Welsh home, reinforced by marriage to a Welsh man – met the criteria of the age for a Welsh painter more closely than did those of many who were included by Mardy Rees in his *Welsh Painters, Sculptors and Engravers*, published in 1912, and in the 'Exhibition of Works by Certain Modern Artists of Welsh Birth or Extraction' organised by the National Museum of Wales in 1913.

10 Given by Spaull, *Women Peace-Makers*, p. 91, but Winifred is clearly the direct source. Stanley's authoritative tone in this conversation was usual: 'It was Stanley, of course, who dominated the company always, for he was … "an authentic great man".' Undated newspaper obituary of Charles Coombe Tennant, written by the Vicar of Aberpergwm.

11 Quoted from the lost diary of Winifred Coombe Tennant in *Swan on a Black Sea. A Study in Automatic Writing. The Cummins-Willett Scripts, Transmitted by Geraldine Cummins*, ed. Signe Toksvig (London, 1965), p. 92, editor's note.

12 The National Portrait Gallery, London, exhibited her work in 1994 in 'Edwardian Women Photographers in the National Portrait Gallery: Eveleen Myers, Alice Hughes, Christina Bloom and Olive Edis'.

13 Winifred's relationship with both her sisters-in-law had soured by the second decade of the twentieth century, and remained difficult.

14 Quoted from the lost diary of Winifred Coombe Tennant, 1902, *Swan on a Black Sea*, p. 11, editor's note.

15 Lodge, *Christopher*, pp. 101-3. At the time of her visit the house was occupied by a

priest, M. L'Abbé, who became a friend and remained so for many years, visiting Winifred at Cadoxton.

16 Dafydd Nicolas, c.1705-74.

17 Winifred Coombe Tennant, 'The Story of Craig y Ddinas', 1953, NLW, BBC (Cymru/Wales) (2A), Welsh Region Scripts, box 38.

18 For the National Pageant of 1909, see Hywel Teifi Edwards, *Codi'r Hen Wlad Yn Ei Hôl* (Llandysul, 1989), pp. 239-83. The reactions to the pageant of the painter Christopher Williams reflect the atmosphere of the period for romantic nationalists, among whom Winifred may certainly be counted. Williams was particularly impressed with the evening performances: 'They seem to me more truly Celtic. You see a group of figures in a strong light, and beyond and around them is darkness – mystery. The evening performances impress me as being more in the minor key, and in this respect in harmony with our Welsh music and also with Welsh art generally, for was not the best work of our greatest artists, G.F. Watts and Burne Jones, also in the minor key?' Edwards, *Codi'r Hen Wlad Yn Ei Hôl*, p. 267.

19 Lodge, *Christopher*, p. 80.

20 Lodge, *Christopher*, p. 95.

21 Lodge, *Christopher*, p. 91.

22 Among Winifred's earliest commissions to artists and craftspeople were those related to the memorialisation of Daphne, in particular the carved tablet and the font cover, symbolising the New Jerusalem, in the Church of St. Thomas the Martyr, Neath.

23 Many years later, Gerald Balfour wrote a detailed account of Winifred's psychic experiences. Gerald William Earl of Balfour, 'A Study of the Psychological Aspects of Mrs. Willett's Mediumship, and of the Statements of the Communicators Concerning Process', *Proceedings of the Society for Psychical Research*, Part 140, Vol. XLIII (May, 1935).

24 Diary, 4 June 1911. Lady Betty Balfour was much involved with the suffrage issue. Again in the company of Betty Balfour, in

1912 Winifred had tea with Ethel Smyth, shortly after her release from Holloway Prison. 'Many tales of Mrs Pankhurst and other prisoners. Are these people drunk with the Holy Ghost?'. Diary, 14 April 1912.

25 The Society had been founded in 1897 and operated under the slogan 'Law Abiding. No Party'.

26 Robert Graves, in *Goodbye to All That* (London, 1929), revised edition 1957, pp. 191-2, remarks upon this sad aftermath of the Great War. Notwithstanding Winifred's revelation of her psychic experiences in *Christopher*, her identification as Mrs Willett remained generally unknown until after her death.

27 *Speeches and Addresses by the late Thomas E. Ellis*, ed. Annie J. Ellis (Wrexham, 1912), pp. 30-1, first published as 'Domestic and decorative arts in Wales', *Young Wales* (July 1899).

28 For a critique of the perception of Welsh visual inadequacy, see Peter Lord, *The Aesthetics of Relevance* (Llandysul, 1992).

29 Winifred Coombe Tennant, review of Arthur Clutton-Brock, *William Morris; His Work and Influence* (London, 1914), published in *The Welsh Outlook* (1914), 408. Although William Morris exerted a great influence on artists and intellectuals of the late nineteenth and early twentieth centuries, not all thinkers of his period in the Socialist tradition in Britain were opposed to industrial methods of production. Neither Kropotkin nor Marx saw machine production as necessarily antipathetic to art. The period in which the ideas of Winifred were forming was, in some ways, becalmed between the aesthetic storms generated by Morris and the later Marxist-Leninist thinkers. In these calm waters Roger Fry came to occupy the most influential position in aesthetics among English-language writers. The original version of Fry's famous essay, 'Vision and Design' (1924), was written in 1912. See D.D. Egbert, 'English Art Critics and Modern Social Radicalism', *Journal*

of Aesthetics and Art Criticism, XXVI/1 (1967-8), 29-46.

30 'How bitterly I regret ignorance of the Welsh language which has been a handicap to me for over 20 years.' Diary, 20 March 1923. Winifred could also have become aware of Matthews' work from his occasional forays in the English newspapers.

31 *Cymru*, ed. O.M. Edwards, 51(1916), 247.

32 'Mr Williams was not commissioned to do it. He merely took sketches for his own amusement, obtaining a special seat at the ceremony through the influence of the late Earl of Plymouth. King George was so impressed with the ceremony that he asked if an artist had been present. My husband was mentioned and commanded to paint two studies from which His Majesty could make his choice.' 'Memoirs of her husband by Mrs Christopher Williams', *Sunday Times*, 8 March 1936.

33 For the artists' colony at Betws-y-coed and the creation of the Royal Cambrian Academy see Peter Lord, *Clarence Whaite and the Welsh Art World: The Betws-y-coed Artists' Colony, 1844-1914* (Aberystwyth, 1998).

34 *Speeches and Addresses by the late Thomas E. Ellis*, pp. 33-4.

35 Most famously, David Cox had suggested the idea in 1848 in *The Welsh Funeral*, and had established it in the mind of the English as well as the Welsh public. The picture became celebrated as an engraving, which Winifred would surely have known.

36 O.M. Edwards, 'Y nodyn lleddf', 1905, in *Er Mwyn Cymru* (Wrecsam, 1922), p. 65.

37 Thomas Matthews, 'Celf yng Nghymru: Arddangosfa'r Amgueddfa Genedlaethol', *Cymru*, ed. O.M. Edwards, 46 (1914), 98, translated from the Welsh. Allusions made much later in Winifred's diary and correspondence suggest that she may have seen the work of John and Innes in London before the Great War.

38 For its possible impact on Christopher Williams, for instance, see Peter Lord, *The Visual Culture of Wales: Imaging the Nation* (Cardiff, 2000), pp. 370-1.

39 John Davies Williams, *Cambria Daily Leader*, 6 December 1911.
40 *The Glamorgan Gazette*, 9 August 1912.
41 NLW Uncatalogued Cymmrodorion material, letter to Sir Vincent Evans, 28 April 1911.
42 In the absence of its own building, both exhibitions were shown at the City Hall in Cardiff.
43 F.P., 'The Peasants of Flanders as painted by Eugène Laermans', *The Welsh Outlook* (1914), 477-8. For Belgian artists in Wales, see Moira Vincentelli, 'The Davies Family and Belgian Refugee Artists and Musicians in Wales', *National Library of Wales Journal*, XXII (1981), pp. 226-33. For Thomas Jones see E.L. Ellis, *T.J.: A Life of Dr Thomas Jones, CH* (Cardiff, 1992).
44 Gwyn Jenkins, 'The Welsh Outlook, 1914-33', *National Library of Wales Journal*, XXIV (1986), p. 465.
45 *Brangwyn in his Studio. The Diary of his Assistant Frank Alford*, eds. Roger Alford and Libby Horner (2004), p. 128.
46 Diary, 26 October 1915. Winifred sat between 11 August and 5 September 1915. Subsequently she met Alford in London and they together chose a frame.

Chapter Two

1 *South Wales Daily News*, 2 August 1918.
2 *Cambria Daily Leader*, 2 August 1918. The closeness of Winifred's remarks to those of Herkomer suggests that she was well aware of his celebrated intervention in Welsh art affairs. Subsequently, Herkomer became much involved with improving the robes and regalia of the Gorsedd, work that Winifred herself would continue after the Great War. For Herkomer and the Eisteddfod see Peter Lord, *Y Chwaer-Dduwies – Celf, Crefft a'r Eisteddfod* (Llandysul, 1992), pp. 60-5. Winifred's most likely source of information about Herkomer would have been Charles Mansel Lewis of Stradey Castle, Llanelli,

a close friend of the painter. However, although Winifred knew many people who moved in the same circles as Mansel Lewis, she does not report that she herself met him. This is surprising, both because of the nature of the social world in which she moved, and the fact that Lewis was a painter of considerable ability. For Mansel Lewis see Stephanie Jones, *Charles William Mansel Lewis: Painter, Patron and Promoter of Art in Wales* (Aberystwyth, 1998).
3 *Cambria Daily Leader*, 1 August 1918.
4 Williams was not an official war artist. See Peter Lord, *The Visual Culture of Wales: Imaging the Nation* (Cardiff, 2000), pp. 354-8.
5 This perception was about to change. Writing in *The Welsh Outlook* in 1918, Isaac Williams, Curator of Art at the National Museum, lent his weight to the process, begun by Thomas Matthews, by which John would become acknowledged in his own country. Williams opened his essay with the observation that 'It is an extraordinary and inexplicable fact that the work of Mr Augustus John is practically unknown in Wales, the land of his birth, from which he has derived so much inspiration'. Isaac Williams, 'Augustus John and his work', *The Welsh Outlook*, V (1918), 201-2.
6 Percy Gleaves to Winifred Coombe Tennant, 2 September 1918, NLW Mam o Nedd Material, 3010. Gleaves also worked on an engraving of the picture, Percy Gleaves to Winifred Coombe Tennant, 6 August 1918, NLW Mam o Nedd Material, 3009.
7 Diary, 24 December 1920. 'CCT' was Winifred's usual diary abbreviation for her husband, Charles Coombe Tennant. Paintings of industrial subjects by Percy Gleaves, exhibited at the Swansea Art Society in 1911, had been noticed favourably by John Davies Williams in the review in which he also first drew public attention to Evan Walters, who was one of his students. Gleaves himself wrote about art and craft in *Wales* in 1913, for the context of which see Lord,

Y Chwaer-Dduwies, p. 68.
8 By way of introduction, Winifred made reference to the new public buildings in Cardiff, which she felt able to describe as 'among the finest in Europe'. *South Wales Daily News*, 2 August 1918.
9 In several references to Alfred Mond in her diary, Winifred gives no indication of having been aware of the remarkable art collection made by his father, the industrial chemist, Ludwig Mond. The collection, mainly of Italian old master paintings, was bequeathed to the National Gallery in London. Alfred Mond generated mixed feelings in Winifred: 'Breakfast. L.G. full of good talk. At 9.30 we all motored off to Llanelly. I picked up Sir Alfred Mond at Morriston – a coarse framed sort of a man but with good brains.' Diary, 10 September 1923. Although straightforward politics partly accounted for Winifred's interest in Mond, certainly the fact that he was a Jew also had a bearing on her conflicting feelings about him: 'Reading Mond's life – passionately interesting his return to the Jew through the Holy Land – the most deeply spiritual experience of his life. I have always loved the Jews and agonized over their martyrdom at the hands of Christians! Lord God of Hosts!' Diary, 8 May 1933. 'Comforted by reading of Alfred Mond's son having yesterday returned to the faith of his fathers, received into Jewry at a Synagogue – Father to son – son to Father – "Spread the Canopy of Thy Peace above us", the Kaddish.' Diary, 16 July 1933. Winifred was fascinated by Jewish people both as a Christian and in the context of the politics of the time. The status of Palestine and the creation of a Jewish state were important issues in the period of her own direct involvement in politics. In the 1930s, Winifred was quick to express distaste for Hitler and to realise the implications of his views for Jewish people. That said, her comments about the many Jewish people whom she observed, whether anonymous individuals or distinguished figures such as Mond and,

later, William Rothenstein, are characterised by the blunt expression of polarities of enthusiasm and of distaste, with specific reference to their Jewishness.

10 Rhiwbina, home to a remarkable group of Welsh intellectuals in the period, undoubtedly inspired Winifred's concept, but at a deeper level it was rooted in her sympathy with the ideas of William Morris. In her review of Arthur Clutton-Brock's book on Morris, Winifred quoted a letter written by him in 1874: '"Suppose people lived in little communities among gardens and green fields, so that they could be in the country in five minutes walk, and had few wants, almost no furniture, for instance, and no servants, and studied the (difficult) art of enjoying life, and finding out what they really wanted; then, I think we might hope civilisation had really begun." Is not this the very inspiration underlying the Garden City movement? And what a different picture it evokes for those who see the Welsh housewife tied like a slave to her cumbrous and ugly furniture and "ornaments," submerged beneath her piles of dust-harbouring labour-consuming household gods!' *The Welsh Outlook* (1914), 408.

11 Welsh Housing and Development Association, *Plans of cottages and living-in quarters for agricultural labourers in Wales* ... (Cardiff, 1918).

12 Diary, 16 November 1918. Daniel Lleufer Thomas (1863-1940) was an original member of the Dafydd ap Gwilym Society (alongside Tom Ellis and O.M. Edwards) at Oxford. He became a barrister and a judge, and distinguished himself by what many people regarded as his sensitive handling of cases which came before him as a result of the Tonypandy disturbances.

13 Abercrombie was of Scottish descent; he had been born near Manchester and at various times lived on the Wirral and at Hafod Wen, Cilcain. Eventually he owned a summer house in Anglesey. His affection for Wales extended to a willingness to involve himself directly in planning issues and in questions of conservation.

Abercrombie's lecture 'The Preservation of Rural England' had led to the creation of the Council for the Preservation of Rural England. Subsequently, with Clough Williams Ellis, he himself founded the Council for the Preservation of Rural Wales. Abercrombie is buried at Rhoscolyn on Anglesey. The National Eisteddfod would continue to provide a public platform for the Welsh Housing and Development Association. In 1923, at Mold, Abercrombie was again a central figure, alongside D. Lleufer Thomas, at a seminar organised by the Cymmrodorion Society. See Lord, *Y Chwaer-Dduwies*, pp. 80-1.

14 Published in *Transactions of the Honourable Society of Cymmrodorion* (1918), pp. 239-43.

15 Winifred noted the parliamentary vote on the issue of women M.P.s in her diary for 24 October 1918: 'The Division in the House last night surprised even me. In favour of women M.P.s 274 – against 25. The power of the vote begins to tell. "I must reign until I have put all things under me". It is a great victory, and I did not expect to see it in my lifetime – but oh! At what cost it has been bought!! Europe bathed in blood!' Winifred was identified as a potential parliamentary candidate by the National Union of Women's Suffrage Societies in November and was invited to stand. She declined on the grounds that she had no chance of being elected if she stood under the banner of the NUWSS. Tokenism was of no interest to her. She believed that the only way to get women elected was 'by getting women adopted by the Political Parties as official candidates'. Diary, 1 November 1918.

16 Williams description of Watts is given in Jeremiah Williams (ed.), *Christopher Williams R.B.A. An Account of his Life and Appreciations of his Work* (Caernarfon, n.d.), p. 46. For Williams in the context of Welsh national art in the period, see Lord, *Imaging the Nation*, pp. 330-6 and 356-8. Watts was the most important of

those English painters who were co-opted for Wales by the intellectuals of the national revival. His is the biggest entry in Mardy Rees, *Welsh Painters, Engravers and Sculptors*, exceeding that of Burne-Jones. Typical of Winifred's diary reflections on her frequent visits to Compton, often in the company of Gerald Balfour (who had been painted by Watts in 1899), was that of 20 March 1912: 'Spent the morning at Compton. Increasing feeling of the greatness of Watts – the greatness of his soul! Saw the beautiful Endymion, and the Slumber of the Ages.'

17 Gwilym Davies later became heavily involved with the international peace movement and achieved distinction by writing the initial document on which the constitution of UNESCO was based. See Ieuan Gwynedd Jones (ed.), *Gwilym Davies, 1879-1955* (Llandysul, 1972). Winifred wrote an account of the 1921 meeting of the Welsh School of Social service at Llandrindod: Gwytherin, 'The Welsh School of Social Service, 1921', *The Welsh Outlook*, IX (1922), 9-11.

18 A Spaniard, 'A Diary of the Eisteddfod', *The Welsh Outlook*, V (1918), 301.

19 NLW Mam o Nedd Material, 3728. The essay was translated into Welsh by John Eilian and published in *Corn Gwlad* in 1949.

20 The other women involved were Lady Penrhyn, Lady Mostyn, Lady Howard and Miss Stepney-Gulston. For the contentious question of the robes and a thorough description of Winifred's long relationship with the Gorsedd, see Emyr Wyn Jones, 'Winifred Coombe Tennant: "Mam o Nedd" mawr ei nodded', *Y Traethodydd* CLI (1996), no. 636, 40-53; no. 637, 85-103; and 'Ychwanegiad', *Y Traethodydd* CLII (1997), no. 639, 48-52. See also Emyr Wyn Jones, 'Winifred Coombe Tennant a'r Eisteddfod', *Y Traethodydd* CLIII (1998), 216-45. Emyr Wyn Jones wrote without the advantage of reading Winifred's diary.

21 He was rejected for active service and employed as a camouflage painter. Nevertheless, he duly received his service

medal, an event noted by Winifred in her diary, 18 July 1920.

22 Diary, 6 May 1920. On his death in 1951 Winifred noted in her diary that she had first seen him when he was under twenty, that is before the Great War.

23 Diary, 10 May 1920. Given Winifred's status and her long established habit of frequenting the Glynn Vivian Art Gallery, it is surprising that this appears to have been the first occasion on which she met William Grant Murray.

24 Clive Bell, *Art* (London, 1914). Bell's relationship with Vanessa Stephen, who he married in 1907, brought him into the Bloomsbury Group. He was an associate of Roger Fry, whose enthusiasm for modern French art he shared and helped to spread among the intellectual community. His elitism in matters of art reached its peak with his volume *Civilization* (London, 1928), which argued that the survival of civilized society depended on the existence within it of a leisured class. For Bell's 'Metaphysical Hypothesis' see especially *Art*, pp. 68-70. Winifred's copy (a 1920 edition) is inscribed 'A Merry Xmas and a Happy New Year. Evan J. Walters', the Christmas in question being, apparently, 1925. Winifred notes her reading of the book in her diary the following year. For Bell in a broader social context of relevance to the views of Winifred, see D.D. Egbert, 'English Art Critics and Modern Social Radicalism', *Journal of Aesthetics and Art Crticism*, XXXVI/1 (1967-8), 29-46.

25 Winifred pasted to the back of the frames what appears to be her own record or recollection of Walters' interpretation of his drawings. The texts are given in full in the Catalogue Raisonné

26 *Cambria Daily Leader*, 25 November 1927.

27 After the conference Winifred noted in particular the 'excellent speech from a Labour woman, Councillor Rose Davies of Aberdare'. Diary, 8 May 1920. Subsequently Winifred worked with Davies in committees of the Welsh School of Social Service.

28 Diary, 16 July 1920. The poet 'AE'

was George William Russell, 1867-1935, whose first volume, the writing of which was encouraged by Yeats, was *Homeward. Mystical Verse* (1894). The poem remembered by Winifred was 'The Vesture of the Soul', for which see A.E., *Collected Poems* (London, 1926), p. 89. Winifred's fondness for Russell is of interest beyond her taste for the poetry. Russell was a notable Irish Nationalist, who published extensively on the arts in Ireland and on public affairs.

29 Winifred's judgement of Williams is less clear. To meet Matthew Arnold's condition for the living of a 'mature life' the editor of the *Cambria Daily Leader* would have required to manifest both the Jew and the Greek in the quality of his journalism. Matthew Arnold, *Culture and Anarchy* (1869). The antimony of Hebraism and Hellenism is elaborated in Chapter IV.

30 For the Eisteddfod exhibitions and reactions to them see Lord, *Y Chwaer-Dduwies*, pp. 76-8.

31 As a strong advocate of Home Rule for Wales, Winifred volubly supported William Llewelyn Williams in the debate on the subject within the Party. She regarded him as 'a great and an honest man', Diary, 9 August 1920. Williams had opposed compulsory military service and supported conscientious objectors during the Great War. His views ultimately led him to break with Lloyd George and in 1921 he fought the Cardiganshire seat against an official Liberal candidate, an election campaign in which Winifred played an active part, though on the side of the official candidate.

32 Diary, 5 August 1920. Winifred's relationship with Charles was sometimes difficult in this period. Matters were exacerbated by the difference of twenty-two years in age between them. Charles suffered increasingly from deafness and Winifred was not always the most tolerant of partners under these circumstances.

33 'I am translating Cezanne's life to Evan Walters in the evening. Cezanne – so

much of a boor seen from outside, so much of a King seen from within!' Diary, 6 August 1920.

34 Diary, 13 August 1920. In an undated letter Peter Keenan informed Winifred that he had been working recently both in Wales and in Ireland.

35 Diary, 25 October 1920. Winifred was depressed by the visit: 'What a prison those country houses in lonely situations have been for generations of women!' Algernon Walker-Heneage was the nephew of the industrialist Graham Vivian. Shortly after the painting of the picture he took over the family house of Clyne Castle, on the death of Dulcie, sister of Graham Vivian, and added the Vivian surname to his own. Walker-Heneage-Vivian was subsequently painted by Margaret Lindsay Williams.

36 Presumably Lodge had brought with him what Winifred described as Eddington's 'address' on the subject of the structure of stars from Cambridge. The material was published in 1926 as *The Internal Constitution of Stars*.

37 For George Maitland Lloyd Davies (1880-1949), see E.H. Griffiths, *Heddychwr Mawr Cymru, George M.Ll. Davies* (2 vols., Caernarfon, 1968).

38 Diary, 26 November 1920. Notwithstanding the doubts that Winifred had expressed so recently about Lloyd George, arising from government policy in Ireland, it was on this visit to London that she became a regular visitor to Downing Street and a confidant of the Prime Minister.

39 Edgar Jones, 'A Welsh Artist. The Work of Mr. Fred Richards, A.R.E.', *The Welsh Outlook*, IV (1917), 310-13.

40 Fred Richards, *Report on the Teaching of Art in Welsh Intermediate Schools* (London, 1918), pp. 6-7.

41 Richards, *Report*, p. 8.

42 Richards, *Report*, p. 24. The influence of Ruskin and the Arts and Crafts movement was as strongly manifested in Richards' practical work as in his ideas, especially in his book design and illustration. For a

summary of Richards' career, see Seiriol Davies, 'Fred Richards: Arlunydd ar Wasgar', *Catalog Celf a Chrefft, Eisteddfod Genedlaethol Casnewydd, 1988*, pp. 43-4.

43 Gwytherin, 'Cardiganshire, February, 1921', *The Welsh Outlook*, VIII (1921), 107-9. The village identified by Winifred as 'Llanfair' was, perhaps, Llanfair Clydogau.

44 Irene White, *The Ladies of Gregynog* (Cardiff, 1985), p. 19.

45 Moira Vincentelli, 'The Davies Family and Belgian Refugee Artists and Musicians in Wales', *National Library of Wales Journal*, XXII (1981), 231

46 George M.Ll. Davies lived in a cottage at Tregynon, on the Gregynog estate, between late 1920 and spring 1922. His impressions of developments there are of interest, given the received wisdom about the virtues of the Davies sisters, their charitable works, and their art collecting: 'The nicest thing that I remember of Gregynog was not its riches but that Gwen got up to have breakfast with me at 7a.m. once. Something in us craves to be "personal to someone". Think of the horrors of Gregynog, the toadying, the coldness, the insincerity, the tyranny of little agents and secretaries, the family feuds, the harm done to Colleges and Chapels by their benefactors.' Given in Griffiths, *Heddychwr Mawr Cymru, George M.Ll. Davies*, p. 142.

47 Gwendoline Davies was a musician, and music provided a further point of contact between her and Winifred. For instance, on 20 March 1921 they lunched in London, before going together to the Temple to hear the Bach *St. Matthew Passion*. Three years later they both attended the Harlech Festival, organised by Walford Davies: 'At Harlech vast crowds – got our seats with difficulty in the castle under a great awning of green and white striped canvas. The whole place packed – grand Hymn singing, Welsh folk songs and then orchestral music. Overture of the Magic Flute and some of Beethoven Symphony 8. Tea with Miss Davies of Llandinam at the Castle Hotel.' Diary, 26 June 1924.

48 Diary, 14 August 1922. Winifred arrived in Geneva on 3 September and attended the Assembly until 29 September. She then travelled in Switzerland before going to London on 22 October, breakfasting with Lloyd George alone in the Cabinet Room the next day. Subsequently Winifred addressed many meetings on the subject of the League of Nations and the peace movement, and also published on the subject. See, for instance, Mrs Coombe Tennant J.P, 'The Future of the League of Nations', *The Welsh Outlook* XI (1924), 178-80, part of an address delivered at Llandrindod in April, 1924.

49 Diary, 23 August 1922. The reference to Llandudno is to the conference of the Welsh National Liberal Council, where Winifred had spoken at length to George M.Ll. Davies, no doubt mainly on the subject of Ireland, with which he was deeply involved. At the Liberal Party conference in London on 21 January 1922, Winifred moved the Irish resolution.

50 Diary, 24 October 1921: 'Delegates had just arrived for the fateful Conference which decides tonight whether the Conference will go on the basis of fealty to the King or whether it will break up on the demand for a Republic. We walked past the doors leading to the Cabinet Room, detectives everywhere, and rows of hats and coats.'

51 'Received from Sir Alfred Cope a precious picture of my beloved Mick, Michael Collins, as he lay in death, a colour print from Lavery's painting – God bless him – "Love of Ireland". He deeply affected the course of my life. It is good to have this from his friend Alfred Cope.' Diary, 12 July 1923. Sir Alfred Cope (1877-1954) was a civil servant, appointed by Lloyd George, who became an under-secretary at Dublin Castle. He won the confidence of the Irish side and played a central role in the 1921 negotiations.

52 Diary, 16 November 1922. Winifred came bottom of the poll. The Labour candidate, James Wignall, formerly of Swansea, took the seat.

53 Gwytherin, 'The Welsh School of Social Service, 1921. An Impression', *The Welsh Outlook*, IX (1922), 10.

54 Diary, 10 August 1922. The chaired bard was John Lloyd-Jones (1885-1956), originally from Dolwyddelan and formerly a student of John Morris-Jones at Bangor. By 1922 he was Professor of Welsh and Celtic at University College Dublin, where he spent his entire career.

55 Diary, 11 August 1922. Sir Henry Wilson was shot in London by two members of the Irish Republican Army on 22 June 1922. Reginald Dunne and Joseph O'Sullivan were hanged for the shooting on 10 August 1922.

56 Diary, 17 November 1923. Nevertheless, she took an active part in the campaign, speaking on behalf of many candidates, including Winston Churchill at Leicester. Only eight women were elected. At the end of the year Winifred 'Wept bitter tears at the powerlessness of Women to mould this cruel heathen-minded civilization – so called – of Europe'. Diary, 25 December 1923.

57 For a detailed account of the exhibitions in the decade 1920-30 see Lord, *Y Chwaer-Dduwies*, pp. 73-96.

58 Alan Llwyd, *Gwae fi fy myw: Cofiant Hedd Wynn* (Barddas, 1991), p. 290.

59 W.H. Jones to Winifred Coombe Tennant, 14 August 1924, Swansea Museum, box 200, item 17.

60 Swansea Museum, box 201, item 19. Among the pieces Winifred sent to be copied was a piece of an old bedgown handed down in her mother's family. Pryce Jones were able to get the pattern copied by an unidentified manufacturer.

61 Caroline A.J. Skeel, 'The Welsh Woollen Industry in the Eighteenth and Nineteenth Centuries', *Arch. Camb.* LXXIX, 7th series, vol. IV (1924) 1-38, with comment by A.H. Dodd and a response from Skeel, 391-5.

62 David Reynold, the Rural Industries Board, to Winifred Coombe Tennant, 26 October 1928, NLW Mam o Nedd Material, 3133.

63 'Speaking in May last at the Rotary Club, Cardiff, Mr Waterhouse [Mr T. Waterhouse, President of the Welsh Textile Manufacturers Association] said that in his opinion the time had come for an effort to produce Real Welsh tweeds from the best wool grown in Wales, standardized in quality and protected like the Scotch tweeds by a National Trade Mark.' Skeel, 'The Welsh Woollen Industry in the Eighteenth and Nineteenth Centuries', 38.

64 The weaver was Thomas James, Lerry Mills, Talybont. Winifred Coombe Tennant to K.L. Kendrick, NLW Mam o Nedd Material, 3558. No contemporary record survives of Winifred meeting Lewis Jones of Lampeter c.1918.

65 'Motored with Gaggi and Zanga and CCT to Ewenny and bought delicious Pottery at the little local Pottery, gay in colour and good in shape. On to the Priory, a noble Norman church full of beauty and interest.' Diary, Thursday 26 April 1923. Winifred visited the pottery twice in 1925 and again in 1927. For the history of the pottery, see J.M. Lewis, *The Ewenny Potteries* (Cardiff, 1982).

66 Winifred Coombe Tennant, 'Beautiful Things Made in Wales', *Cambria Daily Leader*, 18 October 1928. As an example of the economic potential of craft industries, Winifred drew attention to the fact that the 'quilted bed-covers made by the Rhondda women have been an instant success when first shown in London last week, and orders are coming in rapidly'. Among other responses to Winifred's article was one from K.L. Kendrick of Birmingham, representing the Distributionist League. The League was in the process of compiling a 'directory of small craftsmen' and Kendrick sought the addresses of the craftspeople mentioned by Winifred in her article. Winifred Coombe Tennant to K.L. Kendrick, NLW Mam o Nedd Material, 3558.

67 Winifred's surviving correspondence with Peate does not commence until 1947. On 28 July 1947 Peate wrote to Winifred to say that he had no example

of the work of John Davies (presumably a slip for Owen Davies) and in particular the white wool rugs, a specimen of which 'I should dearly love to have'.

68 For the renewal of tradition at St David's in Winifred's period see Peter Lord, *The Visual Culture of Wales: Medieval Vision* CDROM (Cardiff, 2003), 'Time Galleries: The Church and Modern Welsh Identity: St David'. After visiting the Cathedral on 22 June 1929 Winifred wrote: 'I would see Rome in possession of all this again and all these angular Puritans all Catholic, but time never flows backwards'. I am grateful to Dr John Morgan-Guy for drawing my attention to the work of Anson, and for his thoughts on the wider context of Winifred's 'Catholic nostalgia', as he describes it. Dr Morgan-Guy points out that similar revivalist tendencies were manifested in England. For instance, in the same period the re-creation of the shrine of Our Lady of Walsingham was underway.

69 Ifan Kyrle Fletcher to Winifred Coombe Tennant, 16 November 1927. Winifred was in touch with Fletcher from at least as early as February 1927. Kyrle Fletcher was the son of the art dealer and antiquarian John Kyrle Fletcher, who had published on several aspects of Welsh culture, including Pontypool Japan ware, in which he also dealt. His son specialised in selling antiquarian books and had a business address (under his father's name) in Cardiff, as well as in Newport. Ivan Kyrle Fletcher had wide and cosmopolitan connections. He commissioned a coloured bookplate from Edward McKnight Kauffer, an American-born designer, who made a successful career in London after the Great War. He was the main poster designer for London Underground in the 1920s and 30s. Winifred kept a copy of his Ivan Kyrle Fletcher bookplate.

70 Eric Gill, *Christianity and Art* (Capel-y-ffin, 1927), p. 8.

71 Gwytherin, review of *The Necessity of Art* by Clutton Brock, Percy Dearmer, *et al.* (Student Christian Movement, 1924), *The Welsh Outlook*, XI (1924), 168.

72 Diary, 8 October 1924. The Cathedral was badly damaged during the Second World War and the relief burned.

73 Diary, 19 and 20 November 1924. In 1925 Williams borrowed the picture to include in the loan collection which he organised for display at the Pwllheli National Eisteddfod.

74 Diary, 25 and 26 November 1924. Gaggi was Winifred's mother, Mary Richardson. Percy Moon Turner was associated with the Independent Gallery.

75 Diary, 9 December 1924. On 20 March 1923 Isaac Williams wrote in pursuance of an offer made by Winifred to fund the purchase of Walters' 'portrait of the blind man'. Presumably the date on the letter is a mistake for 1925, though it may possibly relate to an earlier painting. NLW Mam o Nedd Material, 3149. *The Blind Pianist* was not bought by the National Museum. It remained in Walters' studio until his death, following which it was given to the Glynn Vivian Art Gallery.

76 Isaac Williams to Winifred Coombe Tennant, 12 October 1925. Winifred would maintain her interest in Gregynog. She spent several days there in the company of the Davies sisters in March 1926, for instance. She took the opportunity to inspect the work of the press, 'type cast, sheets printed, cut, sewn, bound and every process hand done by expert craftsmen. The joy of work, as Ruskin saw it – I had it there before my eyes. Maynard the Master Printer, a young man, originally a painter, does some of the wood cuts. Everything interested and delighted me!' Diary, 19 March 1926.

77 Diary, 20 October 1925. Winifred was in the habit of describing any modernist pictures which she did not like as 'Cubist'.

78 'In the morning the cases containing the pictures I bought in Paris and the easel arrived. Phillip and Hubert unpacked them under my eye, set up the easel in the drawing room and by lunch time 'L'Enfant aux Canards' was gloriously rejoicing my soul, the sunlight filtering

through the fig leaves on to the ducks, the boy, the flower pots – such indescribable joy.' Diary, 21 November 1925.

79 Isaac Williams to Winifred Coombe Tennant, 28 September 1925: 'Of late, I have felt, and felt most strongly, that what we need in Wales is a real live Art Circle, embracing the work and principles of the National Art Collections' fund and the Walpole Society – with a central committee and branches in every county of Wales. As soon as I have thoroughly thought out such a scheme, I should like to talk it over with you and one or two other Welsh Art Enthusiasts and take steps to put it into operation … We *must* have a representative body of strong standing, if necessary, to *force* the claims of Art in Wales. Don't you think so?' Nothing seems to have come of Williams' proposal.

80 *South Wales News*, 4 March 1926.

81 *Cambria Daily Leader*, 10 February 1926.

82 Ifan Kyrle Fletcher, 'The Appreciation of Art in Wales', *The Welsh Outlook*, XIV (1927), 264.

83 Ifan Kyrle Fletcher to Winifred Coombe Tennant, 14 November 1927.

84 The initial English exhibition of the pictures was at Stockport in 1927. Winifred's aspiration to donate the collection to the National Museum was not fulfilled. The only donations of French works that she made were of two bronze plaques, which she bought on a visit to the Paris mint in 1927: '… saw the most magnificent series of medals, plaquettes etc., both historical and modern. Bought 8 of the modern ones, two I intend to give to the National Museum at Cardiff. We have nothing to touch the work of these modern French sculptors and gravers'. Diary, 2 June 1927. Given the widespread recognition afforded William Goscombe John as a medallist, Winifred's opinion of the relative quality of French and British medallists is surprising. She may have been unaware of his work in the field or simply have dissented from the conventional high estimation in which

his work was held. She had admired his equestrian statue of Viscount Tredegar in Cardiff. However, in 1924 she saw for the first time John's statue of Tom Ellis, whom she revered: 'After lunch motored to Bala – very lovely at its lake. We walked about the little town and I gazed in reverence at the rather ugly statue of Tom Ellis'. Diary, 27 June 1924.

85 In the early 1870s the coalfield was disrupted by two serious disputes in three years, but these were followed by the heroic rescue of fourteen entombed miners at the Tynewydd pit, near Porth in the Rhondda. The situation at Tynewydd, which took ten days to resolve, was the subject of detailed and extensive press scrutiny, with both *The Graphic* and *The Illustrated London News* sending their own artists to provide a visual record of the events. Public interest was made more intense by the fact that the same colliery community had suffered 114 deaths a decade earlier. For the evolution of the visual imaging of the miner, see Peter Lord, *The Visual Culture of Wales: Industrial Society* (Cardiff, 1998), chapter 3, 'The Imaging of Social Trauma'.

86 Michael Holroyd, *Augustus John: The New Biography* (London, 1996), p. 441.

87 For the film, see *David Lloyd George. The Movie Mystery*, eds. David Berry and Simon Horrocks (Cardiff, 1998).

88 *Western Mail*, 29 August 1925, p. 6.

89 Diary, 8 July 1925. A brief obituary of Martin was published in the *South Wales Evening Post*, 18 December 1943. It gave his age as 'about 64', and noted that 'His subjects and media were rather grim, and one of his best-remembered pictures was a very striking one of Canaan, Foxhole, which was purchased by Mrs. Coombe-Tennant'. The picture is no longer in the Coombe Tennant collection.

90 *South Wales Evening Post*, 18 December 1943. Martin's picture was 'a little shot at Relativity in paint, the car stationary, and the scenery shooting past; the foreground, naturally, is something of a blur'. George Martin to Winifred Coombe Tennant, 9

January 1926. Martin sold the picture to Winifred for £3, hoping that was not too much to ask.

91 Evan Walters painted an oil sketch of a Gorsedd procession, which is almost certainly the 1925 Proclamation Ceremony. Crawshay is clearly identifiable in the picture.

92 For the Swansea and Cardiff stations see John Davies, *Broadcasting and the BBC in Wales* (Cardiff, 1994), pp. 1-38.

93 In a letter to Winifred, written 19 December 1949, Grant Murray recalled the incident in a slightly different way, having apparently forgotten her close involvement at the time: 'A day for judging was fixed, and Clausen arrived and settled all the awards – John arrived the following day and reversed all Clausen's decisions with the result that all the prizes were divided'.

94 Unidentified newspaper, 1926. The writer's observation that Richard Wilson represented a radical tradition reflected Ruskin's construction of the painter as the founder of English landscape painting and a pioneer in the direct observation of nature. Ruskin's view of Wilson was unchallenged at the time and, since it affirmed the Welsh painter's status in English art, was particularly popular amongst Welsh intellectuals. In a letter of thanks to Winifred, Clausen made oblique reference to the difficulties he had encountered at Swansea. He thanked her for her 'kind hospitality which made my stay a very pleasant one, and a compensation for the very tiresome business of trying to make just awards'. George Clausen to Winifred Coombe Tennant, 23 July 1926, NLW Mam o Nedd Material, 2977.

95 Unidentified newspaper, 7 August 1926.

96 Unidentified newspaper, 26 July 1926.

97 *Cambria Daily Leader*, 29 June 1926, and an unidentified newspaper of 2 July 1926. The art critic of *The Observer*, P.G. Konody, was unusual in expressing enthusiasm for the picture.

98 Evan Walters to Winifred Coombe

Tennant, undated. A part of this statement was published in the *South Wales News*, 16 November 1927.

99 Gwenallt, from *Credaf* (1943), translated as 'What I Believe', *Planet* 32 (1976), 1-10.

100 Winifred Coombe Tennant to John Davies Williams, 30 April 1928.

101 Winifred Coombe Tennant to John Davies Williams, 30 April 1928.

102 Cedric Morris to Winifred Coombe Tennant, undated c. October 1928.

103 William Grant Murray to Winifred Coombe Tennant, 19 May 1931.

104 Evan Walters to Winifred Coombe Tennant, undated but late October or early November 1927.

105 Diary, 9 November 1927. Following this meeting Winifred wrote an article about Walters for the *Cambria Daily Leader*, describing their relationship. *Cambria Daily Leader*, 25 November 1927.

106 Diary, 2 December 1927. For the ancestors of Cedric Morris in the context of visual culture see Lord, *The Visual Culture of Wales: Industrial Society*, pp. 54-5 and 70-1.

107 Cedric Morris to Winifred Coombe Tennant, 5 December 1927.

108 Cedric Morris to Winifred Coombe Tennant, 12 December 1927.

109 Diary, 2 September 1928. No meeting with Morris in May was noted by Winifred in her diary. She spent only 3 May in London, *en route* for the Continent. She did not return until June.

110 Tate Gallery, Cedric Morris Papers, Morris to Lett Haines, 27 July 1928.

111 Location unknown.

112 William Grant Murray to Winifred Coombe Tennant, 17 November 1927.

113 Archie Griffiths to Winifred Coombe Tennant, 11 March 1928. Griffiths' reference to being at Cadoxton Lodge 'again' appears to be a slip. He had not visited Cadoxton Lodge at this date.

114 William Rothenstein, Foreword to *Catalogue of Paintings, Drawings and Etchings by Archie Griffiths, A.R.C.A.* (Swansea, 1928).

115 Archie Griffiths to Winifred Coombe

Tennant, 8 December 1928.

116 The oil painting was shown at the Glynn Vivian exhibition and at Griffiths' subsequent exhibition in London in 1932, but is presently untraced. Winifred regarded the drawing as 'a lovely thing, which I rejoice to have', Diary, 10 December 1928. However, Isaac Williams of the National Museum, who had been contacted by both Winifred and Grant Murray, was unenthusiastic about Griffiths. Although he saw the 1928 exhibition of Griffiths' work at the Glynn Vivian Art Gallery, he confused the painter with Vincent Evans, reporting to Winifred that he had 'bought one of Mr Griffiths' etchings shortly after he went to New Zealand'. Isaac Williams to Winifred Coombe Tennant, 1 December 1928.

117 George M.Ll. Davies to Winifred Coombe Tennant, 31 December 1929.

118 George M.Ll. Davies to Winifred Coombe Tennant, 31 December 1929. Davies' perception of the work of the Quakers and other groups was not shared by all. For Bryn-mawr and the controversy surrounding such charitable interventions, see Lord, *The Visual Culture of Wales: Industrial Society*, pp. 200-203, and Peter Lord, *The Visual Culture of Wales: Industrial Society* CDROM (Cardiff, 2000), 'Visual Journeys: Art for the People: The Settlement Movement'.

119 *Cambria Daily Leader*, 6 June 1929. The review was printed under the headline 'Buy a picture a year!' and attributed to 'An occasional contributor'. Winifred could not refrain from remarking that *Swansea from Richmond Road*, 'full of delicate mother-of-pearl tints, has just been bought for a well-known collection'. The acquisition of Grant Murray's Gorsedd pictures for Swansea proved contentious, because of the price asked by the painter, but the pictures were eventually purchased.

120 Diary, 3 August 1929. Walters had recently completed a portrait of Macdonald, immediately prior to his election victory and the installation of the Labour government.

121 Winifred Coombe Tennant, 'A Boy as Future Citizen', in Mrs A. Hutton Radice, *Home and School* (London, 1926).

122 Diary, 29 September 1930. Indicative of Winifred's longing for France in 1930 is a note to herself written in French on an invitation from the Swansea Art Society to open their annual exhibition. Winifred declined the invitation because the opening was to take place on the day she planned to leave for Paris.

123 Diary, 29 May 1930. The reason for the visit was to leave a picture at the National Museum for cleaning. Winifred had bought the picture, which she had hoped was a Richard Wilson, at a 'tumble down shop' in Eton for £8.

124 William Grant Murray to Winifred Coombe Tennant, 27 July 1930. However, there is no record of the Glynn Vivian Gallery acquiring the picture, or any other by Martin.

125 K.W. Hancock to Winifred Coombe Tennant, 31 May 1930: '… when a painting is sold to the only patron of the Fine Arts of Wales, whose activities in such matters are spoken of wherever I have been, then the pleasure of the sale becomes an honour and a privilege'.

126 Diary, 2 July 1930. Harry Hall taught jewellery and sculpture at the School of Art. In the catalogue to the 1930 exhibition of the Swansea Art Society, from which Winifred bought Hancock's *Still Life*, she marked two works by Janes as 'bad'. George Davies was George M.Ll. Davies.

127 William Grant Murray to Winifred Coombe Tennant, 19 May 1931. Grant Murray was undecided on the question of whether the Slade or the Royal Academy would suit Janes best, and he intended Hancock (whom he thought the more promising) for the Royal College, along with Thomas. J.H. Govier was a newer student, very promising but something of a puzzle to his teacher: 'His work is not the least bit like himself – nothing to say and yet his work is so assertive and fearless'. In addition to

supporting the students at the School of Art Grant Murray and Winifred endeavoured to engage the University College more heavily in art in the town. In February 1930 Grant Murray wrote to Winifred about a reception he had hosted at his house for interested professors, among whom was Saunders Lewis. Grant Murray reported that 'he looks a poet, dreamer and artist – he knew everything in the Gallery – had seen every special exhibition since he came 5 years ago. He was quite enthusiastic on Art matters'. William Grant Murray to Winifred Coombe Tennant, 27 February 1930.

Chapter Three

1 William Grant Murray to Winifred Coombe Tennant, 1 October 1931.
2 William Grant Murray to Winifred Coombe Tennant, 14 October 1931. Chapman and Clement earned their livings as graphic designers, or 'commercial artists' in the parlance of the period. They had been contemporaries at Swansea School of Art during the Great War.
3 *Herald of Wales*, 5 March 1932.
4 William Grant Murray to Winifred Coombe Tennant, 22 February 1932.
5 Myfanwy Lumsden (daughter of Geraint Goodwin), interview with Peter Lord, 7 July 2006. The *Sunday Dispatch*, 18 October 1931, reported that Griffiths had been 'on the verge of poverty'.
6 John Davies Williams, 'The Artist of the Welsh Mines. Rhys Griffiths and his work', *Herald of Wales*, 3 December 1932. The mural was destroyed in the 1960s. It is known only from the photograph published with Williams' newspaper article, which probably reproduces the cartoon, rather than the mural itself.
7 Winifred was possibly aware of this project, since she talked with Jones in the period in which the planning was underway: 'Called on Mrs Tom Jones,

wife of ex Secretary to the Cabinet, and found Tom in bed with neuritis – Hearing that I was there he sent for me and I had the joy of half an hour's talk with him … a unique human being. Spoke of his two recent articles in *The Times* on Welsh miners and conditions in Glasgow, of public affairs, books, people. Elfyn his adored boy of about 12 or 13 killed by a car Xmas Eve some years ago. I thought of that and of Daphne.' Diary, 15 March 1932.
8 'The critic of *The Studio* once spoke of "near genius" and compared him with Blake. And one cannot apply to Blake any of the ordinary tests. One has to say he is a mystic and leave it at that.' Geraint Goodwin, 'An Artist of Vision. The Work of Rhys Griffiths', *The Welsh Outlook*, XIX (1932), 80.
9 Thomas Jones, *Catalogue of Paintings, Drawings and Etchings by Rhys Griffiths, A.R.C.A.* (London, 1932), foreword, no pagination.
10 Unidentified newspaper, April 1932, private archive.
11 The picture was painted on canvas in London. It did not arrive at the gallery until May 1934. 'Archie Griffiths' mural decoration for the Gallery – "Coal Mining" arrived a few days ago but is not yet in position. It is fairly good – better than I expected but not a masterpiece.' William Grant Murray to Winifred Coombe Tennant, 28 May 1934.
12 The commission took a long time to complete. The painting was finally exhibited at the London Portrait Society exhibition at the New Burlington Gallery in London in April 1935. Winifred regarded it as 'a *very* fine thing'. Diary, 26 March 1935.
13 On 14 October 1935 the *South Wales Evening Post* reported that 'Since she has moved to Portland Place, every Sunday is "open house" to the Welsh students in London', but there is no evidence in Winifred's letters and diaries to confirm that this was the case.
14 In fact Godfrey was not yet twenty. Among those young painters with whom he exhibited the most illustrious would

prove to be Mervyn Peake. In its National Eisteddfod supplement, the *Western Mail*, 3 August 1934, published an article by Godfrey, with a photograph of the painter.
15 Kenneth Hancock to Winifred Coombe Tennant, 2 September 1932. The adjudicators were Margaret Lindsay Williams and Goscombe John. Hancock's defensive comments about Richards' painting remaining Welsh, notwithstanding its modernism, suggest that he may have surmised, correctly, that Winifred would not approve. Winifred was sufficiently involved with Hancock to have recently assisted his father, an employee of the Great Western Railway, in a dispute with the company about his enforced redundancy.
16 Winifred bought examples of lace mainly from antique shops outside Wales. She became particularly interested in a contemporary lace maker, Mrs Allen of Beer in Devon. In 1939 she drew her work to the attention of the Queen, with the intention of gaining patronage and publicity, so as to help preserve the practice of the craft.
17 Diary, 6 January 1932. Maurice de Vlaminck, 1876-1958, was perhaps the most radical painter collected by Winifred. Notwithstanding his name (his father was Flemish), Vlaminck was French. He was self-taught as a painter, and for a time shared a studio in Paris with André Derain. From 1904-7 he was prominent in the Fauvist movement, which sought to liberate colour from its purely descriptive function. He worked in England in 1911. In addition to his painting, he also wrote, publishing both articles and novels.
18 Diary, 6 and 8 August 1934. At some time after this visit to Cadoxton Lodge a decision was taken to demolish the house. Cyril Fox and Iorwerth Peate visited in December 1936 to advise on the preservation of some of the features: 'The lovely lead pipes and the plaster ceiling are to go to the N. Museum of Wales when the old place comes down'. Diary, 25 December 1936.

19 *Western Mail*, 8 September 1934.

20 'Madam, I do thank you for your letter. I would have wrote to you yesterday but I was away from home very sorry to say I have no patterns in large plad patterns I do chiefly make shirtings and plain tweeds. The most work I does in weaving is making flannel for the miners and they do keep me rather busy thanking you very much for your kindness for writing to me.' Charles Powell to Winifred Coombe Tennant, 5 August 1924, Swansea Museum, box 201, item 13.

21 Winifred Coombe Tennant, 'Vanishing Looms of Wales', *Western Mail*, 15 August 1934.

22 The Rhondda weavers were a part of the Maes-yr-haf settlement, with which Winifred's old friend George M.Ll. Davies was closely associated. They were described by the journalist Gareth Jones in an article in the *Western Mail* on 25 April 1933: 'We enter the room where women are weaving. We examine the rugs and the cloth they make. The work is striking. The patterns have an artistic value which contrasts with many factory products. There is an individual note about each design'. Jones had been a friend of Alexander Coombe-Tennant at Cambridge, and Winifred also came to know him and his parents. His death at the hands of Chinese bandits in August 1935 caused her great distress. She described him as 'learned, eager, brilliant'. Diary, 29 July 1935.

23 M. Ceri David to Winifred Coombe Tennant, 27 August 1934, NLW Mam o Nedd Material, 2988.

24 Diary, 4 September 1934. The factory may have been Gwenffrwd, with which she had been in touch ten years earlier.

25 William Grant Murray to Winifred Coombe Tennant, 16 April 1935.

26 Isaac Williams to Winifred Coombe Tennant, 16 April 1935.

27 Byng-Stamper, and her sister, Caroline Byng-Lucas, another of those involved, were cousins of Cedric Morris.

28 The organiser of the 'Art for the People' exhibition was the Secretary to the BIAE,

William Emrys Williams, a Welsh person with a liberal agenda similar to that of Jones and Morris. For a wider discussion of the period, see Peter Lord, *The Visual Culture of Wales: Industrial Society* (Cardiff, 1998), pp. 224-35.

29 Thomas Jones, *Leeks and Daffodils* (Newtown, 1942), p. 205. The 1936 BIAE expedition into Wales was not repeated for four years, when an exhibition which included the work of J.D. Innes, Augustus John, David Jones, Evan Walters and Morland Lewis toured venues in the south. With the support of Thomas Jones it was funded jointly by the Pilgrim Trust and the Treasury.

30 For the genesis of the Exhibition of Contemporary Welsh Art and its consequences see Lord, *The Visual Culture of Wales: Industrial Society*, pp. 205-8; Peter Lord, *The Visual Culture of Wales: Imaging the Nation* (Cardiff, 2000), pp. 380-1.

31 Evan Walters to Winifred Coombe Tennant, 19 August 1935. Walters was suffering from a heavy cold at the time of the broadcast, and so his text was read on air by an actor. Its content was discussed in detail by John Davies Williams in *The Herald of Wales*, 7 September 1935, p. 1.

32 NLW J.W. Jones papers, 3619, translated from the Welsh. Timothy Evans was born in Dyffryn Conwy. He had first exhibited at the Llanelli Eisteddfod of 1895, at which Herkomer caused a stir with his negative criticism of both the status and quality of the art on show. Evans was undeterred, and subsequently took many prizes for painting at National Eisteddfodau. He developed his career in London and in later life became somewhat embittered about what he regarded as the lack of recognition afforded him in Wales. See many references in Peter Lord, *Y Chwaer-Dduwies. Celf, Crefft a'r Eisteddfod* (Llandysul, 1992), and Peter Lord, *Clarence Whaite and the Welsh Art World. The Betws-y-coed Artists' Colony 1844-1914* (Aberystwyth, 1998), pp. 157-9, 185.

33 Tate Gallery, Cedric Morris Papers, 8317.1.4, item 91. At Swansea the

exhibition was shown in the Deffett Francis Gallery, the Glynn Vivian being fully booked.

34 Morris would soon be in touch with an educational settlement at Gwernllwyn House, Dowlais, where he would establish art classes. For these, and the subsequent involvement of Cedric Morris with painters in Wales, see Lord, *The Visual Culture of Wales: Industrial Society*, pp. 208-14 and 224-30, and Peter Lord, *The Visual Culture of Wales: Industrial Society* CDROM (Cardiff, 2000), 'Visual Journeys: Art for the People: The Contemporary Welsh Art Exhibition'.

35 D. Kighley Baxandall, 'Cyfraniad Cymru at Gelfyddyd Heddiw', *Tir Newydd*, 2 (1935), 3, translated from the Welsh.

36 *South Wales Evening Post*, 11 September 1935.

37 Walters informed Winifred of his new style of painting, shown in his latest exhibition, in a letter dated 11 November 1936: 'I have changed my style in this show. All the works were painted within 10 weeks. It is a new theory which I will explain to you when I see you. I don't know how it is going, I have not been down for a few days, but I do not expect to sell much, if any, from this show – since it is something new and people will have to get used to things'.

38 Diary, 11 October 1935. It is not clear whether this was the first occasion on which Winifred met Caradoc Evans. The writer was a close friend of Evan Walters, who certainly discussed his work with Winifred. In 1933, for instance, Walters wrote to her about Evans' new book *Wasps*. For the picture of figures on a beach, which was, in fact, by Will Evans, see under William Grant Murray in the Catalogue Raisonné.

39 *South Wales Evening Post*, 12 October 1935.

40 However, there is no work by Janes in the Coombe Tennant Collection.

41 William Rothenstein to Vincent Evans, 29 June 1933, NLW Vincent Evans Archive.

42 *South Wales Evening Post*, 23 April 1935.

43 For the work of Vincent Evans see Lord, *The Visual Culture of Wales: Industrial Society*, pp. 174ff. and Lord, *The Visual Culture of Wales: Industrial Society* CDROM, 'Visual Journeys: The Swansea School: Vincent Evans'.

44 Diary, 9 August 1935. The chaired bard was E. Gwyndaf Evans.

45 Diary, 9 August 1935. Winifred's admiration for T.E. Lawrence was expressed later in her search for the portrait of him made by Augustus John, which she eventually found in New York. She endeavoured to persuade Cambridge University to buy it, but failed. Winifred's visit in 1935 to the birthplace of Lawrence was immediately followed by a second pilgrimage. She visited St. Asaph in search of the workhouse in which her brother-in-law, H.M. Stanley, spent his childhood: 'Saw the grim workhouse where that deserted child had known Hell and my heart went out to Stanley as I had known him – that "tamed and shabby tiger" in the clutches of Richmond Terrace. His nightmare childhood stamped its wounds on him for life – and was both the genesis and the explanation of his lonely bitter love-seeking icy-reserved character'. Diary, 13 August 1935. On 19 August 1935 Winifred visited other sites associated with Stanley.

46 Mary Clarke Pierce-Serocold, née Richardson, Winifred's mother, died on 22 August 1935.

47 Albert Evans-Jones, Cynan (1895-1970), was a leading figure in the National Eisteddfod and in Gorsedd y Beirdd for many years. He had won the Chair once and the Crown three times, most recently in 1931. Winifred admired him greatly.

48 Diary, 16 July 1937. William Crwys Williams was Archdruid until 1947. In the election for the post Winifred voted for Wil Ifan.

49 Diary, 6 August 1937. Howell Elvet Lewis (1860-1953) was among the most distinguished literary figures of the period, renowned as a poet but in particular as a writer of hymns. Winifred was saying her farewell to him as Archdruid. Despite his failing sight he continued to serve as minister of Tabernacl, Kings Cross, in London, until 1940.

50 Diary, 23 April 1936. On 6 February 1936 Winifred had met Jones 'On a Cymmrodorion Deputation to Distressed area show at Charring X underground', along with other prominent members of the London Welsh establishment, including G. Hartwell Jones and Wyn Wheldon, as well as her friend Geoffrey Crawshay.

51 Diary, 3 August 1937. The *South Wales Evening Post* carried obituaries and tributes for several days after its first report of the death of John Davies Williams on 11 September 1936. Williams had died on 10 September in a fall near the summit of Clogwyn. Williams (1878-36) had begun his working life as an errand boy in the office of the *Cambria Daily Leader*. He became its editor during the Great War and edited the *South Wales Evening Post* when that paper absorbed his own. He was an energetic supporter of theatre, as well as of the visual arts, in Swansea. Although a Welsh-speaker, he was an Elder in the English Presbyterian Church, Alexandra Road. He had a great love of hill walking and climbing.

52 Diary, 3 August 1938. Winifred was among those who lobbied successfully for Huw Menai to be granted a Civil List pension in 1949.

53 Diary, 3 August 1938. Winifred duly took the work of the painter to the Wertheim Gallery, where she discussed its potential, but the disruption of her life by the war appears to have put a stop to her efforts to promote him. The painter has not been identified.

54 Whilst expressions of distaste for what she regarded as the ugliness of the industrial townscape are not unusual in Winifred's writings, they are rarely extended to include the people. Such general expressions of distaste occur almost exclusively in the period when Winifred experienced intensely conflicted feelings immediately before her decision to leave Wales: 'Into Neath paying bills, its dirty mean streets filled with ugly mean-looking people … I long for colour, light and warmth … must I always live here?' Diary, 1 January 1930.

55 As a result of her work for the Society Winifred became particularly friendly with Lord Ivor Churchill, whose collection of French pictures, including Cezanne and Vlaminck, she greatly admired. William Rothenstein was also involved with the Society.

56 'Private view at Curtis Moffatt Gallery in Fitzroy Square. My Vlaminck well placed, and marked as uncatalogued. Oswald Mosley and Lady Cynthia, Austen Chamberlain, Margot Asquith-Oxford, Lady Diana Cooper and many others there.' Diary, 1 January 1932.

57 Diary, 5 and 6 July 1936. St. Isaac's Cathedral, built in 1858, had been converted into a Museum of Atheism.

58 Winifred wrote her account of the visit in a diary which has not been located. The *Western Mail*, 8 May 1937, carried a summary account. According to the newspaper, Winifred's visit to the tomb of E. Harold Jones (1877-1911) was undertaken at the request of his mother.

59 Winifred Coombe Tennant to William Grant Murray, 9 January 1940, Glynn Vivian Art Gallery archive.

60 Winifred Coombe Tennant to William Grant Murray, 29 January 1940, Glynn Vivian Art Gallery archive.

61 The story of Henry's escape is told in Major A.S.B. Arkwright, M.C., *Return Journey. Escape from Oflag VIB* (London, 1948).

62 Winifred Coombe Tennant to William Grant Murray, 11 December 1949, Glynn Vivian Art Gallery archive.

63 For a brief account of representations of the Croes Naid at Windsor, and the context in which they were made, see Peter Lord, *The Visual Culture of Wales: Medieval Vision* (Cardiff, 2003), pp. 251-2. Winifred's full account is Winifred Coombe Tennant, 'Croes Naid', *National Library of Wales Journal*, VII (1951), pp. 102-15.

64 In January 1950 Alexander left Cottesmore Gardens to live independently close by. By this time he had returned to his work in the City, and continued to care assiduously for his mother until her death. Following his return from the conflict in Palestine, arising from the establishment of the Israeli state in 1948, Henry also shared Cottesmore Gardens with his mother. He left in 1952. At the end of his army service, Henry became a Roman Catholic, and then a monk at Downside Abbey.

65 '[Augustus] John no doubt wouldn't sit and, anway, when sober?' Winifred Coombe Tennant to William Grant Murray, 5 April 1940 and 4 May 1940, Glynn Vivian Art Gallery archive.

66 Jenkin Evans had undertaken at least one paid commission by this time, to sculpt the only Welsh-born President of the British Dental Association. Winifred's initial attempts to interest further potential sitters were unsuccessful but following the Huw Menai bust Evans received several commissions. His winning submission to the 1938 National Eisteddfod had been a bust of Gwili, which was cast in bronze and loaned by the Gorsedd to the National Museum.

67 Jenkin Evans to Winifred Coombe Tennant, 8 October 1946.

68 Vincent Evans to Winifred Coombe Tennant 6 May 1950; Evan Walters to Winifred Coombe Tennant 11 May 1950. Winifred kept a press cutting on the subject of Jenkin and Vincent Evans exhibiting together at the Royal Academy in 1947, but still appears not to have made the connection with the painter she had met before the war and who reintroduced himself at Evan Walters' private view.

69 'One thing that has rather changed the situation is this appointment of David Bell – I expect that you have heard that the Arts Council has appointed more staff for Wales with David Bell as Art Officer. That's probably a good thing (I haven't met him yet). But if they are going to expand in Wales then there isn't so much room

for the expansion we foresaw in the Federation work. They are the official people with the money and the staff to do the job, and it looks as if eventually they will do it.' Esther Grainger to Cedric Morris, Tate Gallery Cedric Morris Papers, 8317.1.1, item 1263.

70 Lord Ivor Churchill to Winifred Coombe Tennant, 18 January 1951.

71 Tate Gallery, Cedric Morris Archive, 8317.3.1.2. A.G. Tennant-Moon was from Cardiff. He studied at the Royal College of Art. He had introduced himself to Winifred, 'against the rules of etiquette', in a letter dated 9 April 1938. For Josef Herman, see Nini Herman, *Josef Herman: A Working Life* (London, 1996). He had been established at Ystradgynlais since 1944. Ivor Williams was the son of Christopher Williams and earned a living as a portrait painter in a conservative manner which, privately, Cedric Morris disparaged. At the time of the broadcast he was based in Wales.

72 Tate Gallery, Cedric Morris Papers, 8317.1.1270, undated, but 1946.

73 Winifred Coombe Tennant to William Grant Murray, 7 February 1948, Glynn Vivian Art Gallery archive.

74 Ralph Edwards, 1894-1977, was a joint-author of *The Dictionary of English Furniture* (Country Life, 1924-7), and several other volumes on the subject. He also wrote about painting, in particular on the 'conversation piece' genre.

75 For a passionate exposition of Peate's view of the relationship between art, craft and the common people, see his essay 'Pobl Gyffredin' [Common People] in Iorwerth C. Peate, *Sylfeini* (Wrexham, 1938). For the post-war debate on the issue, see Lord, *Y Chwaer-Dduwies*, pp. 107-14.

76 Winifred Coombe Tennant to William Grant Murray, 25 February 1948, Glynn Vivian Art Gallery archive. Winifred quotes Psalm 60, v. 8: 'Moab is my washpot; over Edom will I cast out my shoe: Philistia, triumph thou because of me.'

77 Diary, 5 December 1948. Rhys and

Roberts were nearing the end of their marriage. They were divorced in 1949. Winifred's relationship was renewed two years later, and subsequently through occasional correspondence: 'Keidrych Rhys rang up to ask if he could come and see me. I had only met him once before, when he came with his wife Lynette Roberts one evening, a trivial woman, who has now run away from him. He came at 4.30pm and he left at 7.15pm. Interesting, as much of his talk was the length of his visit. Left me very weary, for I had done a hard day's work before he came. I liked him, something genuine and almost childlike in him, overlaid with much living in dark and desolate places of life, yet essentially I felt he was sound and at heart untarnished'. Diary, 27 August 1950.

78 Koppel's work at Dowlais was much admired by David Bell, and provides an example of the contrasting attitudes within the art establishment to the democratising spirit of the period. In 1947 Bell publicised the work at Dowlais by organising the exhibition 'Some Pictures from a South Wales Town', in which pictures painted by amateurs and professionals were shown together. By contrast, John Steegman at the National Museum did not approve of Koppel, and would not buy his work for the national collection.

79 Kyffin Williams died at the age of 88 in 2006. Ralph Edwards to Winifred Coombe Tennant, 13 February 1948.

80 Kyffin Williams to Winifred Coombe Tennant, 4 October 1950. Winifred's respect for Kyffin Williams was occasionally dented. In 1951 she saw ' hideous and badly painted Kyffin Williamses' at a Society of British Artists exhibition, which depressed her. Diary, 27 November 1951.

81 Winifred Coombe Tennant to William Grant Murray, 25 February 1948, Glynn Vivian Art Gallery archive. For the career of John Elwyn, see Robert Meyrick, *John Elwyn* (Aldershot, 2000).

82 Diary, 18 July 1949. Cemlyn Jones, another friend of Winifred's, was the

buyer for CASW. The Tredegar public gallery was the Working Men's Institute.

83 Winifred Coombe Tennant to John Elwyn, 29 August 1950, NLW 23531C, f. 31.

84 Winifred Coombe Tennant to John Elwyn, 15 June 1950, NLW 23531C, f. 25.

85 Winifred Coombe Tennant to John Elwyn, 23 December 1951, NLW 23531C, f. 51.

86 Winifred Coombe Tennant to John Elwyn, 11 August 1948, NLW 23531C, f. 6.

87 Winifred Coombe Tennant to William Grant Murray, 12 May 1949, Glynn Vivian Art Gallery archive.

88 Winifred Coombe Tennant to William Grant Murray, 20 July 1950, Glynn Vivian Art Gallery archive.

89 Winifred Coombe Tennant to John Elwyn, 6 July 1950, NLW 23531C, ff. 22-3. 'To the Redfern Gallery, to see for the first time, paintings by Ceri Richards. One of the selecting committee chosen for the National Eisteddfod, at Caerphilly. [I] was horrified at the hideous confused jumble of extreme cubist compositions. Just stark madness to me, abstract and totally unrepresentational art. I cannot believe this is in the true line of true art. He was trained at the Swansea art school, but I do not remember his name, I think he never was at Cadoxton.' Diary, 31 May 1950.

90 *Llawlyfr Arddangosfa Celfyddyd a Chrefft, Eisteddfod Genedlaethol Frenhinol Cymru Caerffili, 1950*, Foreword by Iorwerth C. Peate, p. 5.

91 Winifred Coombe Tennant to William Grant Murray, 13 August 1950, Glynn Vivian Art Gallery archive. Winifred received a brief post-mortem account of the selection from Cedric Morris, who 'thought the standard was pretty high – you should have seen what we did not select – it was very difficult and I expect there is much heart-burning among the rejected, but can't be helped'. Cedric Morris to Winifred Coombe Tennant, 24 September 1950. In the same letter Morris commended Glyn Morgan to Winifred, as 'the best of the young Welsh painters'. The other Welsh student of

Morris, Esther Grainger, had been the secretary of the Art and Craft Committee at Caerffili. Winifred had seen her work at the Heal's exhibition and had, in fact, once met her, when she awarded her a prize at Howell's School in Cardiff. Grainger reminded Winifred of this event in a correspondence mainly concerned with Winifred's efforts to ensure that Jenkin Evans' sculpture was shown at Caerffili.

92 *Western Mail*, 8 August 1950, reporting Peate's speech at the opening of the Craft and Art Exhibition.

93 Winifred Coombe Tennant to D.H.I. Powell, 29 November 1950.

94 Winifred Coombe Tennant to Augustus John, 29 August 1950, NLW 22786D, f. 70. In a letter written to her two days earlier, John Elwyn commented on the selection of 'a Polish painter from Ystradgynlais'. John Elwyn to Winifred Coombe Tennant, 27 August 1950.

95 Unidentified press cutting, Exhibition Files, 'Miners at Ystradgynlais', 1948, NLW Welsh Arts Council Archive. In a letter to John Elwyn, NLW 23531C f. 50, Winifred stated that she had seen Herman's first London exhibition. However, this was at the Lefevre Gallery in 1943, and it seems unlikely that Winifred had, in fact, visited the show. From 1946 Herman exhibited regularly at Roland, Browse and Delbanco though, again, if Winifred did see his work there before 1950, no note of it survives.

96 Winifred Coombe Tennant to John Elwyn, 21 August 1951, NLW 23531C f. 50. Winifred pointedly remarked to John Elwyn that she did not follow David Bell in his admiration for Herman. On 8 October 1951 Winifred visited Herman's exhibition at the Rowland Browse and Delbanco Gallery in London. She found 'the drawings clever but repulsive, the oils so dark I could scarce make out what they portrayed'. One factor in Bell's promotion of Herman as a Welsh painter was certainly the high regard in which he was held in England, though John Berger would provide an exception to the

generally positive critical response there.

97 Evan Walters to Winifred Coombe Tennant, 7 February 1948; Diary, 22 February 1948.

98 John Harris, afterword to Caradoc Evans, *Morgan Bible and Journal 1939-44* (Aberystwyth, 2006), p. 192. Marguerite published her novels under the names Countess Barcynska and Oliver Sandys. Marguerite and Winifred seem to have become confused over the picture which they inspected together in 1935. It was not *The Eton Boy* but Walters' portrait of Alexander.

99 By this time Winifred had decided to bequeath her collection of Welsh pictures to Henry. 'Henry and I spent a long time going through the Welsh collection, which will be his when I am gone. He found great pleasure in many of the pictures, Evan Walters, Will Evans, Cyrlas Williams and others. Woke in me many memories of the twenties, of Cadoxton and days when the children were young there. Diary, 26 August 1950. After Winifred's death, as a monk at Downside, Henry could own no property, and so the pictures, with the French collection, passed to Alexander.

100 In a letter to Iorwerth Hughes Jones, written in 1945, Iorwerth Peate reflected sadly on the matter: 'Caradoc Evans picture came before our Committee when it was first painted, and they were foolish enough to turn it down because it was Caradoc!!! Perfect stupidity, of course, and the picture is one of Evan Walters' main masterpieces. I wonder if you could get it again as a gift? The composition of our Committee has changed quite a lot since those days …' Iorwerth Peate to Iorwerth Hughes Jones, 17 February 1945, NLW 20015D.

101 Winifred Coombe Tennant to William Grant Murray, 11 December 1949, Glynn Vivian Art Gallery archive.

102 Diary, 8 December 1949. The line quoted by Winifred, which she also deployed on her first meeting with Euphemia Lamb on 5 June 1952, is from Robert Browning, 'Memorabilia'.

103 Winifred Coombe Tennant to Augustus John, 9 November 1950.

104 Winifred Coombe Tennant to William Grant Murray, 21 February 1948, Glynn Vivian Art Gallery archive.

105 'I am painfully aware of my dilatoriness in producing the landscape for the Civic Centre Collection in Swansea. I intend going to Wales soon to spend some weeks painting'. Augustus John to Winifred Coombe Tennant, 24 August 1939.

106 Winifred Coombe Tennant to Grant Murray, 26 July 1948, Glynn Vivian Art Gallery archive. 'Berlin cum Cripps' had caused the fall in prices, according to Winifred. Stafford Cripps was the Chancellor of the Exchequer.

107 Winifred Coombe Tennant to Grant Murray 6 January 1949 and 15 February 1949, Glynn Vivian Art Gallery archive. The reputation of Gwen John had developed slowly and quietly, as compared to that of her brother. It would appear that, notwithstanding her frequent visits to Paris, Winifred was only vaguely aware of her work until after the Second World War.

108 Winifred Coombe Tennant to William Grant Murray, 15 February 1949, Glynn Vivian Art Gallery archive. Augustus John's observation is quoted in a letter from Grant Murray to Winifred, dated 22 February 1949. Clearly, Winifred and Grant Murray had discussed John's surprising opinion at an earlier date.

109 Winifred Coombe Tennant to William Grant Murray, 16 February 1949, Glynn Vivian Art Gallery archive. Edwin John was trying to make a career as a painter. Two years later Winifred inspected a 'dullish show' of his watercolours at the Beaux Art Gallery in London. Diary, 18 April 1951.

110 Winifred Coombe Tennant to William Grant Murray, 25 February 1949, Glynn Vivian Art Gallery archive. Among the 'crowd' at the Tate Gallery was John Steegman. William Rothenstein, Winifred's old friend and father of John,

the Director of the Tate Gallery in 1949, had died in 1945. Alongside work by Innes, it was one of William's pictures which had most attracted Winifred on her visit. She was much taken with 'a strangely vivid and interesting picture by Will Rothenstein – "The Dolls House". Lady Rothenstein said it was painted in Normandy and the two figures in it were John and herself'. Diary, 24 February 1949.

111 Winifred Coombe Tennant to William Grant Murray, 22 April 1949, Glynn Vivian Art Gallery archive.

112 Winifred's letter requesting John's help in acquiring an Innes had included a characteristic expression of her opinion on the subject of Ceri Richards. The letter found John in the south of France. 'So Cubism has reached Wales', he observed. 'It's dead here long ago'. Augustus John to Winifred Coombe Tennant, 4 July 1950.

113 'I feel terribly weary, but for tea came Brian Rees, the Neath boy who is an art student from the Swansea Art School [now moved] to the Camberwell one. He brought a lovely gouache drawing of Aberdulais Aqueduct which Alexander had commissioned, and with which he is much pleased – paid £4 for it, at which Brian is much pleased.' Diary, 13 January 1951.

114 Glyn Morgan to Winifred Coombe Tennant, 4 November 1950 and 31 October 1950.

115 Diary, 16 June 1951. Winifred was introduced to Thomas by Bernice Evans, whom she had met at a dinner in celebration of Huw Menai. Evans, who came from Port Talbot, had also trained at the Slade School of Art.

116 Manuscript draft. Place of publication untraced.

117 Diary, 18 March 1951. On the same day Winifred sent a similar account of events to Iorwerth Hughes Jones in Swansea. The letter, and others from Winifred to the same correspondent on the subject of Evan Walters, were published in Iorwerth Hughes Jones, 'Evan John Walters and his Patron Mrs Winifred

Coombe Tennant, Cadoxton Lodge, Neath', *Gower*, XVIII (1966), 23-8.

118 Diary, 22 April, 1951. Winifred corresponded with Augustus John on the subject of Evan Walters at this time. John's response was characteristic of his tendency to occasional outbursts of identification with Wales: 'Having been absent lately I only now receive your bad news with respect to Evan Walters and Mr Grant Murray; two nasty blows for our country … I am in the throes of painting a huge Welsh composition, against time. I fear it cannot be done …' Augustus John to Winifred Coombe Tennant, 9 April 1951.

119 Winifred Coombe Tennant to David Bell, 11 May 1951. Rollo Charles was assistant to Steegman.

120 Diary, 4 September 1951. The question of the Walters bequest rumbled on until 1955, when it was agreed that the pictures not taken by the Museum be distributed to galleries throughout Wales. Winifred was able to select the pictures she had been promised by the painter shortly before his death. They were her last Walters acquisitions. She chose three watercolours, which she regarded, with some justification, as 'superb examples of his work'. Diary, 29 May 1955.

121 Ralph Edwards to Winifred Coombe Tennant, 28 May 1952. Edwards could not 'go all the way' with Winifred in her high estimation of the painter. Displaying remarkable indifference to Winifred's feelings, in his letter Edwards immediately proceeded from Walters to discuss the Davies bequest, which was 'by far the most important the Museum has ever received'.

122 Ogwyn Davies, interview with Peter Lord, 20 January 2006, The National Library of Wales, National Screen and Sound Archive of Wales. Beryl Davies remembered that 'We had a lot of Brownie points after that', in Ystalyfera.

123 *The News Chronicle*, 19 February 1952, and G. Cyrlas Williams to Winifred Coombe Tennant, 23 February 1952.

124 BBC publicity material for 'The Legend of Craig y Ddinas'. The script is NLW BBC (Cymru/Wales) (2A) Welsh Region Scripts, box 38, 17 October 1953. The Arthurian legend at the centre of the script was gleaned by Winifred, like much of her local knowledge, from D. Rhys Phillips. Winifred was in frequent contact with Phillips in the 1920s, and assisted him with information from the Tennant family archives while he was writing his *History of the Vale of Neath* (Swansea, 1925).

125 Winifred was gracious in her letters to Bell on the subject, but was, in fact, highly irritated. Bell's estimate had been exceeded by a second valuation given by the Leicester Galleries, but Kenneth Clarke took a more conservative view: '... found David Bell waiting for us on the pavement, outside the gallery door. He took us up and I saw the Innes that Lady Howard Stepney and Marged had always promised I should have, at between £50-£130, and which [was] filched from me, by having it valued in London by the Leicester Gallery at £275. The Glynn Vivian paid £250 for it and, on applying to Arts Council for a grant towards purchase, Sir Kenneth Clarke refused — said price too high for the picture. It is a small, lovely picture of Arennig seen in evening light, and I remember it from more than 30 years at Cilymaenllwyd'. Diary, 24 October 1953.

126 Note written by Winifred Coombe Tennant in September 1951.

127 Diary, 19 September 1953. The six works by Condor bought by Winifred have not been included in the catalogue raisonné of the Welsh collection. They are: *The Buddha*, lithograph heightened with chalk, 12×18; *Voyage de Plaisir à Dieppe*, 1901, pastel 8×10; *Stella in a Spanish Shawl*, pastel, 22×16; *Invitation to a Fancy Dress Party at the Artist's Home*, 1905, lithograph, 6×10; *Souvenir de Rejane (Souvenir de Ballet)*, oil, 15×19; *Painting of seven figures*, on silk.

128 Augustus John to Winifred Coombe Tennant, 18 March 1954. The offending article, a review of John's current exhibition at Burlington House, appeared in *The Times*, 13 March 1954. Winifred's indignant response was not published.

129 Diary, 5 June 1952. The sale of *Cloud over Arennig* to Winifred was the second occasion on which Euphemia Lamb had parted company with the picture. The previous purchaser was Lord Howard de Walden, from whom she had retrieved it at some stage.

130 Diary, 1 December 1951. In her diary, 'Martha Martha' or 'Martha-ing' was Winifred's usual short-hand for drudgery. Her note on the life of Condor does not appear to have been intended for publication. It described the purchase of her first work by the painter and gave a synopsis of his career.

131 In 1953 Winifred sought to persuade the Leicester Galleries to give John Elwyn a one-person exhibition, for instance, and she secured for him the patronage of J.T. Morgan of Swansea, who had been a friend of John Elwyn's father. See letters to John Elwyn in NLW 23531C, ff. 59-67.

132 Bessie Evans to Winifred Coombe Tennant, undated but early August, 1951. For the National Eisteddfod at Llanrwst see Lord, *Y Chwaer-Dduwies*, pp. 114-16.

133 Obituary of Bessie Evans, written by Winifred Coombe Tennant and published in the *South Wales Evening Post*, 19 August 1953.

134 Winifred Coombe Tennant to John Elwyn, 10 August 1954, NLW 23531C, f. 69.

135 Winifred Coombe Tennant to John Elwyn, 10 August 1954, NLW 23531C, f. 67.

The Welsh Collection:
CATALOGUE RAISONNÉ

Winifred Coombe Tennant was an enthusiastic cataloguer. She made detailed records of all her collections of Welsh and French paintings, lace and icons. The 'Tennant Collection of Modern Paintings' was begun in December 1924. It included both Welsh and French works but in the late 1920s increasing demand from English art galleries to show the French works alone led to the Welsh collection assuming a separate identity. Winifred continued to revise the catalogue of her Welsh pictures until 1955. The primary source for the present catalogue is, therefore, Winifred's own documentation, to which is added information gleaned from letters and diaries. The catalogue gives details of all the Welsh pictures collected by Winifred, including some which had, in her mind, strong Welsh associations but, perhaps, might not be seen as Welsh today. It also includes modern Welsh pictures acquired by her sons, Alexander and Henry, during her lifetime, since they were bought under her guidance and she included them in her own catalogue.

Most of the pictures survive as a collection, but a few were given away by Winifred or, for other reasons, are presently untraced. These works have been included, based on Winifred's own descriptions. In general the works of Dorothy Tennant bought or otherwise acquired by Winifred (which included both oil paintings and drawings) are not listed, since she regarded them as family pictures rather than as a part of the Welsh Collection. However, Dorothy's portrait of Winifred, painted in 1896, and also the earlier portrait by Olivier, are included, so as to give a complete record of portraits of Winifred in her own collection.

The circumstances surrounding the acquisition of works and biographical details of the painters are given only if they are not adequately described in the main text (to which page references are given), or readily available elsewhere. Following the same rule, pictures are illustrated only if not to be found in the main text. Sizes are given in inches, to the nearest round figure, height before width.

Frank Alford
Recumbent Figure, 1914
Charcoal, 9×12

Perhaps one of a group of
drawings shown to Winifred
by Alford in 1916.

> *Frank Alford dined in
> evening and brought some
> nice drawings. He is going
> to varnish my portrait soon.*
> [Diary, 26 July 1916]

Frank Alford
*Portrait of Winifred Coombe Tennant,
1915*
Oil on canvas, 47×35

This portrait was known to the
family, somewhat unkindly, as
'The Elephant'. See pp. 38, *39*.

For the career of Frank Alford, see
*Brangwyn in his Studio. The Diary
of his Assistant Frank Alford*, eds.
Roger Alford and Libby Horner
(privately published, 2004).

Charles H. Collins Baker
Tyrau Mawr, n.d.
Oil on canvas, 16×24

Exhibited at the New English Art
Club Summer Exhibition, 1918.

Acquired on 12 June 1953 for 8
guineas. The vendor was Robert
E. Abbott, a dealer working from
Barnes, Middlesex, from whom
Winifred made several purchases
in the 1950s.

> *Had a good look at the
> pictures brought by Abbott
> yesterday and decided to
> buy a painting by Condor,
> 'Souvenir de Ballet', figures
> of 2 ballet dancers ... I also
> bought a largish landscape,
> very modern and full of
> brilliant colours, 'Tyrau
> Mawr', by Collins Baker,
> once Director of the National
> Gallery. 'Tyrau Mawr' is in
> the Cader Idris massive above
> Dolgelly and Barmouth ...
> Oh the healing, consoling
> joy of a fine work of art.*
> [Diary, 13 June 1953]

Charles Henry Collins Baker
(1880-1959) was born at Ilminster,
Somerset. He became a painter
of landscapes, but was better
known as an art historian and
administrator. He was Keeper of
the National Gallery, London,
1914-34, and Surveyor of the
King's Pictures, 1928-34.

David Bell
Traeth Mawr, c.1952
Oil on board, 11x14

Exhibited at Swansea Art Society Exhibition, Glynn Vivian Art Gallery, June-July 1952.

I often feel why should I spend all my time and energy on administration when I would rather paint, but apart from the bread and butter position, which is a very real one with me, I do feel that my work for the Arts Council and now for the Gallery have been to some purpose and I don't feel I have wasted my life as I might do if I were merely an indifferent painter. But who shall judge these things?
[David Bell to Winifred Coombe Tennant, 11 September 1952]

David Bell (1916-59) was trained as a painter at the Royal College of Art. He became Assistant Director for Wales of the Arts Council of Great Britain, 1946-51, and Curator of the Glynn Vivian Art Gallery, 1951-9. His book *The Artist in Wales* (London, 1957) was the first attempt since 1912 to survey the field. For Bell's influence on the development of visual culture in Wales see numerous references in Peter Lord, *The Visual Culture of Wales: Industrial Society* and *The Visual Culture of Wales: Imaging the Nation* (Cardiff, 1998 and 2000).

Sir Edward Coley Burne-Jones
Study for the Memorial to Laura Lyttleton at Mells, n.d.
Watercolour, 27x10

Acquired from Christie's, 3 December 1954, for 6 guineas, previously in the collection of the painter's daughter. The picture is presently untraced.

Burne-Jones was claimed as a Welsh painter by intellectuals of the National Revival period. Laura Lyttleton was of particular interest to Winifred as the daughter of Sir Charles Tennant, and one of 'The Souls'. Gerald Balfour had been in love with her, but she married Alfred Lyttleton. She died in 1886.

Ogwyn Davies
The Bar of the Victoria Arms, 1950
Oil on board, 8x12

Acquired from the exhibition of work by students at Swansea School of Art, Glynn Vivian Art Gallery, August 1950, following a recommendation from William Grant Murray. See pp. 189-90, *190*.

Ogwyn Davies
The Mangel Field, 1952
Oil on board, 11x16

Acquired from the painter. See pp. 197-8, *198*.

Ogwyn Davies was born at Trebanos in 1925. He served in the RAF during the Second World War and subsequently studied at Swansea School of Art. For most of his career he taught art at Tregaron School, painting in his spare time. He has exhibited widely, and his work is held in many public collections.

Sydenham Edwards
Suffolk Agricultural Punch Horse and Suffolk Mare and Foal from the Stock of the late Duke of Bedford, n.d.
Watercolour on paper, 9x7

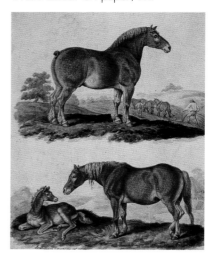

Sydenham Edwards

King Charles dog; La Pyrana dog; Pug dog; Spaniel; ? Buff; ? Buff; Lion dog Buff; Newfoundland dog; Royal Buff, n.d.
Watercolour on paper, 9×7

There is no record of Winifred's acquisition of Edward's pictures, but she probably became aware of the painter's work towards the end of 1925, when Isaac Williams enthused to her about him:

> *[I] have just secured a small collection of animal drawings and an illustrated book by Sydenham Edwards of Usk - date 1800. Until now we had only one example of this remarkable Welsh artist's work in the Museum.*
> [Isaac Williams to Winifred Coombe Tennant, 23 December 1925]

Sydenham Edwards (1768-1819) was born at Usk and became one of the most distinguished animal and botanical illustrators of his day. In the National Revival period he came to the attention of patriotic writers on art. See T.H. Thomas, 'Sydenham Edwards of Usk', *Cardiff Naturalist's Society Transactions*, 43 (1910), 15, and T. Mardy Rees, *Welsh Painters, Engravers and Sculptors* (Caernarfon, c.1912), pp. 38-42.

John Elwyn

Approach to a Welsh Village – Pontrhydyfen, 1949
Oil on board, 12×8

Acquired from an exhibition shared between John Elwyn and Jack Wright at the Paul Alexander Gallery, 1949, 13 guineas. See pp. 174-5, *174*.

John Elwyn

Palm Sunday, 1949
Oil on board, 12×19

Acquired by Alexander Coombe-Tennant from an exhibition shared between John Elwyn and Jack Wright at the Paul Alexander Gallery, 1949. See p. *175*.

John Elwyn

Easter Communion, 1949
Oil on board, 9×12

Acquired from an exhibition shared between John Elwyn and Jack Wright at the Paul Alexander Gallery, 1949. The picture is listed as *April Communion* in the exhibition catalogue. See p. *177*.

John Elwyn

The River Odet, Brittany, 1949
Oil on board, 9×13

Acquired by Henry Coombe-Tennant in 1951, 9 guineas.

John Elwyn
Ilston Chapel, 1953
Watercolour, 5x8

The picture was commissioned for a presentation book about Ilston Chapel on the Gower Peninsula. The painter worked from photographs.

John Elwyn
Manor Deifi Church, 1955
Oil on board, 11x14

Given by the painter, and inscribed by him: 'To Mam o Nedd, with gratitude, and thanks for her help and encouragement, August 1955, John Elwyn. Manordeifi Church, near Llechryd'.

In his last letter to Winifred, John Elwyn wrote of the picture:

> *I painted it at Llechryd on the banks of the Teify river and it may interest you if I enlarged a little on the church itself. The old parish church Manordeifi was built between 1250-1300 about the same time as some of the tales of the Mabinogion were written. In fact the background and the setting of the story referring to Pwyll was in this valley which bears the name of Cych. There was an earlier church on the same site dating back to the 8th century - so it must be one of the early Welsh churches. A most unusual feature in the interior are the old box pews - two of which actually have fireplaces in them. Services are no longer held in the building - but an open air service is held once a year in July when it seems hundreds of people attend outside the fabric. Alun - the Welsh Poet was rector here between 1833-1840 - his grave is marked by a white cross - which is very sketchily stated in the painting to the left of the entrance. The little pink washed cottage no longer is the home of a true blood celt but the shelter to an alien family of Italians - which is yet another indication of the change that is gradually overcoming the Welsh countryside.*

[John Elwyn to Winifred Coombe Tennant, 8 October 1955]

See p. *207*.

For the career of John Elwyn, see Robert Meyrick, *John Elwyn* (Aldershot, 2000).

Will Evans
Stormy Down, 1924
Oil on canvas, 19x25

Acquired at the Swansea Art Society Exhibition, Glynn Vivian Art Gallery, 1925, 8 guineas. See pp. *98*, *99*.

Will Evans
In the Bay, 1929
Oil on board, 12x18

Acquired at the Swansea Art Society Exhibition, Glynn Vivian Art Gallery, 1 June 1929, 4 guineas. See pp. 123, *124*.

Will Evans
Sand Dunes, Kenfig, 1930
Oil on board, 18x22

A long morning's work then after lunch motored into Swansea so see the Swansea Art Society Show - bought a most lovely landscape by Will

Evans of Kenfig Dunes ... How I shall miss all that in London, where prices are so high I can't buy anything!
[Diary, 18 May 1930]

Will Evans (1888-1957) was professionally involved in design in the tinplate industry in Swansea, and worked as a painter in his spare time. He became well-known throughout Wales (he was a member of the Royal Cambrian Academy), but particularly so in Swansea, where he was a prominent figure in the Swansea Art Society and a close friend of William Grant Murray. He had been a part-time student at the School of Art soon after Murray's arrival, and many years later established the Lithography Department there.

Paul Godfrey
Sand Dunes at Morfa, Margam, 1933
Oil on canvas, 20×24
Acquired from the painter, October 1933, 2 guineas.

... to Paul Godfrey's studio. He has some talent and I bought and carried off a lovely oil sketch of the Margam Hills and sand dunes - scenes of days gone by when I was young and the children young and the sun shone and skies were blue ...
[Diary, 29 October 1933]

P.F. or J. Gostas
David Lloyd George as a Young Man, n.d.
Pencil and chalk, 16×13

Acquired December 1953 for 10/-, because of Winifred's interest in the sitter.

Archie Rhys Griffiths
Henry Coombe-Tennant, 1928
Oil on canvas, 22×18

See p. 117.

Archie Rhys Griffiths
Miners Underground, 1928
Oil on paper, 15×11

See pp. 117, *118*.

Archie Rhys Griffiths
Miner Underground, 1928
Chalk on paper, 15×11

Inscribed 'Archie Griffiths drawn at Cadoxton'. *Miners Underground* and the portrait *Henry Coombe-Tennant* were also painted at Cadoxton. See pp. 117, *119*.

Archie Rhys Griffiths
Miners Returning from Work, 1928
Oil on canvas, 20×27

Acquired from Griffiths' one-person exhibition at the Glynn Vivian Art Gallery, November 1928, 10 guineas. See pp. 120-1, *121*.

Archie Rhys Griffiths
Tro yn yr Yrfa, 1928
Charcoal on paper, 15×22

Described by Winifred as 'Miners bearing body of one of their comrades to his home'. This is the drawing for the lost painting of the same name, which was shown in the painter's exhibitions of 1928 in Swansea and 1932 in London.

Archie Griffiths has sent me the drawing from which he painted 'Tro yn yr Yrfa' ... as a gift - a lovely thing which I rejoice to have.
[Diary, 10 December 1928]

See p. 121.

Archie Rhys Griffiths
Child Sleeping (The Cradle), c.1932
Oil on canvas, 20×26

Acquired at the painter's one-person exhibition at the Young Wales Association, London, April 1932. The child is almost certainly Griffiths' daughter, Diana. See p. 137.

Archie Rhys Griffiths
On the Coal Tips, 1932
Lino cut, 12×8

Acquired at the painter's one-person exhibition at the Young Wales Association, London, April 1932, where it was titled *Women Carrying Coal/Merched yn Cludo Glo*. See pp. 137, *138*.

For the career of Archie Rhys Griffiths, see *Tro yn yr Yrfa*, a film by Geraint Ellis (Cwmni Da for S4C, 2006).

Kenneth W. Hancock
Still Life, 1930
Oil on board, 21×24

Acquired from the Swansea Art Society Exhibition, Glynn Vivian Art Gallery, May 1930, £4.

Motored after lunch to Swansea to see Art show - liked a still life by a boy called Hancock.
[Diary, 17 May 1930]

See pp. 131, *132*.

Kenneth W. Hancock
Child Asleep, 1951
Chalk on paper, 15×19

Exhibited at the Swansea Art Society Exhibition, Glynn Vivian Art Gallery, July 1951.

Kenneth W. Hancock (1911-1978) was born in Mumbles. He trained at Swansea School of Art and the Royal College of Art. In 1946 he returned to Swansea as Principal of the School of Art.

J.D. Innes
Seascape, 1905
Watercolour on paper, 7×11

J.D. Innes
Decoration, 1907
Pen and watercolour on paper, 12×24

Exhibition of the work of Innes at the Chenil Galleries, April to June 1923, where purchased by J.E. Slade. Acquired by Winifred from R.E. Abbott in July 1953.

J.D. Innes
Landscape with a Pine Tree, 1909
Pen and watercolour, 11×8

Acquired from Sotheby's, 6 July 1955, from the collection of Mrs A.G. Innes, 4 guineas. The picture was mounted as an oval but had been cut from a larger rectangular original in landscape format. See p. 205.

J.D. Innes
Welsh Mountains, 1911
Watercolour on paper, 10×14

Exhibition of the works of Innes at the Leicester Galleries, February 1952. Formerly in the collection of Lord Howard de Walden. Acquired by Winifred with *Mountains, North Wales*, in September 1951 from the Leicester Galleries. See p. 200.

J.D. Innes
Cloud over Arenig, c.1911
Watercolour on paper, 10×14

Exhibition of the works of Innes at the Leicester Galleries, February 1952. Formerly in the possession of Euphemia Lamb and then Lord Howard de Walden. The picture was acquired for the second time by Euphemia Lamb and finally sold to Winifred after the Leicester Galleries Innes exhibition of 1952. See pp. 203, *205*.

J.D. Innes
Mountains, North Wales, n.d.
Watercolour and pencil on paper, 12×17

Exhibition of the works of Innes at the Leicester Galleries, February 1952. Formerly in the collection of Horace de Vere Cole, then Lord Howard de Walden. Acquired by Winifred with *Welsh Mountains* in September 1951 from the Leicester Galleries. See p. 200, *200*.

J.D. Innes
Mountain Landscape, n.d.
Watercolour on paper, 9×13

Acquired from the Redfern Gallery, 7 November 1953, for £10.

J.D. Innes
Lady at the Piano, n.d.
Ink and watercolour on paper, 8×7

No acquisition details. See p. *202*.

J.D. Innes
The Coast, La Ciotat, n.d.
Watercolour on paper, 10×16

Acquired in December 1951 from the Beaux Arts Gallery. The picture was formerly in the collection of Lord Ivor Churchill. See p. 201.

For John Dickson Innes (1887-1914), see J. Fothergill and L. Browse, *J.D. Innes* (London 1946).

Alfred Janes
Drawing of a Head, 1929
Pencil on paper, 7×5

Acquired from the Swansea Art Society Exhibition, Glynn Vivian Art Gallery, 1929, and donated to the Gallery. Winifred had a high opinion of Janes and saw him occasionally into the 1950s, but she bought no other work by him. See pp. 131, *131*, 133.

Augustus John
Head of a Woman, n.d.
Pencil on paper, 12×8

Acquired from the Beaux Arts Gallery, December 1951, for 20 guineas. See pp. 201, *202*, 203.

For Augustus John (1878-1961), see Michael Holroyd, *Augustus John. The New Biography* (London, 1996).

Gwen John
Kingfisher, n.d.
Pencil on paper, 5×3

Gwen John
Deer, n.d.
Pencil and watercolour on paper, 6×9

Gwen John
Two Women, n.d.
Pencil on paper, 8×6

This group of works by John was acquired from R.E. Abbott, 29 April 1953, who gave the provenance as 'a member of the John family'.

The Gwen John animal drawings were almost certainly done at the zoo. They were among several others of lions, peacocks etc. Although unsigned their authenticity is certain and is guaranteed. I think the bird is a kingfisher. The sketch of the two women is from her studio, I should guess. I am glad you like it.
[R.E. Abbott to Winifred Coombe Tennant, 29 April 1953]

See pp. 202, *203*.
For Gwen John (1876-1939), see Alicia Foster, *Gwen John* (London, 1999).

J.J. Jones
Ynystawe Moonlight, 1926
Oil on canvas, 20×24
Acquired from the Swansea Art Society Exhibition, Glynn Vivian Art Gallery, April 1926, 5 guineas.

Motored to Swansea after tea with Emperors and CCT. Saw the Swansea Art show all hung. CCT wants to buy a small water colour of the old bridge over the Tennant Canal at Port Tennant - I to buy a queer attractive picture buy one J.J. Jones of Morriston of a canal seen by moonlight. price £5.0.0.
[Diary, 30 April 1926]

Derwent Lees
Two Haystacks, n.d.
Watercolour on paper, 9×13

Acquired from R.E. Abbott, November 1953, for 9 guineas. Formerly in the collection of Michael Sadler.

Derwent Lees
Russian Peasants, n.d.
Oil on canvas, 24×16

Bought from R.E. Abbott, November 1953, 18 guineas. See pp. 202, *203*.

Percy Wyndham Lewis
Woman with a Bowl, 1923
Pencil on paper, 26×18

Acquired from R.E. Abbott, April 1953 as *Portrait of a Woman*.

Dr Iorwerth Hughes Jones had encouraged Grant Murray to consider purchasing a picture by Wyndham Lewis for the Glynn Vivian Art Gallery in 1949. Winifred thought the work 'hideous', and concluded her response to Grant Murray's request for an opinion on the work as follows:

I don't advise the Glynn Vivian to spend any money on Wyndham Lewis but should like Dr. I. Jones to buy the drawing of the Artist's wife and present it to the Gallery!! It is an interesting example.
[Winifred Coombe Tennant to William Grant Murray, 12 May 1949, Glynn Vivian Art Gallery Archive]

In the event, it would seem that Winifred's curiosity about Wyndham Lewis had been aroused and, notwithstanding her generally low estimation of the painter, when the opportunity arose she acquired this work.

Lewis had little connection with Wales other than ancestry, but was frequently co-opted by enthusiasts, and was included in the 1935 Exhibition of Contemporary Welsh Art. See pp. 177-8, *179*.

John Linnell
North Wales, 1813
Pencil, 10×17

John Linnell
North Wales, 1813
Pencil, 11×19

John Linnell
Dolwyddelan Valley, North Wales,
1813
Pencil, 9×18

John Linnell
Dolwyddelan, North Wales, 1813
Watercolour, 15×8

John Linell
Near Betws-y-coed, North Wales,
1813
Watercolour, 17×11

John Linnell
Betws-y-coed, n.d.
Watercolour, 14×22

This group of works was given
to Winifred by V.W. Hillier in
December 1953. Hillier had been
given them by Mrs Hewett, grand-
daughter of Linnell. All were
signed by the painter, except
Dolwyddelan Valley, North Wales.
The pictures are presently untraced.

John Linnell (1792-1882) was born
in London and studied under John
Varley. He entered the Royal
Academy Schools in 1805. He
worked as both a portrait and
landscape painter early in his
career but later turned mainly to
landscape. For Wales in his career,
see A.T. Story, *The Life of John
Linnell* (London, 1892).

George Martin
Sabbath in Canaan, 1925
Oil, size unknown

Acquired from the Swansea Art
Society Exhibition, Glynn Vivian
Art Gallery, July 1925, 2 guineas.
The picture was given by Winifred
to Dr Llywellyn Lewis on his
retirement in November 1928.
It is presently untraced.

Winifred became interested in
Martin and sought to acquire
another picture in 1925. As
Martin was an elusive individual
she asked Evan Walters to act as
intermediary:

*I will see that he paints a
good picture about 24x20 -
if it will not be very good I
will make him do another.*
[Evan Walters to Winifred
Coombe Tennant, 18 July 1925]

See p. 99.

George Martin
Speed, 1926
Oil on board, 23×21

Acquired from the Swansea Art
Society Exhibition, May 1926, £3.
See p. *99.*

A brief obituary of George Martin
(c.1879-1943) was published in
the *South Wales Evening Post,* 18
December 1943.

Ernest E. Morgan
*Old Port Tennant Bridge over
the Tennant Canal,* 1924
Watercolour on paper, 7×10

Acquired by Charles Coombe
Tennant, owner of the Tennant
Canal, from the Swansea Art
Society Exhibition at the Glynn
Vivian Art Gallery, April 1926.
See entry for J.J. Jones, above.

Cedric Morris
Birds on the Welsh Coast, c.1928
Oil on canvas, 12×14

Acquired from R.E. Abbott, 7
February 1953, 8 guineas. Winifred
bought pictures by Luard and
Connard from Abbott on the same
visit to his gallery. The picture was
previously in the collection of Mr
Meyerstein, who had bought it at

Tooth's, probably at the Cedric Morris exhibition in March 1930, from which Winifred selected *Llanmadoc Hill, Gower*, for the Glynn Vivian Art Gallery. She had not been impressed by his work at the time.

Two very similar pictures by Morris were reproduced in a BBC schools broadcast pamphlet, Ana Berry, *Looking at Pictures* (c.1928), which was sent to Winifred by the painter in October 1928.

Cedric Morris
Seabirds (Pintail Duck and Tern), c.1928-30
Oil on canvas, 21×27

Acquired 5 July 1955 from R.E. Abbott, 15 guineas. See p. *114*.

For Cedric Morris (1889-1982), see Richard Morphet, *Cedric Morris* (London, 1984).

William Grant Murray
Swansea from Richmond Hill, 1929
Oil on canvas, 33×33

Acquired at Swansea Art Society Exhibition, Glynn Vivian Art Gallery, June 1929, 10 guineas. The title is sometimes given by Winifred as *Swansea from Richmond Road*. See p. *123*.

William Grant Murray
Winter Sunshine, Richmond Road, Swansea, 1929
Oil on board, 18×12

The picture was given to Winifred by the painter when she acquired *Swansea from Richmond Hill* by purchase from the Swansea Art Society Exhibition, Glynn Vivian Art Gallery, 1929. Winifred had written a glowing review of the painter's work in the *Cambria Daily Leader*. See p. 124.

At the opening of the Exhibition of the Works of Past Students of the School of Arts and Crafts at Swansea in 1935, Winifred noted in her diary:

> *Grant Murray gave me a lovely picture of his, which I was unwilling to take but had to accept - figures on a beach.*
> [Diary, 11 October 1935]

Notwithstanding the clarity of the note of this gift and subsequent references in her catalogues to it as William Grant Murray, *The Beach* (Llangan Bay), it seems certain that this picture is the same as Will Evans, *In the Bay*. Although it bears the clear signature of Evans, a label on the back of the picture indicates that it was lent by Winifred as a Grant Murray to the Principal's memorial exhibition in 1951. By 1935 many of Winifred's pictures were kept in store, and it is possible that she had forgotten *In the Bay* in the six years that had elapsed since she bought it. Nevertheless,

how she both lent the picture to the exhibition, and then gained the impression that it was a gift to her from Grant Murray, is a mystery. See pp. 124, *125*.

Herbert Arnould Olivier
Winifred Coombe Tennant, 1889
Oil on canvas, 22×18

Probably painted while the family was living at Cherryhinton, Cambridgeshire. The circumstances of the commission are unknown.

Herbert Arnould Olivier (1861-1952) was born in Sussex and studied at the Royal Academy Schools, where he won the Creswick prize in 1882. During the Great War he painted portraits of French and Belgian leaders, and the celebrated *Where Belgium Greeted Britain, 4 December 1914*, which depicted the meeting of George V and Albert of the Belgians on the last remnant of unoccupied Belgian soil in 1914. See p. 11, *12*.

J. Powell-Jones
The Dawn of Reason, n.d.
Oil, size unknown

Acquired from an exhibition of the painter's work at Spring Gardens, London, in 1926, 6 guineas. Subsequently it was given away by Winifred. Powell-Jones does not figure in discussions of Welsh painting in the period.

Samuel Prout
Mountain Pass, n.d.
Watercolour on paper, 16×23

No acquisition details.

Samuel Prout (1783-1852) was born in Plymouth. His early work was undertaken mainly in the south-west of England, but he moved to London in 1812, where he became a member of the Old Watercolour Society. He toured widely, including to Wales, but is particularly known for his architectural pictures made in France.

Brian Rees
Aberdulais Aqueduct, 1950
Gouache on paper, 8×12

The picture was commissioned by Alexander Coombe-Tennant, £4.

Brian Rees has just called, a shy, quiet boy, at present working on a farm during the holiday - not much time for painting. I summed him up as a painstaking boy with a certain amount of 'flair' liable to be influenced by other workers - I impressed on him the importance of being himself. At the Art Society he exhibited a large oil, very much after 'Petra' by David Jones.
[William Grant Murray to Winifred Coombe Tennant, 22 July 1950]

After Winifred's death Brian Rees (b.1930) attended the Central School of Art in London, where he became involved with printing. Later, he worked at the Woburn Press. See p. 189.

Dorothy Tennant
Winifred Coombe Tennant at Cadoxton, 1896
Oil on canvas, 20×15

See p. 18, *18*.

Henry Tennant
[Augustus Henry Coombe-Tennant]
Archie Rhys Griffiths, 1928
Pencil on paper, 15×11

Drawn during Archie Griffiths' stay at Cadoxton in September 1928. Griffiths has drawn a small demonstration on the sheet. Henry also received help with drawing and painting from Evan Walters, see his *Still Life: Apples and Glasses*, 1926.

Ivor Thomas
Miner Underground, 1929
Woodcut, 6×4

Given to Winifred in December 1929 by George M.Ll. Davies.

There is a young collier, Ivor Thomas, Avondale, Crosshands, who is at present at the School of Art, Swansea. I enclose a wood-cut which gives some idea of his work. Perhaps you may like to see more of it when you are in Swansea.
[George M.Ll. Davies to Winifred Coombe Tennant, 31 December 1929]

See p. *132*.

Norman Tudgay
Building the New Road, 1950
Pen and ink, heightened with
gouache, 7x11

Acquired from the exhibition
of work by students at Swansea
School of Art, Glynn Vivian Art
Gallery, August 1950, following
a recommendation from William
Grant Murray. The picture depicts
a scene outside the Royal
Institution of South Wales.

Cornelius Varley
*Cattle in a River with Herdsman
and Dog*, n.d.
Ink and watercolour on paper,
11x13

Bought in Cambridge, 9 February
1914, 2/-.

*Found an exquisite sepia
watercolour of Cornelius
Varley, which I bought for 2/-.
A scene of cows in a river,
herdsman asleep in the
foreground, fine trees to the
right - such a joy! He was
contemporary with Blake
and brother to John Varley,
Blake's friend.*
[Diary, 9 February 1914]

Perhaps Cornelius Varley
Woodland and Mountains, n.d.
Watercolour on paper, 14x22

No acquisition details. Probably a
Welsh view.

Cornelius Varley (1791-1873) was
the brother of the more celebrated
painter John Varley. Cornelius
became renowned as a maker
of mathematical instruments.

Evan Walters
Weep for Joy, 1915
Pencil and colour wash on paper,
15x9

Acquired from the exhibition of
paintings by Evan Walters at the
Glynn Vivian Art Gallery, 1920.

Inscribed on reverse by Winifred:

*This coloured drawing was
made early in 1915 by Evan
Walters and taken with him
to New York, being brought
back from there in 1919 on
his return to Wales. The main
idea underlying the picture is
that of Love as the source of
deepest joy in life, Joy being
synonymous with Love, and
Love with Joy.*

*The lowest figure represents
Evil in the form of a Devil,
writhing in a final death
struggle, while the woman by
whom it has been vanquished
is seen, sickle in hand, with
triumphant arm uplifted. She
calls upon all womanhood to
weep for joy at evil defeated
and slain.*

*Evil has continually entered
the Garden of Love, which is
also the Garden of Joy, to
destroy it, and evil here
symbolises the lower nature
of man with its lusts and
appetites. The woman's figure
symbolises Love and Joy
grown to womanhood, and
risen in revolt against the
destroyer, sin. In mortal
combat the woman slays the
Devil, thereby liberating the
elemental powers of Nature
that are the appointed*

protectors of the Garden, symbolised in the picture by strange prehistoric beasts that have risen from sea and land, and stand guardian to exclude all further intruders from the sacred precincts of the Garden of Love.

In the upper portion of the picture is seen a group of three figures, Motherhood, symbolised by a mother and babe, sorrowing womanhood, and a figure with drooping head typifying redeemed and liberated womanhood, who weeps for joy at the defeat of evil.

To the left in the lower portion of the picture appears a group of three figures typifying human love, father, mother and child, the parents with arms interlaced, the child, her back turned to the spectator, reaching up both hands towards them, whilst beside the figure of the triumphant woman, who stands with one foot upon the prostrate figure of Evil, are seen two other female forms, one standing and one in an attitude of complete exhaustion after long endurance in struggle.

See pp. 48-50, *51*.

Evan Walters
Study for a Picture, 'Cleanse Me in Great Waters', 1915
Pencil and colour wash on paper, 15×14

Acquired from the exhibition of paintings by Evan Walters at the Glyn Vivian Art Gallery, 1920. Inscribed on reverse by Winifred:

This coloured drawing was made by Evan Walters in New York in 1915 when under the influence of Blake's genius. The immediate source of the inspiration of the picture was the concluding passage of Oscar Wilde's 'De Profundis':
'All trials are trials for one's life, just as all sentences are sentences of death; and three times I have been tried. The first time I left the box to be arrested, the second time to be led back to the house of detention, the third time to pass into a prison for two years. Society, as we have constituted it, will have no place for me, has none to offer; but Nature, whose sweet rains fall on unjust and just alike, will have clefts in the rocks where I may hide, and secret valleys in whose silence I may weep undisturbed. She will

hang the night with stars so that I may walk abroad in the darkness without stumbling, and send the wind over my footprints so that none may track me to my hurt: she will cleanse me in great waters and with bitter herbs make me whole.'
The design shows a waterfall broken by rocks. To the right is a kneeling figure typifying the liberated soul from whom all evil spirits have been swept away by the purifying flood. The spirits of evil are seen, borne downwards, and falling over a ledge of rock, a serpent intertwined among their limbs.

Far below lies a deep abyss of blue water from which the spray is seen rising in white vapour. The great waters which perform the act of purification are the beneficent powers of Nature 'whose sweet rains fall on the unjust and the just alike', who will cleanse in great waters and with bitter herbs make whole the soiled and bruised spirit of man.

See pp. 48-50, *49*.

Evan Walters
Mother and Babe, 1919
Oil on canvas, 18×21

Acquired from the exhibition of paintings by Evan Walters at the Glyn Vivian Art Gallery, 1920, 12 guineas. In the catalogue it is titled *Mother and Baby*.

> *Joy! I can buy Evan Walters' painting of 'Mother and Baby' for 12 guineas - wrote at once and said I would buy it, so tender and beautiful.*
> [Diary, 8 May 1920]

See pp. 48, 52-3, *52*.

Evan Walters
The Sailor, 1919
Oil on canvas, 21×17

Along with *The Collier* and *The Laughing Woman*, acquired from the painter on a visit to his studio at Llangyfelach on 9 December 1924, £3. The sitter was Walters' brother. See p. 86, *86*.

Evan Walters
Winifred Coombe Tennant, 1920
Oil on canvas, 25×20

Painted at Cadoxton Lodge between 24 June and 16 July 1920. Every sitting was documented by Winifred in her diary:

> *Being painted all morning. Evan Walters announced*

at lunch he had decided to change the background of my picture from dull gold to a soft grey. Feel amazed!
[Diary, 10 July 1920]

> *Painted all morning. Evan Walters changed my background: it was thrilling waiting, as I sat for him, to see it done and yet the result invisible to me until rest time. Then I saw how wonderful had been the effect. It has added a distinction and a refinement to the picture - it is all together satisfactory.*
> [Diary, 11 July 1920]

See pp. 53-6, *55*.

Evan Walters
Charles Coombe Tennant, 1920
Oil on canvas, 24×20

Walters began the portrait on 4 August 1920. See pp. 57-8, *58*.

Evan Walters
Alexander Coombe-Tennant, 1920
Charcoal on paper, 21×15

Probably the first of the two charcoal drawings of Alexander Coombe-Tennant made at Cadoxton Lodge on 10 and 13 August 1920, while preparing to paint *Dominoes*.

> *Evan Walters decided on the pose of the group picture of Emperors and self. He did a wonderful charcoal of Alexander's head - beautiful and entirely like him.*
> [Diary, 10 August 1920]

See p. 57.

Evan Walters
Alexander Coombe-Tennant, 1920
Charcoal on paper, 19×13

Drawn on 13 August, with
the portrait of Winifred, below.
See p. 58.

Evan Walters
Mam o Nedd, 1920
Charcoal on paper, 15×11

Drawn on 13 August, with the
portrait of Alexander, above.
See p. 58.

Evan Walters
Augustus Henry Coombe-Tennant,
1920
Charcoal on paper, 21×15

A preparatory drawing for
Dominoes. See p. 60.

Evan Walters
Oliver Lodge, 1920
Charcoal, size unknown

Much talk with O[liver] L[odge].
Evan Walters did a charcoal
drawing of him in the
music room while I
read Eddington's
address on the interior
substance of the stars
aloud ...
[Diary, 29 August 1920]

The picture is untraced,
perhaps having been
taken back to Cambridge
by the sitter.

See p. 59.

Evan Walters
Dominoes (Mrs Coombe Tennant
and Her Sons, Alexander and Henry),
1920
Oil on canvas, 60×50

Exhibited Royal Academy, 1922.

Walters began work on the
picture on 7 September 1920 and
had substantially completed it by
19 January 1921. He made some
small alterations on 9 July 1921.
Winifred's intention was to leave
Dominoes to the National Museum
of Wales. It was, in fact, given to
the Glynn Vivian Art Gallery in
1957. See pp. 57-60, *61*, 63.

Evan Walters
Garden at Cadoxton Lodge, 1920
Oil on board, 15×13
Sometimes known to Winifred as
In the Garden, Cadoxton Lodge.

Evan Walters
The Laughing Woman, 1924
Oil on board, 15×12

Along with *The Collier* and *The Sailor*, acquired from the painter on a visit to his studio at Llangyfelach on 9 December 1924, £3. See p. 85, 86.

Evan Walters
The Collier, c.1924
Charcoal on paper, 17×15

Along with *The Sailor* and *The Laughing Woman*, acquired direct from the painter on a visit to his studio at Llangyfelach on 9 December 1924, £3. Winifred noted that *The Collier* was a 'Study for a head in his large oil painting of "Miners on Strike"'. The date on the drawing is in Walters' hand, but is illegible. See p. 86.

Evan Walters
The Gorsedd Procession, 1925
Watercolour on paper, 15×22

The picture probably represents the procession to the Proclaimation Ceremony for the National Eisteddfod at Swansea in 1926, which took place in Singleton Park in July 1925. The mounted figure in the centre is Geoffrey Crawshay, the Herald Bard. Winifred, as Mistress of the Robes, is probably the figure in green robes, foreground to left of centre. The same event was depicted in a series of oil paintings by William Grant Murray.

Reached Swansea at 10.30. Got Geoffrey's green Ribbon, met Archdruid and Pedrog and Gwalter Dyfi in circle at noon, lunched with Mayor, then to Robing Room. Robed, heading the Procession, in front of the Gorsedd Banner.

Stood in torrid heat for over half an hour waiting for Mayor's procession, we forming in behind it. Long march to Singleton. Then I with Pedrog took part in initiation of Geoffrey and later in his installation as Herald Bard ... The Gorsedd Rite continues - the men and women are faded away one by one - new one's take their places. The One remains, the many fall and pass. Dream-like the whole seemed to me - ghosts more real than flesh and blood communed with my yearning, longing, grieving heart. Some day I shall reach their peace, their rest and their triumph. He who works shall rest and he who reigns shall rest. A heavy thunder storm cut short the Ritual and we hurried to Singleton. Garden Party given by Mayor. I got Cynan and Geoffrey together and they started on the possibility of dreaming up a form of Ritual both verbal and otherwise ...
[Diary, 2 July 1925]

See p. 99.

Evan Walters
Still Life: Apples and Glasses, 1926
Oil on board, 18×12

Painted as a demonstration for Winifred's children:

A day of joy! Evan Walters came to start the Wise One painting in oils ... In the Music Room they sat peacefully together painting a blue and white bowl containing oranges. W.O.'s quite good for a first attempt, Evan Walters joyfully bold and strong. Lunch. More painting. Then E.W. painted a vase and a glass for W.O. to see. All this I watched breathlessly. [Diary, 20 April 1926]

Evan Walters
Still Life of Fruit in a Bowl, 1926
Oil on board, 9×11

Clearly, the picture was painted on the same occasion as *Still Life: Apples and Glasses*.

Evan Walters
Gerald, 2nd Earl of Balfour, 1926
Oil on canvas, 30×25

Evan Walters
The Rt. Hon. David Lloyd George, 1926
Oil on canvas, 29×22

Commissioned by Winifred following an offer from Walters to paint the picture gratis, if she could persuade Lloyd George to sit. The sittings began in late December 1924 but the picture was not completed until July 1925. Winifred paid Walters £25. See pp. 94-5, *95*.

Evan Walters
Poster for the National Eisteddfod at Swansea, 1926
Lithograph, 40×25

See pp. *101*, 102.

Evan Walters
Elfyn, c.1927
Oil on board, 16×12

Acquired at the one-person exhibition of the work of Evan Walters at the Dorothy Warren Gallery, 1927, 16 guineas.

The sitter may be the son of Thomas Jones, killed in a motor car accident a few years later. See p. 111, *111*.

Evan Walters
Llangyfelach, c.1927
Oil on canvas, 16×20

Exhibited at the one-person exhibition of the work of Evan Walters at the Dorothy Warren Gallery, 1927. Acquired privately after the exhibition, 14 guineas.

In the Glynn Vivian gallery hangs one of his loveliest things, his Llangyfelach. I never look at it without envying Mrs Combe Tennant its possession, for it might have been mine, had I been more courageous; the good lady from Neath stood aside until I had made up my mind. It is a small canvas, but everything in Llangyfelach I love is there - the deep roads between the hedges, the emerald-green fields, and their crazy patterns.

It is so alive with beauty that I wonder why all the world does not see it with my eyes .... But it does not!

I took a Swansea man, whose opinions on literature I respect, to see it the other day. I told him that the essence of Evan Walters was there. He is a man of blunt language, and while Evan Walters himself would have rejoiced in the strength of his adjectives, perhaps the people who read this may be pained if I were to record it. Its effect, in short, was that he wouldn't hang it in his back-kitchen were it offered him! Such is the blindness of some of us when we are asked to step out of the rut in which we live.
[John Davies Williams, 'The Art of Evan Walters', *Herald of Wales*, 20 June 1931]

See pp. *110*, 112.

Evan Walters
Courting, c.1927
Oil on canvas, 20×27

Exhibited at the one-person exhibition of the work of Evan Walters at the Dorothy Warren Gallery, 1927. Acquired privately after the exhibition, 16 guineas.
See pp. *110*, 112, 167, 243.

Evan Walters
Sketch for the Portrait of Henry Coombe-Tennant, 'The Eton Boy', 1929
Oil on canvas, 22×9

Wise One's portrait started. At 2.30 he posed against a background of trees and Evan Walters did an oil sketch of him - very promising I thought - though whether he will get Wise One's extreme refinement and distinction into the picture I don't know. Squaring the sketch out on the collosal canvas on which the portrait is to be painted.
[Diary, 4 August 1929]

See pp. 124-28, *126*.

Evan Walters
Portrait of Henry Coombe-Tennant, 'The Eton Boy', 1929
Oil on canvas, 91×36

The portrait was commissioned in May 1929, and painted through the month of August of the same year. On completion Winifred paid Walters £150. It was exhibited at the Royal Academy in 1930.

Henry's portrait is in Royal Academy. Heard by evening post from Evan Walters that the portrait of Henry in Eton clothes has been accepted, and hung in Room X under the title of 'Eton Boy: Eton and Harrow Match 1929'. I am pleased! It is a notable picture. It will help Evan Walters, and I rejoice. The painting of it on the lawn here last year seems a long time ago.
[Diary, 30 April 1930]

See pp. 124-8, *127*.

Evan Walters
Sketch for the Portrait of Alexander Coombe-Tennant, 1933
Oil on paper, 23×16
See p. 139.

Evan Walters
Portrait of Alexander Coombe-Tennant, 1934
Oil on canvas, 91x36

Exhibited at the London Portrait Society , New Burlington Gallery, April 1935.

> *Went to Private View morning and afternoon. In afternoon Zanga [Alexander] arrived to see himself given the place of honour, at the end of the big room with the King relegated to a side wall. The Portrait looks very well.*
> [Diary, 1 April 1935]

See p. 139, *139*.

Evan Walters
Elfed, Archdruid of Wales, 1937
Charcoal on paper, 22x15

The picture was given to Winifred by Erma Meinel on 15 November 1953. It is one of two drawings made by Walters for a National Museum of Wales portrait series, the other being in the Museum. Winifred was a great admirer of Howell Elvet Lewis, the Archdruid Elfed:

> *Took the Emperors to the afternoon service at Zoar where the Archdruid was to preach. He read - divinely - a wonderful passage by Paul ...*
> [Diary, 31 August 1924]

Presently untraced.

Evan Walters
The Apples, c.1950
Oil on board, 16x20

Acquired from the exhibition of the paintings of Evan Walters at the Alpine Gallery, London, in May 1950, 15 guineas.

> *Evan Walters supped. I have bought the picture Henry so much liked at his recent exhibition, for 15 guineas, in place of 25 guineas asked. A still life of apples and a knife lying on a table, with a mysterious huge ghost apple in the fore-ground, double vision. Lovely colour and, apart from the ghost apple, which I personally hate, a fine thing.*
> [Diary, 28 May 1950]

See p. 183, *183*.

Evan Walters
Untitled, 1950
Oil on canvas, 24x20

No acquisition details.

Evan Walters
Roses, 1950
Oil on canvas, 16x20

No acquisition details.

Evan Walters
Sketch for the portrait of Winifred Coombe Tennant, 1950
Oil on canvas, 12x10

Walters' first attempt at this portrait, begun 16 June 1950, was abandoned.

> *Evan Walters started painting a small head of me on a small canvas, a new canvas. The one he had started before I could not endure, far too long a head for the canvas on which it was painted. I find it tiring sitting for just over an hour. Evan stayed to tea - like old times to have him in the house.*
> [Diary, 28 August 1950]

See p. 184, *184*.

Evan Walters
Winifred Coombe Tennant, 1950
Oil on canvas, 12x10

Exhibited Royal Society of Portrait Painters, Royal Institute Galleries, November-December 1950, and galleries outside London till August 1951.

After lunch, to private view of the Royal Society in the Royal Institute Galleries, and my portrait by Evan Walters was hung near the one Augustus John in the show. I like my Dutch-style portrait, and it looks very well in the gallery. [Diary, 21 November 1950]

See pp. 184, *184*, 196, 203, 244-5.

Evan Walters
Landscape with Panels in Foreground, 1950
Oil on canvas, 25×20

No acquisition details.

Evan Walters
Self Portrait, n.d.
Oil on board, 15×12

No acquisition details. However, the picture was certainly acquired in the painter's lifetime. See p. *109*.

Evan Walters
The Ploughman, n.d.
Oil on canvas, 24×18

No acquisition details. The double-vision style of the picture dates it to 1936 or later.

Evan Walters
The China Cat, n.d.
Oil on canvas, 27×20

No acquisition details.

Evan Walters
Nativity, n.d.
Charcoal and watercolour on paper, 21×29

No acquisition details.

Evan Walters
Woman at the Fireside, n.d.
Oil on paper, 15×23

No acquisition details.

Evan Walters
Still Life: Blue China and White Egg-cup and *Still Life: White China*, n.d.
Watercolour on two sides of paper, 10×14

A wonderful small still life, painted on both sides, one of a jug and dish of food on a table - and on the reverse a lovely still life of plates - dishes on a table - some in vivid blue.
[Diary, 29 May 1955]

Winifed noted in her catalogue that she thought these 'the finest watercolours Evan Walters ever painted'. They were given to Winifred by Erma Meinel on 26 May 1955.

Evan Walters
Still Life: Blue China and Still Life: Blue China and White Jug, n.d.
Watercolour on two sides of paper, 10×14

There are two similar pairs of watercolours painted on both sides of a sheet in the Welsh Collection, but only one pair is listed in Winifred's own catalogue.

See p. *194*.

Evan Walters
Landscape: Hills beyond Llangyfelach, n.d.
Watercolour and charcoal on paper, 15×22

Given to Winfred by Erma Meinel on 26 May 1955.

A strange pale landscape of a wide stretch of country, hills seen beyond a range of valleys, a great sense of space and

expanse of hill and vale, said to be of hills behind Llangyfelach, his near Swansea house.
[Diary, 29 May 1955]

Evan Walters
Landscape: Country Road, n.d.
Watercolour and charcoal, 21×14

Given to Winifred by Erma Meinel, on 26 May 1955.

A landscape of a country road up a steep hill, crowned with a dark boss of wood - above a lovely huddle of village houses.
[Diary, 29 May 1955]

Evan Walters
Flowers in a Vase, n.d.
Watercolour on paper, 30×21

No acquisition details.

Evan Walters
Still Life: Flowers, n.d.
Oil on canvas, 24×20

No acquisition details.

Evan Walters
Still Life: Apples and Candlestick, n.d.
Oil on canvas, 20×24

No acquisition details.

Evan Walters
Near Swansea, n.d.
Oil on canvas, 12×15

G.F. Watts
Study for Hope, c.1865-70
Oil on canvas, 26×20

Acquired from Christie's, February 1952. The picture had been bequeathed by Watts to Mrs Lilian Chapman, thence to H.C. Green, Guidford. Shown at the Arts Council exhibition of the work of G.F. Watts at the Tate Gallery, 1954-5.

Winifred frequently expressed her admiration for Watts. She had been a regular visitor to the Watts Museum and Chapel at Compton in Surrey from before the Great War. In that period Watts was considered by patriotic intellectuals to be a Welsh painter. See p. 45.

Archie Williams
Hillside Houses, c.1950
Gouache on paper, 10×14

Acquired from the exhibition of work by students at Swansea School of Art, Glynn Vivian Art Gallery, August 1950, following a recommendation from William Grant Murray.

Evan Williams
Caernarfon Castle, c.1860
Oil on canvas, 24×20

Acquired in London in 1939 for £1.10.0.

In afternoon looked in at Foster's and saw a good reddish picture of Caernarvon Castle catalogued as 'Unknown Castle Scene'. I left a bid of 30/- on it, thinking to give it to L[loyd] G[eorge] or some Welsh gallery.
[Diary, 23 May 1939]

Heard that the picture at Fosters had been knocked down to me for 30/-.
[Diary, 24 May 1939]

Evan Williams (1816-78) was born in Lledrod, Cardiganshire. He was both a painter and a minister in the Calvinistic Methodist denomination. As a painter he is best remembered for his portraits of distinguished individuals such as Ebenezer Thomas, 'Eben Fardd', but in his lifetime was also known as a painter of landscape. He was the first person to write substantial essays on visual culture in Welsh. See Peter Lord, *The Visual Culture of Wales: Imaging the Nation* (Cardiff, 2000), pp. 238-9 and 292-3.

J. Cyrlas Williams
Ogmore Castle, 1926
Oil on board, 12×13

Acquired at the National Eisteddfod Art and Craft Exhibition at Swansea, 1926, £5.

I came across him in this way. I went in with Clausen who was staying with us when he came up to adjudicate in the Art Section, National Eisteddfod, Swansea 1926, and walking round the exhibition I saw a picture in the Castle Competition which made me say as I looked at it 'That is

first rate. No one could have painted that who hadn't worked in Paris'.
[Winifred Coombe Tennant to J.D. Williams, 30 April, 1928]

See pp. 105-6, *106*.

J. Cyrlas Williams
Paris, 1926-8
Oil on canvas, 15×18

Acquired from the painter's studio, with the following three pictures, 15 April 1928, £10.

Jack goes to the Grande Chaumière in the mornings and to Collarossi's in the afternoons, up to the present he has not been successful in his search for a studio. He hopes to share a studio shortly with two or three others ...
[Gwladys Williams to Winifred Coombe Tennant, Paris, 28 December 1926]

See p. 107.

J. Cyrlas Williams
The Dark Boats, Martigues, 1927
Oil on canvas, 18×21

See p. 107, *107*.

J. Cyrlas Williams
Boats, 1927
Oil on canvas, 18×21

J. Cyrlas Williams
Model in a Studio, 1928
Oil on canvas, 18×21

J. Cyrlas Williams
Henry Coombe-Tennant, 1928
Oil on canvas, 24×20

Jack Cyrlas Williams (painter of my Castle picture) came over from Porthcawl to do an oil sketch of Henry - blessed sight of easel and oil paints in Music Room ...
[Diary, 27 April 1928]

The sketch is finished - a clever, strong, downright piece of painting - not a very good likeness ... The sketch is to go to the Swansea Art Society's show next month, such fun, also my 'Dark Boats' picture. Cyrlas Williams is tremendously encouraged at all this and I am so glad that I had this picture done.
[Diary, 28 April 1928]

See p. 107.

Kyffin Williams
Llynau Cwm Silyn, 1948
Oil on canvas, 20×27

Acquired from the painter in November 1950, £25.

Started in dense fog at 10a.m. for Highgate to see Kyffin Williams' pictures in Hampstead. Visibility almost nil, we crawled on and, finally, came to the house. Saw some 30 or 40 pictures, many of them fine. I bought one, a dark North Wales mountains, with a lake in the foreground ... for £25. A superb painting. Kyffin, small, emaciated (tb), and entirely delightful, much interesting talk. The two pictures he is sending to the Leicester Gallery soon, very fine, especially one of Hafod Fawr, Festiniog Mountains - farmstead and fields - but I liked my picture best of all, very North Wales of very

North Wales. Drove slowly through the fog past Highgate Cemetery, where is an empty tomb.
[Diary, 26 November 1950]

Kyffin Williams
The Wave, 1950
Oil on canvas, 18×24

Acquired from 'Artists of Fame and Promise' exhibition, the Leicester Galleries, August-September 1950.

Henry drove me to the Leicester Galleries, where saw two John Elwyns, better than those at Caerphilly, and saw two superb Kyffin Williams, one of which I felt I couldn't live without, 'The Wave', a seascape, 30 guineas. Bought it for myself ... I saw some lovely pictures in the gallery, but 'The Wave' exceeded them all. Has not yet been shown, but one of the Directors got it up for me to see. Back to Cottesmore Gardens for tea, my heart thrills with joy when I think of 'The Wave'.
[Diary, 14 August 1950]

See pp. 172-3, *173*.

Kyffin Williams
Group of six watercolours and drawings, c.1951

Llyn Idwal from below the Devil's Kitchen, Penyroleuwen on the right and Foel Goch on the left
Wash

Penygaeri, one of the highest points of Mynydd Mawr between Brynkir and Llanaelhaiarn, Caernarvon
Guache

Llyn y Cau, Cadair Idris, Sketch for the picture in the National Library, Aberystwyth

Mountains above Pen y Groes, Caernarvon

Y Cnicht seen from Garreghylldrem. From the road near Aberglaslyn to Penrhyndeudraeth

Y Cnicht
Watercolour

Acquired 27 February 1952 from the painter, 20 guineas, all presently untraced. *Y Cnicht*, the largest of the group, was bequeathed to Elizabeth Joyce Hooper after she saw it at Cottesmore Gardens in January 1953.

Joy!! Kyffin Williams. Brahms! Kyffin brought me his portfolio of watercolours and drawings. What a feast! I had asked him to choose only scenes in Wales and especially mountains. I chose

6 - glorious things - the largest of Cnycht. Others of mountains in North Wales - one in Anglesey ... Oh what a joy they will be to me.
[Diary, 27 February 1952]

Kyffin Williams
Lliwedd, 1951-2
Oil on board, 11×15

Shown in Williams' one-person exhibition at the Leicester Galleries, February 1952. The gift of the painter.

Drove back at 5.50p.m., then came Kyffin Williams ... We went over his six watercolours, now in their mounts and framed. One, a dark scene full of snow and mountains. They are a noble company. He brought me, as a present, the lovely small oil in the Leicester Gallery show, 'Lliwedd', no. 6 in the catalogue. Wonderful greens, Snowdon peaks from near

Penygwryd. Oh! the great joy of Art, the release from earth into a world of beauty and imagination and freedom. I have some wonderful pictures.
[Diary, 12 March 1952]

Kyffin Williams
The Glyders, 1951-2
Oil on board, 9×16

Acquired from Williams' one-person exhibition at the Leicester Galleries, February 1952, £21.

Kyffin Williams
Skye from Harris, 1954
Oil on canvas, 18×22

Exhibited at the Leicester Galleries, December 1954, but acquired on 14 January 1955 from the artist, 20 guineas. The full title of the picture, as given to Winifred by Williams, was *Distant View of Skye from Tarbert in Harris*. The hills are Quirang and Storr.

It gives me such pleasure to see the illustration of one of your pictures in today's Times, and a good notice of the show. I succeeded in getting there and particularly admired the one picture illustrated, 'Llanllechid' ... I wanted you just to know this. So fare you well.
[Winifred Coombe Tennant to Kyffin Williams, 10 December 1954]

I went down to the Leicester Galleries the day before it closed and the picture of Skye from Harris had not been sold. Am up here [Menai Bridge] for a holiday - no painting but a few days hunting. Am off to Penygwryd tomorrow to hunt on the Glyders. Shall take a sketch book and make notes.
[Kyffin Williams to Winifred Coombe Tennant, 3 December 1954]

See pp. *206, 207*.

INDEX

Winifred Coombe Tennant.